WOMEN
WHO
dream

WOMEN
WHO
dream

LISTEN TO THE LIFEGUARD

kate butler
BOOKS

First Edition

Copyright © 2022 Kate Butler Books

www.katebutlerbooks.com

All rights reserved.

ISBN: 979 8 9881314-1-0

Design by Melissa Williams Design
mwbookdesign.com

This book is dedicated to you. We see you, we feel you, we relate to you, and we connect with you, because . . . we are you. At the core we are more alike than we are different. We are beings of light and love who deeply desire to make a positive influence in the world with our unique type of brilliance. The pages of this book promise to fill you with the wisdom, insights, and inspiration that will align you further with your soul's path. Our hope is that the vulnerability and authenticity of these stories will remind you deeply of who you are and inspire you to rise up and shine your light in the world.

It is your time. It is our time. It is time.

Enjoy the unfolding . . .

table of contents

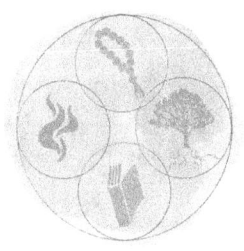

BORN FOR THIS

Maya Comerota

It's Saturday morning in Elkins Park, Pennsylvania. I'm nine years old, and I've just arrived at my friend Jillian's house.

"C'mon, let's go!" I call.

"Coming!" she calls back as she runs down the steps with her sweatshirt and backpack. "I was getting supplies."

She and I were like a female Tom Sawyer and Huckleberry Finn that summer, heading out first thing in the mornings on long adventures that would keep us out until after dark.

We'd fill our backpacks with blankets, Archie Comics, snacks, sandwiches, and apple juice boxes, then take off for the magical wonderland in the woods behind our neighbors' backyards.

We'd climb trees and take turns swinging on the rope above the creek while imagining we were anyone we wanted to be.

We'd play, build castles and forts, then fall over exhausted onto a bed of leaves, panting heavily and giggling from our effort.

When we'd finally come back to Jillian's house, we'd run upstairs to begin our musical escapades.

After dressing up and doing each other's makeup and hair like Madonna and Debbie Gibson, we'd sing "Cherish," "Like a Prayer," and "Electric Youth" at the top of our lungs.

We'd stay up late and then call into the pop radio station, Eagle 106.

"You have reached Eagle 106. What's your name and song?"

"This is Jillian calling from Elkins Park. I want to request 'One More Time' by Timmy T. and give a shout-out to my girl, Maya, who is here with me!"

I would let out a squeal with her as we both jumped up and down. We were on the radio, just like we knew we would be!

There was nothing we couldn't do. No one we couldn't be . . .

Adventurers. Explorers. Pop singers. Broadway stars. Makeup artists. Actresses. Dancers. Teachers. Doctors.

We believed whatever we dreamed, whatever we imagined, we would be.

I was going to live a legendary life full of incredible musical adventures, jet-setting around the world to impact lives *and* have an incredible husband, three kids, a puppy, and a beautiful home.

Twenty-five years later, after following all the rules I thought I was meant to follow, working hard to get good grades, and working even longer and harder at work, I wasn't a singer, Broadway star, or a doctor. But I was making an impact, building billion-dollar brands and supporting hundreds of thousands of patients around the world as the director of Latin America for a Fortune 100 Biotech company.

I was flying first class to Guatemala, Mexico, Colombia, Brazil, and Argentina where I would stay at the St. Regis for weeks at a time with my own personal butler, concierge, driver, and security detail to take me to and from the hotel and office.

I had married James, a gorgeous, adventurous, six-foot-five Australian with long brown hair and an accent that would make any woman swoon.

We knew we'd get married the moment we met. Our beautiful wedding was held in Antigua, Guatemala, in a fifteenth-century monastery, lit by two thousand candles.

It seemed like a fairy tale.

2

We moved to a beautiful condo in Chicago and later bought a lake house and a boat. We weren't often home at the same time because of our work schedules, but we would meet in different locations around the world. I had recently found out I was pregnant with our first child.

I'm sure from the outside looking in, I seemed to have it all.

But deep down inside, I felt something was missing. I wanted *more.*

I would think, "Maya, how can you possibly be unhappy? You have a great career. You have a gorgeous husband. You get to travel and stay at the most beautiful places. You're going to have a child. You have a dream life."

I could hear how ridiculous it sounded. But the feeling wouldn't go away.

Nine months later, after receiving *another* promotion, I was sitting in my closet on a conference call with my boss at 10:30 p.m., whispering so I wouldn't wake up James who was asleep in the bedroom.

My boss said, "Maya, this launch is huge. We can count on you to get this report to the team by ten a.m. tomorrow, right?"

"Umm . . . sure. Absolutely. Whatever you need!"

What?! I was 225 months pregnant, ten days overdue, and scheduled to get induced into labor in less than twelve hours!

But I *never* let anyone down. Plus my boss had told me she was crazy for hiring me when I was seven months pregnant, and I wanted to prove she'd made the right choice.

So eight hours later, I was on the delivery table, strapped into that contraption that shows how big your contractions are on a video screen, but I was not paying attention. All my focus was on a different screen: my Blackberry.

I felt a little guilty for working right then, but there were things I had to get done before this baby came.

My contractions aren't off the charts yet. I still have time, I thought to myself.

James starts to walk over, I'm sure to take my Blackberry away from me.

"Please. I just need to send these last two emails. You don't understand. I can't let the team down."

I was going to show everyone that I could handle it all. Career. Baby. Family. All of it.

Uh-huh. Right.

After two additional promotions, I was taking Ritalin for ADHD and Lexapro for depression to help me focus through long workdays and to help me feel not so "blue" day after day after day.

One beautiful Sunday afternoon, I was typing away in my office. Hunter was three years old, playing downstairs with his nanny. And I was upstairs working.

I'd been working fourteen-hour days for years. I'd worked every weekend for the last six months.

All I wanted was to go downstairs and play with Hunter, but I felt stuck and chained to my computer.

Bing!

A text from work. I needed to get out of here and clear my head.

"Hunter, Mommy will be home in an hour." I ran out the door and jumped in my husband's truck.

Twenty minutes later, I was stopped at a red light thinking, *How did I get here? I can't even remember driving the last twenty minutes.*

Then *CRASH!*

A huge black SUV crashed into me.

The car started to spin. Everything turned into slow motion. I saw scenes of my life pass before my eyes, both from the life I've lived and the life I had yet to live.

I see my funeral. James and Hunter are so sad.

I see James looking into my eyes with so much love on our wedding day. He hasn't looked at me that way for so long.

I see Hunter's birth and again feel the rush of love I felt when I promised to love him forever unconditionally.

I see all the moments I felt unloved because I compromised myself, apologized for myself, or sacrificed myself.

And I see myself as that little girl running carefree through the woods, climbing trees, singing songs, being anything and anyone she wanted to be.

I knew there was more to life than the one I'd been living.

I knew there was more to *me* than the woman I was being.

There was someone I was created to be, and I hadn't become her . . . *yet.*

But I *wanted* to be her! I *wanted* to feel alive, vibrant, passionate, brave, bold, wild, and free—the way I know each of us is meant to feel. The way we were born to be!

"God, please let me live through this. If I make it out alive, I promise I will be the person you created me to be. I will discover who that is and I will be her."

By the time the police arrived twenty minutes later, I was embracing the woman driving the SUV.

Both our cars were totaled, yet neither one of us had a scratch on us.

Six months later, I handed in my resignation. I was free for the first time. Free to be me, Maya.

Not Maya, director of Latin America, or Maya, global head of innovation. Just Maya.

I wasn't exactly sure who she was yet, but I couldn't wait to meet her and discover why God put her on this Earth.

Slowly I let go of the titles, the roles, the expectations.

I let go of the medications.

I let go of my car, the boat, the lake house.

I let go of my regrets and I started to dream a new dream.

I dreamed of being in love with life and in love with my husband again.

I dreamed of playing and laughing with Hunter.

I dreamed of leading and inspiring women around the world to live the lives they were born to live.

I knew that I had to *become* her first before I could inspire others. I had to first *be* the woman that *I* was born to be.

So I began living that dream.

It wasn't easy. I lost investments. I lost businesses and business partners. I lost some friendships. My relationship with my husband was in turmoil. I even asked for a divorce. But every time things got hard, or I fell down, I would hear the words,

There is someone you were created to be.

You are here for a reason.

You are born for this.

Today, over two million people have been impacted by my messages, events, and programs. I speak on the world's largest and most prestigious stages supporting people to be who they are uniquely created to be and to share their gifts with the world.

But I never forget that before I could share my story and support others to change their lives, I had to dare to dream and first transform my own.

For 2022, I wanted to dream even bigger and bolder and welcome even more freedom, passion, prosperity, joy, and vitality into my life.

My company was poised to double in size, and I am about to expand my team, launch new programs, write another new book, and teach on new stages.

But what I was most looking forward to was doing Everesting 29029 with James. Together we were going to climb twenty-nine thousand twenty-nine feet, the equivalent of Mount Everest, in only thirty-six hours.

We were going to train for six months and cross the finish line together. It was going to be a family vacation with Hunter waiting for us at the finish line. I could already see James giving me a big hug and kiss when we crossed the finish line with our family and friends shouting and cheering for us in the background.

This was going to be especially meaningful because just five years before, I had asked James for a divorce.

We hadn't been happy for many years. We had tried to make it better for so long, and I wanted us both to be happy . . . finally. Even if it meant letting each other go. I knew I needed to let go of our relationship so I could make room for the passionate, joyful, loving relationship we both deserved.

Months later, as James was packing his things in boxes and preparing to move into an apartment nearby, he looked at me and said, "Do you think it's possible we could stay together?"

I paused.

I mean, I believe *anything* is *possible*. That *is* what I teach.

"Dream the impossible dream no matter what."

But this?

We'd been trying to make it work for so long, and it just wasn't. I knew it was time to let it go. I knew that would be the most loving thing for us to do.

"Anything is possible," I said, "but I don't think it's likely."

"I see us together, Maya. That is what I want," James said. "You, me, and Hunter, walking together hand in hand. You're wearing a white dress. I see it so clearly. What do I do with that vision?"

I considered what he was asking.

"Hold that vision then," I said through tears, "but without attachment to me or the outcome."

My vision was of a passionate and loving marriage with a husband who could be my best friend. Someone who would laugh with me and celebrate me being the me I was born to be. I wanted a marriage that would be a true example of what marriage should be, for Hunter and for others. I wanted us to be incredible parents together. I didn't want Hunter seeing two roommates as his parents and believing that was what marriage was. My vision seemed so far from the couple that James and I had become.

But I held on to my vision of the marriage I truly desired and James held on to his.

We leaned into each other, day by day, moment by moment until my dream and his dream merged into one. We didn't force it. We simply became our own dreams. We made choices and decisions in alignment with what we desired and the people we were born to be. I didn't know if we'd stay together and neither did he. But after walking through the fire of difficult conversations, decisions, and actions, we fell in love again and became the couple we both wanted to be.

Doing Everesting 29029 was going to be the culmination and celebration of our journey. The odds of finishing are about 60 percent, but I knew with 100 percent certainty James and I were going to cross that finish line!

Then a few months ago, I was driving Hunter to school. We were belting out songs from Disney's *Encanto* when I began feeling nauseous.

"Mom, what's wrong?" Hunter asked.

"I don't know, little guy. I have never felt this way before."

"I'm sorry, Mom. I hope you feel better! I love you!" Hunter closed the door to walk into school.

When the door banged shut, I remembered . . . there was one other time I felt like this . . . eleven years ago . . . when I was pregnant with Hunter.

I stopped at the Walgreens to grab two pregnancy tests.

Pregnant.

Pregnant.

I stared at them. Uncertain how to feel.

James was working in Virginia.

"We're pregnant," I told him over the phone.

After a slight pause, he said, "Yaaaaaaaay?"

He was trying to sound enthusiastic, processing the news just like I was.

I burst into tears.

This can't be, I thought. *Things are finally back on track. We have big plans this year. The company's growing, I'm speaking all over the country, people are counting on me, we're doing Everest 29029, we are planning on moving and taking vacations as a family. How are we going to do it all if I'm pregnant and have a baby?*

When Hunter was a baby, it was hard! I was working fourteen-hour days and weekends. I did the best I could. I hired help, but my heart broke every time I couldn't play with him and every time I had to travel. The stress of it all came flooding back.

Could James and I survive another baby? We'd talked about it once years ago, but because of our strained relationship, it didn't make sense for us to have more kids.

Will James want to have a baby now?

Over the next twenty-four hours, I experienced every emotion possible, but I couldn't discern how I really felt.

Then I paused and asked, *What would you really love, Maya? If you could dream any dream, what would it be?*

I saw a vision of our family. Of a beautiful baby girl laughing and giggling with us. I saw all the love and joy that she would bring. I saw her gazing at Hunter with her big, beautiful eyes, totally in love with her big brother, and I saw Hunter tickling his little sister. I saw all of us, including our puppy, Coco, going to the beach, the park, and on vacation together. I saw graduations, Thanksgivings, Christmases, weddings, and grandkids. I saw us traveling the world *together* as a family, dreaming our biggest dreams and doing it together. And I saw the impact that this little baby and her big brother would have on the world simply by being who they were born to be.

I called James the next day.

"I think God is laughing at us right now. I think he's saying, 'Maya, James, this is everything you have been asking for. You wanted more love, more laughter, more joy, more fun, more play, more impact, more adventure. Here you go! Your relationship is better than ever, you're in love, you're being who you were born to be. Everything you desire is coming true in the most miraculous of ways. And it is *easy!*"'

James and I both laughed while sensing the truth in it all.

As I sit here typing, there's a little human growing inside me. She chose us, and we chose her.

One of my favorite authors is Henry David Thoreau. Many years ago, he decided to do an experiment with life. He went into the woods to live for two years, two months, and two weeks because he wanted to learn what life and the woods had to teach him. He wanted to be sure that he didn't come to the end of his life only to discover that he had not yet truly lived.

I didn't want to come to the end of my life and discover that *I* had not yet truly lived.

I started to ask myself the question, *What is my bold, brave experiment with life?*

"James, Hunter," I called, running down the stairs into the kitchen to sit down while James cooked dinner.

"What do you think about going on an adventure and doing a life experiment?"

"Oooh, what kind of adventure?" Hunter asked. James shifted his attention from the pan of vegetables over to me as he put his arms around my growing waist and gave me a big kiss.

"Well, what if once the baby comes, we buy an RV and travel around the world together talking to legendary families about what it takes to make dreams come true? Let's make a documentary and create a television show to share the stories of legendary families who support each other's dreams and aspirations."

I was thinking of people like Oprah, Tony Robbins, Dean Graziosi, Mary Morrisey, Bo Eason, Jesse Itzler and Sara Blakely, Sonia Choquette, Jack Canfield and Jamie Kern Lima as well as my colleagues and students from my Born For This and Living Legendary programs who are also extraordinary people doing extraordinary things.

James winked at me, chuckled, and said, "That does sound like an adventure. Let's do it."

Hunter said, "I'm in!"

Bing!

It was a text message from a mentor, Dean Graziosi.

"Maya, let me know if you have a few minutes to chat today."

He invited me to speak at his upcoming event to thousands of mission-driven entrepreneurs.

"I would love to!" I said, honored and blessed that I got to be me and share my heart with the world without compromising anymore.

Hunter called, "Family cuddle!"

James, Hunter, Coco, and I along with our unborn baby girl gathered in the living room.

Hunter whispered to the little baby growing in my belly, "I can't wait till you get here!"

As I lay there with my family, I closed my eyes and knew that I was finally being the woman I was created to be, living the life I was created to live, feeling more alive and joyful than ever, and knowing that this is still only the beginning of our adventures.

I am born for this.

And so are you.

ABOUT MAYA COMEROTA

Maya is a visionary entrepreneur, transformational teacher, and speaker. Maya spent fifteen years in the biotech industry building multibillion-dollar coaching platforms that impacted over 300,000 people worldwide.

After leaving her corporate executive role as global head of innovation, she immersed herself in the study of personal transformation learning from the best of the best in neuroscience, quantum physics, and high performance.

Through her companies, consulting, programs, and live events, Maya has empowered millions of people to achieve new heights of wealth, joy, aliveness, and authentic success.

Maya has been a featured speaker and coach on major media outlets such as NBC, ABC, CBS and has been featured on stages with Dean Graziosi, Mary Morrisey, Bo Eason, among others. Maya was recently invited to train other visionary entrepreneurs on the art and science of turning dreams into reality on Sir Richard Branson's island.

Web: www.mayacomerota.com
Facebook: Maya Comerota
Instagram: @mayacomerota

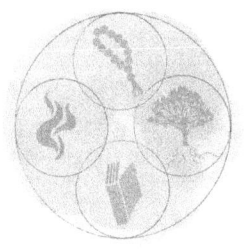

INTRODUCTION

Kate Butler

I was being interviewed for a podcast last week and the host asked me, "Did everyone in your life think you were crazy when you walked away from a successful company you built to pursue your dream?"

I said, "Yes. Until it worked."

***

I always knew I would do something with writing because expressing myself through words always came innately to me. It was not completely out of the question to believe I would write a book one day, although I did not think I would write twelve international best sellers and go on to publish over 400 #1 best-selling authors as well. This is still, in many ways, shocking to say.

I was thirty years old running a business from my home, based on what I had done in corporate. It made great money. I also got to be home with our children. And I was bored out of my freaking mind. I had an awareness one day that I was selling myself short, that I was not put here to run a staffing and recruiting business, that I was meant for more and I was being called to do more. And here's the thing about awareness . . . once you know it, you can't unknow it.

If I was going to scrap this business, if I was going to do it all again, if I was going to build an actual dream . . . I was going to do it differently.

When I was working in a business that was out of alignment with my purpose, it always felt like there was something missing, like I could never do enough, like I always had to push to make more happen.

It was constant pressure . . .

What do I need to do this week?

What needs to happen to meet goals this month?

What do I have to do to complete this project?

What does this client need from me now?

Each week, month, quarter, and year, it seemed like a heaviness clouded over me of goals that needed to be achieved and I needed to make happen, but when the goals were met, there was only brief satisfaction. There was never a lightness. It always felt like I was carrying bricks in a backpack and pushing a bolder up a hill. It always felt like no matter what goals were met, I always needed to make more happen. It didn't bring me happiness. It just made me money. It wasn't fulfilling, it just felt like it was what I had to do.

What if I could have both? What if I created from that place?

I was going to build something that ignited a fire inside my belly every time I opened my email. I was going to create something that others wanted to be part of. I was going to start a movement that had me jumping out of bed in the morning. I was going to create a life I was madly in love with.

I wanted to feel like I *get* to do this each day, not like I have to.

And as soon as I decided this, my next thought was, *but how?* And then, *who are you to create this empire that you long for?*

So I had to decide at that moment: which one?

Which one is it going to be, Kate?

Are you going to choose what you've always known? Or are you going to choose the forest with no path, no trails, and no map? Which one?

If you know me, you know I am not much for camping, or forests, or woods. But this was different. This forest was enchanted. I could just *feel* it.

I shared with you earlier that an awareness revealed itself to me. And once you know, you can never unknow it. And so, I *knew*, I knew that although it did not appear that there was a trail or a path or a guide or a map . . . I had this knowing that I WAS THE MAP. I realized I was born knowing the way. I had a deep knowing that I had everything I needed within myself and I always had.

And with this knowing, I then began to ask, so if I have everything I need . . . then why am I waiting for others to give me the green light on my dreams? Why would I let a publisher decide if my story is good enough to tell? Why would I wait for someone to ask me to speak at their event to share my message? Why am I waiting for someone else to give me the opportunity? Why not just create them myself?

And so I did.

I got into action.

The first thing I did was get clear. And I got clear by getting quiet and by getting that pencil to paper.

I asked myself these questions over and over:

What if I stopped waiting to be picked and I picked myself?

What if I stopped waiting for someone else to invite me to their stage and I built my own?

What if I unsubscribed to gatekeepers and just created my own opportunities?

What would that world look like?

I reminded myself it's right now that we get to taste the coffee and bite into pizza and dive into the water and bake the cookies and hold the hand and feel the sand and bask in the sun and walk in the grass and hike the arch and feel the belly laugh and see the smile of delight and give the kisses goodnight. It's only right now. And even if we have hundreds or thousands of years left, it still won't be enough. Because once we don't have these miracles anymore, we will know, we will *know*, that when we *were* here, we had everything.

The universe had shown me very clearly there was one thing I did not want to be: the person waiting. Because the people who played the waiting game always lost.

So it was time. It was time to dream the dream now. It was time to go for it, to have the journey and allow my God-given map to guide me down my path.

And once I decided, it began to unfold.

The idea for my first children's book came through me, and I felt it right down to my bones. We were on vacation in Aruba, and while sitting on the beach, it all just downloaded. I am not sure where my phone was, but I remember frantically asking my family, "Does anyone have a paper? A pen? I need to write something down right now!" Aunt Penny was back in a flash with a little mini composite book and a pen, which I still have, and I wrote down the entire story of *More Than Mud* right there in that moment.

I had decided I was going to create my dream. My dream was to inspire others to live the life they were meant for. I decided that meant starting with children, my children, my two girls. I wanted to write a book for them, a guide, on how to live a limitless life, but in a language that children could understand. I got into action, and I did this by getting still every morning and connecting into my higher power, and I also did this by journaling each day. And once I got into motion, the rest came. It poured out of me onto the pages. Right there on that beach. And that book went on to be a #1 best-selling book and stayed on the best-seller list for over 100 weeks straight.

This was an opening. I knew it, I felt it, I received it, and I went for it. We must be ready to walk through the openings when they come.

My next children's book was imagined by my daughter Bella when we were on vacation in Florida. She saw what a phenomenal journey it was to create *More Than Mud,* and she had a dream of creating something too. So she began to bounce ideas around. And then this one day, it was all there, it all came together, and we had our second book. Another divine download, just like the first one, right there in that pool in Ft. Lauderdale. *More Than Magic* was created and at five years old, my daughter Bella became a #1 best-selling author—since the story, after all, was hers.

My daughter Livie is now involved in the writing and illustrations of our books. She started with her first #1 best-seller, *Believe Big.* My husband, Mel, works on the back end of our business. We travel together. My girls and I speak on stages together, we do author readings and book signings, we visit schools and are hired for conferences and events. I have created not only my dream business, but my dream life.

I did not wait. I did not wait for the invitation, I did not wait for permission, I did not wait to be chosen.

I CHOSE ME.

I was born worthy. You were born worthy.

I was born with a dream. We deserve to live out our dreams.

I was born with what I needed to live my dream life beyond measure. We all have our own map inside. We just need to be reminded.

When I decided to create a new business and truly go after creating a dream, it was like coming home to myself. I made decisions based on what felt good, not the way everyone else was doing it. I conducted business based on my moral compass and my soul alignment, not based on what had always been done before. The people I surrounded myself with were more about the vibration they brought to the table, not the résumé. The actions I took each day always involved being still, setting clear intentions, acknowledging and appreciating things in gratitude, and getting clear about what I was available for and inviting in. In the past, my daily required actions involved a certain amount of calls, emails, follow-ups, and meetings. I now had new non-negotiable actions because I realized that when you combine the foundation of the energetic alignment to the next action you take, it is magnified exponentially.

This is how I explain what has been built over the last twelve years. This is how I explain the wild success of my books, the outrageous success of the Inspired Impact Book Series, being offered my own TV Show, being featured in an award-nominated documentary alongside some of my well-known mentors, speaking on stage next to the greats of our time, and creating millions of dollars, millions of dreams, and millions of lives touched by waking up each morning and being completely head over heads in love with my life.

This is it.

I decided to dream. I decided to choose me. And when we bet on ourselves, we win.

Every
        Single
                Time.

We are just getting started.
We get to do this.
Your dreams are waiting. ALL OF THEM.
I love you.

Kate

ABOUT KATE BUTLER

Kate Butler is a TV Host, Publisher, #1 International Best-selling Author and Speaker. Kate is the host of the TV Show, "Where All Things Are Possible" which streams on Roku. She is also creator of the *Inspired Impact Book Series*, a #1 International Best-selling Series that has published over 300 authors. Kate focuses on taking your story and bringing it to life in a best-selling book . . . this is her specialty!

As a CPSC, Certified Professional Success Coach, she offers dynamic live and digital programs creating transformational experiences to ultimately help clients reach their greatest potential and live out their dreams, including becoming a #1 Best-selling Author through her mentorship. Kate believes in learning the tools to help create those "Made For Moments" in your life. Her passion is teaching others how to activate their authentic mission, share it for massive impact while also creating a lucrative business.

Kate's expertise has been featured on Fox 29, GoodDay Philadelphia, HBO, PHL 17, Roku the RVN network and many more tv and radio platforms.

Kate offers a variety of free tools on her website to help you get clear on what you want and also to show you the path to make it possible. Visit www.katebutlerbooks.com

Connect with Kate:

Facebook: @katebutlerbooks
Instagram: @katebutlerbooks
Website: www.katebutlerbooks.com

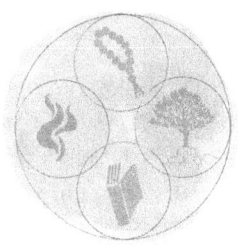

YOU ARE WORTHY

Tracey Watts Cirino

Have you ever had a dream sitting silently in you, but you kept pushing it down?

I know I have, and once I was given permission to fully dream and embrace all that is possible, it was like unleashing a never-ending water tower of hopes, dreams, and possibilities just waiting to be brought to life to share with the world.

If you have ever felt like your dreams have been silenced or you didn't feel worthy of having good things happen to you, let alone actually achieving your dreams or you haven't felt safe and supported to share your dreams, and somehow because of not feeling worthy, you silenced your dreams and shoved them all down so deep you were living a lie instead of the authentic life you were born to live, then this story is for you.

I'm a former award-winning salon owner of a salon that has been named one of the top 200 salons in North America seven different times and a #1 international best-selling author, speaker, digital course creator, and business success coach and trainer. I am a loving wife and mother and the friend you want in your corner to help you believe in the power of your dreams and your greatness.

But it didn't exactly start out this way. When I was young, I struggled with so many challenges and struggles and didn't know why I was different or what was wrong with me.

Later on, I eventually was labeled with dyslexia and severe ADHD. I refer to these as my learning differences because they forced me to create what I now call the "go-arounds," a unique path through learning and living with these differences.

Back then, I felt unworthy of love and true belonging. Greatness of any kind felt like it was unattainable, and I was in pain and living in total frustration and anger most days.

Eventually, all that pain and frustration actually led me to achieve my hopes and dreams once I stopped trying to hide all my flaws, trying so hard to be perfect, and realized there was real beauty in being me—flaws and all.

When I was struggling and trying to cover up all my cracks and imperfections, I was miserable. The more I tried to be perfect, the more life was a struggle only leading me on the journey of suffering analysis paralysis. It left me feeling defeated and truly miserable.

I didn't even love myself, and I didn't even know you were allowed or supposed to love yourself. So I really wasn't that much fun to be around back then.

Have you ever felt that way? So much pain and suffering you felt bad for who had to be around you?

Well, if you have or if you have not, that is where I was.

Over time with my go-arounds, I discovered that achieving your dreams is about progress over perfection and done is better than just another crazy idea that doesn't get accomplished. When we stay stuck in a self-sabotaging cycle of pursuing endless perfection, we tend to cause ourselves so much harm under the surface and limit our abilities to achieve our dreams.

Let's get started at one of the moments when I started having big dreams.

There I was at my very first hair show, and I was sitting in the audience thinking, *Wow, these people are amazing, and they are talking to me directly. Are they living inside my head? Because I have never shared this stuff with anyone. How do they know everything I'm thinking?* I saw so many famous people in the salon industry doing amazing hair on stage, but for some reason, I really connected with Micheal Cole and Geno Stampora on stage, who at the time I didn't know this, but they were teaching us that anything was possible if we just believed. At just sixteen years old, I knew I was born to be on stage and empower people. I didn't know why I felt this way or how it was going to happen. I just knew with every fiber of my being that I was born for that. I remember thinking, *YES, please I want to do that!* Now I wish I could say that it was in this moment everything changed and I knew my calling and everything was smooth sailing from here. But this is real life, and real life is messy, painful, and filled with jagged edges that take us on a real journey of self-discovery. Right?

So let's get into it. At that time I was always told, "Who the F do you think you are? You are so crazy! You can't do that. You are not good enough! You must be crazy! Did you get dropped on your head? How selfish of you to believe you can do anything like that! What is wrong with you? You are not enough! Women are not allowed to do that. Especially women like you who are not that smart."

Have you been told any of these? As a young woman born with a very big dream and huge ambitions, I was often shamed into thinking I was not worthy of my dreams. The truth is, having big dreams made other people uncomfortable.

Fast-forward to a few years later, I was attending yet again another hair show at the Cleveland Convention Center, and I was asked if I had ever thought about being an educator on stage that teaches hair cutting, coloring, styling, and salon business best practices. Guess what my response was. "Yes, absolutely, every day of my life. Sign me up now!"

I practically attacked the man asking me this question.

When I was young, I never had anyone who really understood or even asked about what I was going through or what life was like for me. It felt like I wasn't even worthy of having an idea an opinion or a voice. So I suffered in silence, shoving down my hopes and dreams because I just didn't believe that I was worthy of them.

When I was asked if I had ever thought about being an educator and speaker on stage, I said yes because my intuition had told me years earlier that I was born for this, but I really had no idea what I was getting myself into.

Guess what happened next. They asked me to audition for a spot on the hair design team.

The audition consisted of five intense days of training where they gave you a four-inch-thick manual and basically said, "Here, you have to memorize everything in this so you can start presenting on stage and teaching people how to use these products, how to grow their business, and how to do better haircuts and grow their color business. You must memorize this and present it on stage tomorrow."

At the time I had a limiting belief that I was not a good reader because my backward reading had gone undetected for so many years. I was petrified and pretty much shaking in my shoes. Enter the person who changed everything about my belief process. My first mentor and teacher Mr. Cary O'Brian saw me and shouted it out for everyone to hear.

"Hey, Tracey, do you have dyslexia?" *Um, what is happening here?* I was mortified and petrified all at the same time. I had been hiding my little secret forever. A few teachers had mentioned it to my parents, but they were so busy. We had so many kids in my family that they just kind of were like, "Oh, she'll be fine." That was actually a good thing because that's how I discovered the go-arounds that helped me discover how to learn in layers of auditory, visual, and practical application. It forced me to focus on people and really study their behaviors.

However, having Cary say this at this moment in front of a room of twenty-five people was mortifying. I felt like I was dying.

Then what he said next was what was actually most important . . . "Wow, you're doing so great, and I really like how you are presenting the material. Keep it up. Everyone else, do what Tracey is doing." *Wait what? Is he really talking to me?*

Daily, as we had to read out loud in front of this room, Cary would say, "Wow, Tracey, you're the youngest one here, and obviously, we've already talked about your learning struggles, and look how great you're doing." Every day when I made a speech and gave my presentation, he referenced how great my speech was and made a comment about how if I could do it, anyone can do it—which has sort of been my anthem for life ever since.

Trust me when I say if I can do it, you, my friend, can do it too!

Cary was the first person I've ever met in my adult life who saw me and the shameful secret I had buried deep and was hiding from the whole world and still believed in me anyway.

So at that moment in time, the twenty-five of us got narrowed down to four of us, and within just a few months, we were down to just one. And guess who that was. Yup, it was me.

I somehow made it through the dark valley of feeling small and unworthy because one person saw something and believed in me.

So even if the world tells you that you can't do something—because let's face it, if you have failed English in the past as I had or if you have been told your whole life that you're not a good writer, singer, speaker, or aren't worthy of speaking because no one cares what you have to say or you're hoping and dreaming of being a great speaker presenting on stage or being a published author and you kind of shove those down—you'll realize there are Carys in the world who crack you open and help you believe that everything you have been dreaming about is actually possible. In a world filled with noise and often so much judgment, we are constantly told to stop dreaming and be realistic. We are told to get real.

I used to beat myself up or believe something was wrong with me because I was always dreaming and I had big dreams and huge visions for what life could be. I loved fairy tales and truly believed in the possibility of happily ever after.

How about you? I consider it my personal mission to help others believe in their dreams even if everyone around them tells them it is not possible. Even if they have silenced and shoved these dreams down for years and years.

Dreams are the secret ingredient for the magical recipe for us to grow and create a life we love and become the absolute best versions of ourselves. Dreams are the cure that keep us going on our darkest days when it seems like we can't take one more step up the mountain of life—carrying all of our baggage of old hurts, tears, fears, and unkind words, and maybe even years of disappointment and letdowns. Dreams that we hold in our hearts give us the energy we need to take one more step up the mountain. Believing in what is possible or what could be is all we've got.

No matter where you are today on your climb up the mountain of life, just start from where you are. No matter what has happened and what past hurts make you feel like you are not enough. Start from where you are. If you haven't dreamed in a while, think of one tiny little thing, like a wish, you would like to happen. It could be the smallest thing, no matter how big or small, and write it down and start from where you are.

If no one in your life has ever believed in you or your dreams, my friend, that changes for you today because you now have me, and I want to be your Cary. I believe in you and the power of your dreams.

Even if we have not met yet, I want you to know I truly believe in you and your dreams.

It is that simple and I just do! You deserve everything you've ever wanted or dreamed of simply because you do. This is your birthright. Your dreams choose you for a reason and when it comes to making your dreams come true in your life and in your business, this is my most favorite thing to help you do.

Helping you turn your dreams into your personal reality—whether it is turning that purpose of your dreams into a profitable business or re-clarifying your life so that you can live in better alignment with your dreams—your passion and your purpose is my core genius, and I am just getting started.

Okay, now we have a dream. Now what? Why do you believe in the power of your dreams?

That is the first step that is actually why I was first attracted to the hair and beauty industry because salon and beauty people were always so happy. I had never experienced any other place on Earth like that—better than Disneyland for me. So if you believe that you deserve to achieve your dreams, that's what will happen for you.

Our standards and how things feel are what we truly achieve. I know that things feel right when I am working from my faith and purpose and expanding and growing in the direction of my dream and when I am helping others do this too. It feels as though I'm completely filled with all the god bumps (that is what I call goosebumps) and absolutely exhilaratingly living my absolute best life.

Once Cary showed up for me in a real genuine way and absolutely believed that anything was possible for me, it allowed me to create space and allow so many other hopes and dreams to come to fruition in my life. Accepting that I am guided by God's hand and the universal higher power is always protecting me and leading me in the direction that is best for me and the greater good of all who I have been called to serve is truly me living in pure alignment with my purpose and my mission here on this Earth.

Once I surrender to the idea that things are exactly as they were meant to be, the real magic of dreams coming true actually happens. Even when your current life and circumstances send you on a detour, you will discover more blessings and gifts beyond your imagination and a whole new way of dreaming bigger than you ever thought possible when you believe that you are absolutely worthy.

When we quiet the mind enough to enjoy our breath and our beating heart, we are guided by divinely trusting our own intuition and inner call to go within and experience life in peace and joy no matter what is happening in the outer world. Everything falls into place when we choose inner peace and wellness. The outside world doesn't matter. Loving your life, what you do and how you contribute to the world, is the path that allows us to achieve our dreams from a place of knowing all is well and good within us and within the world.

When I believed it was possible and had the correct recipe, everything worked out in my life and business. That alone with no action will not help you achieve your dreams. Action without intention and true belief that you are worthy and everything is possible will not produce the result you're looking for. Only when you combine a positive mindset, true belief, and knowing that you are absolutely worthy along with the purposeful action and a success strategy and recipe will your dreams come to be.

Once I realized all of this, I realized I had been dreaming too small, though I had achieved quite a bit of success to the outside world. But I still had been suffering unfulfilled and feeling like part of my heart was missing. Once I realized I was called to serve a bigger purpose to help more people than I could from just inside my salon, that's when I sold it, started the Beyond Common Success Coaching and training company, created the Beyond Common Success method, and started speaking and writing because my dream of helping over ten million women achieve the life and business of their dreams was not gonna happen until I started sharing my passion, my purpose, and my story with everyone.

If you're feeling called to do something bigger and follow your dreams, I would love your help to spread the message so we can help ten million women together. If you have a dream in your heart that has been silenced and shoved down for far too long, I would love to be your Cary—the person in your corner who really believes in you and encourages you to follow your dreams and pursue your passions. We only have one life to live, and your time is NOW!

A great first step is to sign up for a Beyond Common Success Essentials training to help you get really clear and really present on where you are and where you want to go. I would love to help you believe in the power of your dreams and help you turn them into your new reality.

With love and gratitude,

Tracey Watts Cirino

This story is about my very first mentor, Mr. Cary O'Brien, who believed in me and saw something special in me when I didn't even know what that meant. There were so many times I wanted to quit and give up, and he encouraged me to keep pursuing my dreams no matter what. He has touched my heart and positively impacted so many lives in the hair and beauty industry and beyond, and I just wanted to honor him in this very special way. To pay tribute to his wife Talisa O'Brien and their four beautiful daughters Sydney, Mia, Chloe, and Isabel so that they know that even in passing, his legacy will forever live on because of all the lives he touched. My life and my purpose were positively impacted when I meet someone who believed in me and that is why I believe in you and the power of your dreams with such passion and conviction because knowing that just one person believes in us makes a world of difference that cannot be measured. It can only be treasured and paid forward by the lives that we have the honor and privilege to impact.

It is my hope that Cary's amazing legacy will live on forever by honoring him here forever in my story for Women Who Dream! Keep Dreaming!

TRACEY WATTS CIRINO

#1 International Bestselling Author and Speaker, podcast host of Beyond Common Business Secrets. As a thought leader, and unshakable optimist dedicated to helping you get out of your own way so you can become the person you most want to be. She is a former award-winning salon owner and most sought-after color transformation expert turned business success coach and strategist. As an all-in, no BS, passionate female business success coach and speaker Tracey loves doing keynotes, hosting retreats, training workshops, masterminds, and lighting up the stage to deliver her Beyond Common Success message of Hope & Possibility. She is Certified in the Canfield Success Principles, John C. Maxwell Certified Speaker, Coach, and Trainer as well as Tony Robbins Business Mastery.

She launched her hairstylist career as a stage artist who worked alongside the salon industry's most iconic teachers when she was just 19 years old. Tracey's business, Lavish Color Salon, is a 7-time winner of Salon Today Magazine's top 200 awards. Tracey then sold Lavish Color Salon to follow her passion and focus full-time on helping motivated business owners align their purpose with their passion and business. Beyond Common Success Coaching and Training, Co. was born and now we get to help more business owners and leaders achieve success and live the life of their dreams. Tracey is a Cleveland, OH native who enjoys a hike or cooking with her kids and her husband with their dog Rocky right at their heels.

To connect with Tracey:

Web: www.TraceyWattsCirino.com/dreambig
Facebook: Tracey Watts Cirino
Instagram: @traceywattscirino
LinkedIn: TraceyWattsCirino
TikTok: @traceywattscirino

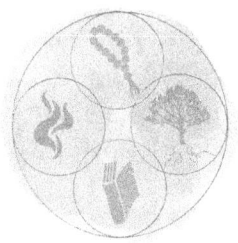

LIVING MY DREAM THROUGH THE FEAR

Ellen M. Craine

"Don't be pushed around by the fears in your mind. Be led by the dreams in your heart."

—Roy T. Bennett

M y eighteen-year-old son, Michael, is a pediatric cancer thriver, diagnosed at age eleven. I am not naïve enough to think that we are among the lucky. In the beginning, I felt fear at everything my son endured. I felt fear over whether he would survive the treatments, let alone the cancer. We were fortunate to incorporate integrative medicine, including mistletoe therapy, into my son's treatment plan. I believe, as do his doctors, that it helped him have fewer complications and bounce back more quickly from his chemotherapy. We still have anxiety with every "major" symptom my son has. I am eternally grateful for my son's medical team and their remaining presence to support us on this journey and help us navigate through these challenges.

I do not wish this journey on anyone, regardless of prognosis. I feel the fear and anxiety, but in my heart, I also dream of a world where integrative medicine is available for all pediatric patients and their families as an adjunct to conventional medicine if they want it. Perhaps this is my way of coming to terms with being a pediatric cancer mom. I do not know. What I do know is that I feel a passion or excitement in my gut and heart when I think about helping other families navigate their cancer journey. I try to focus on this dream and not my fear about my son's potential for relapsing or developing another cancer as we navigate "normal" illnesses or symptoms that may crop up.

I strongly believe families should have integrative medicine available to them without the barrier of finances. Juggling finances when you have a sick family member is a given unless you can afford to take time off work, have a great support system, and the list goes on. It has become a passion of mine to provide resources to my son's outpatient team through education so they can offer these services to other children and their families. To support this dream, my family has established a fund at my son's treating hospital, Beaumont Children's Hospital in Royal Oak, Michigan. Michael's doctor has discretion to use this fund to help children get integrative medicine consultations with the naturopathic oncologist at the hospital. The fund is set up to even help pay for some of the services that may become part of a child's treatment plan.

There are now salt lamps and essential oil diffusers in each outpatient pediatric private infusion room. To my son's doctor's credit, she did fellowship training through a program put on by Beaumont Hospital. I am honored because she has shared that I was a big influence in her decision to take this training and to make some changes in the way things are handled in the outpatient setting for her patients. I was fortunate enough to be a guest lecturer on two different occasions discussing oncology.

It is my dream and passion to continue this work supporting those who want guidance and need help with where to look for a complementary approach to healing emotionally and physically, regardless of prognosis from a pediatric cancer diagnosis. I do not wish this journey on anyone, but having lived through it, and being a social worker, I am uniquely qualified to provide coaching and support to someone who wants it. I believe it is a higher power within me that allows me to push through and toward this dream of helping others on their journey. I can honestly say that I may not know exactly how someone feels or what their specific journey is like for them, but I can share my experiences and my journey.

About two years after Michael's journey began, and just when we thought we would start to be living a more "normal" life, my husband, Marty, was diagnosed with Stage IV inoperable glioblastoma. He died April 26, 2016, six weeks after his diagnosis. Admittedly, I am not sure I have found my passion or dream around this one. It was definitely harder to navigate the medical system when it comes to integrative medicine. I still struggle to know why the Universe has "gifted" me and my sons with this challenge. I imagine that will eventually come to me. What I do know is that my passion to make the world a better place for my family and others has not died. I am grateful for that. Maybe that passion is enough of a takeaway from Marty's death. Time will tell.

Moving forward five and a half years later, I thought my sons and I were finally gaining some peace in our life. This did not eliminate the grief we each felt with Marty's absence, or the anxiety with every challenge Michael faced, but we slowly started to feel that we could have dreams for our lives and move toward them.

Halloween weekend, 2020, everything started to change. I found a lump in my left breast. Admittedly, I may have felt something smaller a couple of weeks before but minimized the whole thing. Somewhere deep in my gut, I knew it was cancer.

The next week, I saw my gynecologist, had my mammogram and ultrasound, then a biopsy the following Monday. The results came in. I had Stage II breast cancer, invasive ductile carcinoma. I would be looking at a treatment plan that included eighteen rounds of chemotherapy, surgery of some kind, and possible radiation. I was overwhelmed, to say the least, and could not imagine how I would get through everything. Keep in mind, this was all during COVID, and I had to navigate this on my own—no one could come to appointments. Marty was not there to support me. I have friends, and some excellent ones at that, but that is not the same as having a significant other who can hold and comfort you any time of the day or night.

Additional testing and meetings with a breast surgeon and oncologist followed. Following an MRI, one of the last pieces needed before surgery, a Stage 0 cancer was found in my right breast. By Thanksgiving, I had a port placed in my chest to receive my chemotherapy every twenty-one days until what felt like forever. I could not believe what was happening. The good news appeared to be that there were no lymph nodes on either side that were affected. At this point, I had already had six rounds of chemotherapy with lots of side effects.

I began seeing my treatment in phases. All the testing was one phase. There were a lot of ups and downs throughout this process for me and my kids. I (and we) survived that! My initial six rounds of chemotherapy with the harshest drugs I would be given was another phase. This was very difficult for my twenty-two-year-old, who had already been through so much losing his dad and dealing with his brother's cancer. Matthew now had to be a caregiver for me and his brother while going to school at home, online, during the pandemic.

Surgery was my next phase. My surgeon was recommending a double mastectomy. I was having a hard time wrapping my head around this news. On the one hand, I understood where she was coming from with both breasts being affected by a different type of cancer. On the other hand, a double mastectomy? I hoped I could just have a double lumpectomy and breast reduction at the same time.

One question remained, and it was a big one: did I have any gene mutations that gave me a pre-disposition to breast cancer? This was a concern since my dad had had pancreatic cancer diagnosed at the age of eighty-two, and his mother was diagnosed with breast cancer when she was sixty-three. There is no known family history of ovarian cancer. I was fearful of finding out I had a gene mutation, not fully understanding the power it would give me if I did. I prayed I was negative and could have the surgery I really wanted. I asked the Universe to guide me to make the best decision for me and my sons.

The genetic testing process included a phone consultation (due to the challenges of COVID) with the genetics counselor and a blood test. After a couple of weeks, I learned that I was BRCA1 and BRCA2 (the most commonly known gene mutations) negative! I was thrilled. Then, the genetics counselor shared that they found I have a newer gene mutation called PALB2. Wait, what? This gene mutation had only been tested for since around 2014–2015. It is linked to pancreatic, breast, and ovarian cancer in women. There is a link with this gene mutation for pancreatic and breast cancer in men as well.

According to the PALB2 interest group, with this gene mutation, there is a 13 to 21 percent chance of breast cancer by the age of fifty and a 44 to 63 percent chance of breast cancer in cisgender females by the age of eighty. For cisgender males, the chance of breast cancer is less than 1 percent by the age of fifty and around 1 percent by the age of eighty. In the cisgender population, there is a 12 percent chance of breast cancer for females over our lifetime. By the age of eighty, people have around a 5 percent chance of getting ovarian cancer and around 2 to 3 percent chance of getting pancreatic cancer with this gene mutation. Cisgender females have an approximate 2 percent chance of getting pancreatic cancer without the gene mutation. At this time, there is no known increased risk for prostate cancer or colon cancer for anyone.[1]

Following my double mastectomy, I learned there was no

1— PALB2 Interest Group, "About the PALB2 gene," PALB2.org, accessed June 28, 2022, www.palb2.org/about-the-palb2-gene/.

cancer in the tissue analyzed. In addition, all of my lymph nodes removed out of an abundance of caution were also negative for cancer. I did not need radiation. So grateful! Finishing my eighteen rounds of chemotherapy December 9, 2021, was the end of another phase in my journey!

It will have been eighteen months since my journey with breast cancer began by the time this chapter is published. One takeaway from this first year of being a cancer patient is that knowledge is power. Getting a cancer diagnosis is scary, but do not give up on your dreams and passions for your life. Learning all you can about your family history and genetic predisposition can be a big help in treatment planning. It may even be lifesaving.

In my breast cancer journey, I incorporate a lot of complementary medicine into my self-care. I learned and did as much as I could before I was diagnosed and continued to do so during treatment. I honestly believe that in spite of all the challenges during treatment, I did as well as I did because of what I did. I am confident that I did not cause my cancer; I was just more susceptible to it because of my genetic makeup. However, I believe in my heart that taking control of my life the best I can is important. It is about even taking just five percent more responsibility each day for my life. For me, this means taking supplements, making sure I am drinking enough water, getting adequate sleep, meditating, exercising, eating as healthy as I can, journaling, asking for help when I need to (something I am learning how to do), having a positive mindset, participating in personal growth training, seeing a therapist, and, yes, giving myself mistletoe injections.

The adult cancer world is harder to navigate than the pediatric cancer world. My dream/passion is to make this world a little easier to navigate by being a coach, educator, and support person for those who want it. I hope by sharing my journey and educating others about the importance of knowing family history and our genetics, I am making a positive impact on at least one person's life.

I am lucky to be looking at my life from the other side of a cancer diagnosis. As I do that, I see helping others on their journey as a piece of my journey moving forward. I believe in the importance of facilitating and having authentic conversations with others on these difficult topics is the key to moving forward in life in a more positive way. I provide individual and family support, so reach out if you need help facilitating these authentic conversations with yourself or with family members or friends. I can be reached at ellen@crainecounseling.com.

I have made an agreement with myself, my children, and others, that I will be around on this earth for at least another thirty years. First and foremost, that is my dream and passion regardless of all the others. I intend to do everything within my power to make that agreement become reality. A good friend of mine shared a message she received from my husband when I was diagnosed, and I still carry it with me today. It said, "I am the captain of my ship." I believe that I am and that we all can be. I look forward to helping you figure out how to be the captain of your own ship.

For more information about mistletoe therapy, visit www.believebig.org.

ABOUT ELLEN M. CRAINE

Ellen M. Craine is in private practice as a licensed clinical and macro social worker in the state of Michigan. She owns Craine Counseling and Consulting Group and has over twenty-five years of experience working with couples, families, groups, and individuals in a variety of capacities.

Ellen M. Craine is an effective trainer and educator. She teaches a variety of continuing education classes around ethics for social workers, including informed consent and telehealth, subpoenas, loss and grief, custody and co-parenting issues, and success principles for social workers and others. You can see a full list of her offerings and upcoming events on her website at www.crainecounseling.com.

Ellen M. Craine had her master's degree in social work from the University of Michigan. [CC1] [e2] [e3] In addition, she has a certificate from the Institute of Integrative Nutrition in Health Coaching and is a certified trainer in Jack Canfield's Success Principles.

Ellen M. Craine is a #1 International Bestselling Author in *Women Who Empower*, the seventh book in the Impact Book Series with Kate Butler.

Ellen M. Craine is a co-associate producer of the documentary, *Authentic Conversations: Deep Talk with the Masters*. This documentary is the first in the documentary series and is written, directed, and produced by LA Emmy nominated Dr. Angela Sadler Williamson.

You can learn more about Ellen M. Craine on her website: www.crainecounseling.com

Facebook group: Living through Loss and Grief
Facebook page: Craine Counseling and Consulting Group
LinkedIn: Ellen Craine
Email: ellen@crainecounseling.com

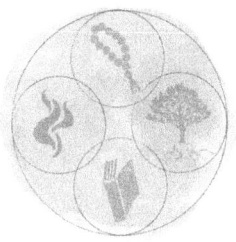

DAYDREAM BELIEVER

Addy M. Kujawa, CAE, DES

"To achieve your dreams, work is required. Suffering is optional."

—Jack Canfield

I grew up in a small, small town. The same town my parents, and their parents, had lived their entire lives. I dreamed of leaving and living in some far-off, distant place. I wanted to be rich and live big and large and loud, and I knew that wasn't going to happen in my little town in Wisconsin.

It was a beautiful, sunny, summer day, and my mom and I were going garage-saleing! I was excited because we were looking for new clothes for my new middle school. I had to move schools, and I was leaving my good friends behind, but it was all right because they were all just a short walk away. The new school was bigger and had art and band and even a real wood shop. I was going to take classes to learn how to cook and bake and sew and make notepads, and I was so excited. We found a beautiful blue dress with flowers and ruffles along with a few other things, and we headed home. I was happy and ready.

Standing at my locker on my first day, I fumbled with the combination. It was the first time I'd had to use a locker, and

I was worried I was going to be late to my first class. I looked around to see kids heading to classes.

To my left, there was a beautiful blonde girl watching me. I smiled quickly and got back to my locker. I heard her call out to me, so I turned to look at her again. She said, "Hey, where'd you get that dress anyway?"

Immediate panic. I was not going to tell her I got it at a garage sale. "Penney's!" I shouted.

She stared at me. Her head tilted and her arms crossed and a smile slowly crept across her face, and she said, "Oh, I don't think so. I think you got that at my garage sale."

And I was crushed. Mortified. Why did I say anything at all? What an idiot! And of course, of course, she had to call me out. Why am I so stupid? Why do I have to be here? I want to go back to my old school. At least everyone there knew what was going on. They knew my family's situation. I went about my day and noticed stares and whispers and laughter. How did everyone hear about it so quickly? There's nothing I could do. I had to keep going, walking through long hallways and sitting through even longer classes. I set my jaw, feeling naked and embarrassed and like I just wanted to hide.

That winter, I was walking home from school one day, and I was so cold and my backpack was so heavy, and on top of that, I was lugging my tenor saxophone home for practice. I walked looking down at the ground for the most part, occasionally looking up when crossing streets. As I crossed the next street, I saw in the distance a thin figure all dressed in black standing at the bus stop. I had a moment to decide whether I was going to turn left or continue on my way which would take me right past him. I looked to my left, and it's uphill. I couldn't do it. I was already loaded down and so tired. I kept going. I thought it would be fine.

As I got closer, I saw he was watching me. And as I got closer, he just kept watching me. *Do I turn around?* I couldn't get any distance because of the snow piled along the sidewalk. I kept going. Trudging. He started to make comments. "Hey, pretty girl." "Hey, girlie, whatchyou carrying?" "You look nice." "Wanna keep me company?" I kept going. *Why is it taking so long? Why can't my legs move any faster?*

And then I heard it. The worst sound in the world. His throat scraped and then he was spitting, and I felt it land in my hair with a soft but weighty thump. *Ohmygodohmygodohmygod. He. Spit. In. My. Hair. What do I do? What can I do?* I kept going. I hunched over further, hunkering down into my coat even more, hiding as best I could. *Keep going, keep going, keep going, keep going.* I was so angry and so hurt and the tears streaming down my face froze in place and I felt all alone.

Left. Right. Left. Right. And he was hollering at me, but he wasn't coming after me and that's all I cared about. I kept going and eventually I got home. My mom was furious. She wanted to kill him. I just wanted it out of my hair. It was frozen and I didn't want to touch it. I headed to the kitchen, dropping things as I went until I could lean my head into the kitchen sink and run warm water through my hair and keep running warm water until I felt certain it wasn't there anymore and I could scrub and scrub it out. *It's so gross. I'm so gross. Of course I deserve this.* I was bottom of the barrel at my new school. I was the odd duck.

Feelings of worthlessness, fear, loneliness, and desperation for external validation began there and followed me.

The next summer my family went on a trip to Chicago with my aunt and uncle and their kids. We visited a restaurant . . . Ed Debevic's. That was a magical experience for me. Why? Well, at this particular restaurant, the wait staff are rude. Like, really rude. Throwing straws, snarky comments, smart-ass replies to questions. As a kid, to see my parents and my aunts and uncles talked to that way was shocking! And funny! And then, at one point, the entire wait staff got up on all the countertops and the ledges between the seating areas and rocked out—dancing to a song. The entire restaurant was engaged in the performance, and in that moment, I knew I was going to live there one day. People that lived here lived the way they wanted to; they talked the way they wanted to. At that age, I imagined everyone in Chicago must be like this and so that became my dream. To live in Chicago and be free.

I went back home, went to school, graduated, and got married. I agreed to move to an even smaller town if we would eventually move to a bigger city. After four years and still no move, among other things, we parted ways. I took a year to get myself back to rights, and then I made my first big leap. The first time I really felt like I was showing up for myself, and I was going to do what I wanted to do, and nobody was going to tell me otherwise or get in my way.

I had a month to get everything squared away to attend the University of Madison. Due to my divorce and my own fears and embarrassment, I couldn't get the financial aid to work out. With the prospect of college dwindling and the rent coming due, I applied at all the temp agencies I could find and took any job I could fit into my schedule. My sister suggested a part-time job at her favorite restaurant, Noodles and Company, if they offered free meals to employees like many restaurants did. I applied and began as a busser so I could eat. She was right, a free meal every shift! I worked really hard, and was eventually promoted to manager, and was able to quit my other temporary jobs. Except for Kohl's—the deals on clothes and shoes I was privy to while working returns at the service counter were too good to pass up, so I continued to pick up shifts there.

I worked six days a week at the restaurant, and they were long shifts. I hired so many college kids. I fired someone for the first time and the second time. I caught kids drinking on the job. I started smoking just to get a break. I picked up shifts at the other restaurant that was downtown. I scrubbed the ins and outs of freezers and storage lofts and disgusting coolers. I mopped floors and plunged toilets. I opened up the restaurant so the grease traps could be emptied. That smell sticks with you; it is beyond anything I had ever experienced up until that time—and I grew up in farm country.

I loved working in the restaurant industry. After about two years, one of my best team members and friend told me she had been offered a job in college after graduation. I bemoaned the fact that I would never get there, sad to be left behind, and she blithely responded with "Why don't you come along? I could use a roommate!"

I canceled my lease and moved in with another friend to finish out my notice. While apartment hunting in Chicago, we found an absolutely perfect unit in a building on the north side. Close to the lake, on the rooftop level with a pool, outdoor access, two bedrooms, and our own patio. Located just a couple blocks from the "L," it was convenient to most anywhere in the city. We put down a deposit, and moving day was set.

I applied to temp agencies and restaurants. The first place I applied? Ed Debevic's of course! I was brought in for two interviews but didn't get the job. Devastating at the time. I was eventually offered an administrative assistant position with a nonprofit and I grabbed it. It wasn't what I wanted at all—the role, the salary, or the location. But it would pay the bills, and I would be able to eat, barely, so I took it.

I had a demanding, visionary boss and a huge workload. I loved what I was doing though. I worked hard. Between being afraid of disappointing or upsetting my boss and wanting and needing validation and the thrill of success, I would sometimes go in at 8:00 a.m. on Monday morning and work all the way through until 5:00 or 6:00 p.m. on Tuesday. Through the night, yes. Exhausted, I would go home and sleep, just to repeat that for Wednesday and Thursday. I knew most of the security guards from arriving early morning, leaving so late at night, and all my weekend treks into the building. I was driven and passionate and wanted more. I was in the Big City, but barely making ends meet.

After several years and two promotions, my manager was let

go. I was already helping out with those responsibilities and helped write the position description for a new hire. Handing in the finished document, the head of the department said to me, "Don't even think about going up for this job. The CEO will never consider you because you don't have a degree." I hadn't actually even considered going up for it, so I was completely blindsided. I turned around, embarrassed, and walked out. During my commute home that evening, my face was hot, tears flowed, and I struggled to shake the embarrassment. Those feelings evolved into frustration, and then anger. Suddenly I was yelling to myself, "Why not me?! I'm already doing a lot of it! I am so good enough!"

At home that night, I opened up my laptop and updated my cover letter and resume to match the position description I had finished earlier that day, and I submitted it to HR. I was sick with anxiety for days, but then my boss interviewed me. And then, I got the job! I continued to work hard and had the longest tenure in the department.

I always had of goal of making, and then continuing to make, twice my age in salary, so when I was thirty, I wanted to be making $60,000 and so on. I was getting close to that not happening, and I knew that any further promotions or career moves would require a bachelor's degree. I had been told often that the manager role I had earned was the last one I would be able to get based on experience only. I had earned my associate's after high school but had opted out of any further education at that time to get into the workforce as quickly as possible. I had taken a class here and there as I could but was still a year and a half away from fulfilling the credits I needed. It was always in the back of my mind, and then I had my first baby, and then my second.

Home with my second baby, on maternity leave, I decided now was the time to jump back into my degree and get it done. I'm not sure why I expected to have extra time while on maternity leave considering I hadn't had any with my first baby and I could only take seven weeks. I got it in my mind though, and so I filed all the paperwork and started classes.

I took class after class after class with very few breaks to finish as quickly as possible. I did finish and began applying for my next big role: my first lead staff position! I was terrified but determined. I interviewed for many roles and lost many roles. Eventually though, I was offered the lead role for an organization that had three staff, and I was absolutely thrilled. I've been there for twelve extremely rewarding years.

I think back to that young girl often with her big dream and her struggle with her self-worth. A short story allows for only so much to be shared, and I shared two of my most poignant memories out of hundreds that took a toll on me growing up. Just as you have many, I'm sure. All the things that happen in a person's life and the things you have overcome to be where you are. They matter and they are meaningful. And I also feel strongly that while they are meaningful, your past absolutely does not dictate your future.

Whatever dream you are dreaming, let it bloom and blossom in your heart and soul. Napoleon Hill said in his book, "Whatever your mind can conceive and believe, it can achieve."[1] **Your** mind. Not your mom's or your dad's or your sister's or your wife's or your husband's mind. Yours. You are the most important component of that sentence. It doesn't matter what others think or how they feel. It only matters what you believe and think and feel. Believe in you and your dream and work for it. Make them come true. That's what I did. And so can you.

> *"Make a conscious effort to surround yourself with positive, nourishing, and uplifting people—people who believe in you, encourage you to go after your dreams, and applaud your victories."* —Jack Canfield

---

1—Napoleon Hill, Think and Grow Rich (Meriden, Connecticut: The Ralston Society, 1937)

ABOUT ADDY M. KUJAWA, CAE, DES

With over twenty years of executive leadership for professional associations and organizations, Addy is today the CEO of the American Alliance of Orthopedic Executives as well as The Radical Change Group. She is a certified Jack Canfield Success Principles trainer, certified association executive, and certified digital event strategist.

In addition to her job, she has been a frequent speaker presenting on a variety of topics including personal branding, strategic planning, how to sell, how to negotiate, creating your true life destination roadmap, getting from where you are to where you want to be, goal setting that actually works, and much more.

She considers herself a personal and professional development junkie, constantly learning and trying new things.

Addy, as a consummate cheerleader and creator of safe places, has a life purpose to share with others her transformation of her life's events, from tragic and tragedy to appreciation and fulfillment, in hopes of inspiring and motivating them to see new possibilities and to believe in pursuing their own dreams.

To book Addy as a speaker or to work with her, you can contact her directly using the information below.

Web: theradicalchangegroup.com
Email: addykujawa@theradicalchangegroup.com
Mobile: 847-624-2339
Facebook: TheRadicalChangeGroup
Instagram: @theradicalchangegroup

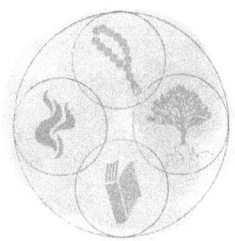

THIS IS *NOT* HOW MY STORY ENDS

Christina Macro

My life began in turmoil, literally. When my mother was eight months pregnant with me, she fell down a flight of stairs into our unfinished basement through the bulkhead door so prevalent of the tiny Cape Cod cottage-style homes of the neighborhood in which we lived. She tossed me around in her belly all the way down ten stairs, then landed on the cold cement floor where she passed out. My father found her when he arrived home from work while my older brother screamed bloody murder in his crib. It was a scene from a tragic movie, thankfully without the tragic ending. My mom told me that story much later in life on one of our girl's week trips to Antigua, and she told me that it was that day that she knew I would be special. When I was born, she said she looked in my eyes and called me her little fighter.

We grew up poor. I mean dirt poor. My mom was a single mother raising four kids on a hairdresser "salary." She survived on tips, her income each year teetered around $16,000 a year. With that, she paid the mortgage, utilities, and fed four kids. With a little over a thousand dollars a month, it is a total miracle that we all survived. We learned to be thankful for the basic things in life like heat and a roof over our head. There were no frills in our family, and as the only girl, I wore my brothers' hand-me-downs, from their sneakers to their underwear. I would pretend to be sick on gym days because I imagined the self-inflicted horror and embarrassment that would come with my changing into gym clothes in the girls' locker room. I had nightmares every night before gym days that all the girls would discover me sporting my brother's tighty-whities. I remember not being able to participate in class trips or events because my mother just could not afford the additional expense. I would pretend that I simply forgot the permission slip rather than admit that my family was poor and having heat was a higher priority than my taking class field trips. The number of days I spent in the supervised homeroom crying because I could not participate outweighed the number of days that I felt a sense of belonging.

Even in my mother's belly, I experienced firsthand the cycle of being knocked down and dragged through the mud to pull myself up by the bootstraps, dust myself off, and search for ways to see the good, remain positive, and just be happy. I mean, after all, I was a product of a terrible fall in utero and I survived that—what could possibly be worse? I knew that I had this internal strength, and it was inherent in me. It was. It just was.

When I graduated from high school, I had this burning desire to get far away from home to go and conquer the world. I wanted so much for myself, and I knew that the only person who could get me there was the person staring back at me in the mirror. And off I went to the world before me. No matter what lay ahead, I wanted to have a positive impact on my life and in the world. I had big dreams for myself without the means, the tools, the financial support, nor mental capacity to create the path . . . and so it was. Throwing caution to the wind, off I went to conquer my dreams. *Broadway, here I come!*

And not even six years after graduating from high school with a dream in my heart and a skewed vision for sight, there I was stuffed in the bottom of the life barrel of tragic events, failing miserably while digging my way up and out. I never went to college—I got married young and had a baby instead. Now without my son's father to support me and him, I landed on my own father's doorstep with his new family. With my eighteen-month-old baby and the contents of our life that fit in a rented passenger van, I had not a pot to piss in nor a window to throw it out of. To say that I was at my most vulnerable is an understatement. My father took me in without question. I was in enormous financial debt from mounting medical bills for my son's health issues. I was wet, cold, tired, hungry, and desperate for a way out of the mess I was in at the tender age of twenty-three. I was frantically searching for answers to a life that continued to hand me lemons with no way to make lemonade.

After moving in with my father and his family in Syracuse, I started a career as a waitress in the hotel industry. I worked three jobs when my son was a baby; yes, three. I would take the bus to a law firm during the day and work there opening files and answering phones, get back on the bus home after my day job, kiss my son, have some dinner, and change for my night job as a waitress. And on the weekends, I bartended.

This was not the life I dreamed of. Not in any way, shape, or form. I was living the *furthest* from my dreams. Sad, lonely, alone, longing for love, longing to belong, wishing I fit in, trying to care for a sick child, trying to earn a living. Trying to dig myself out emotionally; I didn't know where I belonged in the world, but I knew it was not at the bottom of that barrel.

I was broken, bruised, lifeless, and living. Barely. But I never stopped believing in me. I knew in my heart that my life experiences at that point were building a foundation for me. A foundation for greatness.

Cesare Pavese once was quoted to say, "We don't remember days, we remember moments."[1] I recall vividly the moment I

1—Cesare Pavese, Goodreads quotes, accessed June 28, 2022, https://www.goodreads.com/quotes/329380-we-do-not-remember-days-we-remember-moments-the-richness.

packed my life in the back seat of my sportscar for a promotion in Washington, DC. This was four years after I had landed on my father's doorstep. I had worked my way up the corporate ladder in the hotel world; I was on my way to an executive position with a hotel in a major metro market. I drove down the GW Parkway from upstate New York and watched with childhood wonder as I drove by iconic monuments like Arlington Cemetery and the Washington Monument. I had arrived. I was in the big city, and my next chapter, filled with hope and expectation, had finally begun. I had picked myself up and brushed myself off. I felt like I was finally advancing my dreams as I had intended. Somehow, in my mind, I knew that my dreams were about creating a life for my son that was in complete contrast to my childhood.

I worked in the hotel industry for ten years, I hit the proverbial glass ceiling set as high as possible for a woman without a degree. I went back to school and earned my network engineering certifications, then off I went to the IT industry; I spent two years working my way up *that* corporate ladder and achieving titles and benefits that small-town girls without a degree could only fathom. We hit the dot-com boom, and I was without a job. I went back to school, this time obtaining my real estate license.

I can clearly recall my first day at my first brokerage. We were in a training class and the instructor asked everyone to go around the room and share their first-year vision in their new career. Each agent stood up and said things like "I want to help people" or "I love houses" or "I want to learn how the industry works." I was the very last person in the entire room of over fifty new agents to speak. I stood up with all the conviction of a seasoned real estate veteran and said, "I am going to sell ten million dollars my first year." I will never forget the look on the instructor's face as her eyes rolled almost completely back in her head. She asked me why I had this particular dream. And with all the clarity in the world, I said, "Look, I don't want to sell real estate for the money. I want to sell real estate because I want to advocate for people and teach them what the home-buying/home-selling experience should be and what an agent's role is in a real estate transaction. But let's be clear here, I am not independently wealthy, and frankly, I don't even know how I'll afford my first year in business. But I do know this: I have a vision for myself, and I know that if I focus on being the best agent I can be *for* my clients, then the money will follow." Again, she rolled her eyes. I settled almost $10M my first year. I moved on in that industry to earn awards and accolades galore.

Excellence, it seemed, was within my grasp. This financial vision was fostered from my desire to provide a lifestyle for my son that *I* only ever visualized. I finally had the ability to control my own destiny—as my father said to me, "The harder I work, the luckier I get." And I knew in that moment that even without the degrees or the family coat of arms, I *could* get myself places and sail past the industry statistics. I was the one percent.

In my ten years in production, I created financial stability for the first time in my life for me and my son. And then the real estate crash happened. It was about that time that I grasped the reality that I had been living a lifestyle no one could sustain long term. Earning a six-figure income and saving only a fraction meant that when the market crashed, I also faced a financial crisis. And again, I was looking at life through the bottom of the life barrel trying to, once again, dig my way up and out. My 401(k) went from stable to abominable. I started to blow through savings at an alarming rate to maintain my lifestyle. I started to live on credit. And I was sinking quickly. I was crashing hard and fast alongside the real estate market. I had to change course. I found myself once again in survival mode and forging a trail with rewritten dreams consisting of a new career path. I was still focused on my son and ways to build a life for him. My dreams were still about him and ways I could provide for him financially and emotionally.

So, having the foresight to see what was happening in the market, I earned my broker's license and started to hit the streets to advance my career in leadership. I had missed leadership, so the timing was perfect. I was offered a position as a managing broker with a steady salary, benefits, and a more stable schedule. By this time, my son was in his first year in college and I was paying in full for his education. I got down to brass tacks, built a budget, started selling off things, reduced my lifestyle, gave up the shopping trips, repurposed everything, and paid all my debts. Every last one. And I learned how to live within my means, save, balance, and reduce to a lifestyle focused on needs versus wants while staying committed to supporting my son's almost-adult life.

Once I pieced myself back together from the real estate crash and a terrible divorce, I rebuilt my life, got myself stable, and did everything to continue to focus on my son's stability. It was when he earned his MBA and moved to Chicago with his girlfriend that I began to unravel. And unravel I did, slowly and without any indication of the pain and hurt of being knocked down that was the history of my life experience.

They say that sons are your sons until they marry their wife. This realization hit me hard. It was unfolding before my eyes. I spent my life focused on providing for him. From the moment that child was born, my dreams were actually dreams for his happiness. While this was not necessarily intentional, it was real. Palpable. And who I became. Every day of my life was intensely fixated on ensuring his happiness. Until he left. Without warning and without an ounce of preparation for the thick wall of sadness about to smack me upside the head, he was gone.

When you live your life in a space where your dreams are built around fighting hard every day to provide a lifestyle far removed from your own, it is a fall from grace that can only be described as a poignant and perceptual free fall from a hundred-story building. Sadly, the free fall is one that moves slowly and deliberately in a way that you don't feel until you land on the cement in a million tiny pieces with no emotional glue to put yourself back together.

The year 2016 was the year that began this free fall for me. It was a year. I was fired from my job. Two weeks later, my mom quickly and unexpectedly died. And two months later, my son got married. I suffered losses at the hands of life and God; my coping mechanisms were on overdrive from July of that year. My internal mechanisms were working against me. My body began the debilitating process of dealing with depression and loneliness. I found myself stressed nonstop. I was dealing with the financial burden of my mother dying alongside the emotional trauma of my entire life purpose being stripped from me. All in a matter of weeks.

Just when I got my act together and was ready to heal over the loss of my mother, my father up and died. This went on for another year . . . loss, sadness, depression, grief.

The day after my father died, I laid in bed looking at the ceiling of my bedroom. For the first time in a long time, I cried. I don't cry. I internalize just like my mother. I breathe. I focus forward. I walk, I read. I listen to others. I volunteer. I escape the internal demons. But on this day, I cried. I begged for forgiveness for whatever I had done in my past leading to this intense sadness. I begged karma to back off. I begged my father to stop being mad at the life he chose. I prayed that my mother would not be mad for decisions I made. I cried for the loss of my son. I cried for all the events in my life that required me to be strong. I prayed for strength. I wished for angels to watch over me. I prayed for forgiveness like I had never prayed before.

I wanted clarity and to be whole. For one fucking time in my life. Once. To not deal with being kicked in the teeth. To just have a day without sadness and grief. I was tired of suffering. And tired of suffering at the hands of others.

That very morning, and for the first time in over three years, I stripped myself naked and stepped on the scale. I thought I was seeing things. I had gained almost 100 pounds during the turmoil that was my life. I could hardly breathe when I stepped on and off the scale a number of times hoping that it was just another event in my life that was unreal.

When they say life is a series of ups and downs, I believed it that morning. I reflected on my life to that point and knew that my life was a series of gut punches that required me to reach deep within to get back up. As I stood on the scale, I realized I had not gotten back up since 2011. I didn't sink quickly to the bottom of the ocean floor; I sank slowly and deliberately over the course of 84 months or 336 weeks . . . slowly eating myself to death. Slowly padding layers of protective fat to keep myself from being seen anymore. I was down for the count. And down for good. That same day, I received an email that changed me forever. "Dear Christina, thank you so much for applying for healthcare coverage with our specialized plans designed for the self-employed . . . blah, blah, blah, blah, blah . . . we are sorry to inform you that we cannot underwrite a policy for you due to your weight status considered to be morbidly obese . . ." I stopped at those two words. Morbidly obese. I am morbidly obese? I said it over and over in my head.

The next morning, I awoke with a fire within me that I had not experienced in many years. The flame that breathes life into a decaying spirit and the hopelessness built over years of dejection and grief. I opened my journal that morning and wrote these words: "Things must change." And I then wrote out a list of the things in my life that needed to change starting with my unhealthy relationship with food, my weight, and my stress levels. I knew that I had to start with my weight—I knew that getting my weight under control would positively impact all the other failings of my life.

Finally, I was taking control and succeeding at getting my health back on track and doing all the things that an emotionally healthy person does. Six months later, I was in the hospital with incredible numbness and pain throughout my arms, back, and hands. I was diagnosed with RA, a debilitating autoimmune disease that wreaked havoc on my body and crushed my spirit. My body was failing me. Suddenly, my diet became the most important focus of my life. And my emotional well-being was at the root of it all. I had to find a way to get back up, but this time I could *not* do it alone. For the first time in my life. I needed help. This time, both my mother and my father were not available to call. Or to lean on. I was truly alone.

By the start of 2020, I had lost eighty pounds. I got the emotional support I needed through a therapist and a business coach. I was working toward the next phase of my life. I had just completed my bachelor's degree in real estate completely online; I graduated Magna Cum Laude and won all the awards. I was accepted in the number two grad school in the country for real estate. I was back in production, just earning enough to cover my monthly nut and also have enough to save. My credit scores were back where they belonged, my savings was back to a respectable level, my 401(k) was growing, and I was doing all the things to reduce stress, sadness, depression while avoiding yet another kick in the teeth. Lord knows I had fought my way through so many in my life. I was over it and wanted a month of pure joy. And then . . . COVID.

With RA, I was that person who did not leave the house. I ordered groceries three weeks in advance, only left the house to walk around my own neighborhood, converted my entire life to Zoom calls, conference calls, and remaining in total fear of catching and dying of COVID. But it was the perfect year to earn my master's degree at a school that was fully online. I mean, we were all stuck inside. I made the best use of my time by studying. And study I did! I graduated top in my class and won all the awards for my cohort. I was selected to compete in a development project competing with schools like Wharton and UNC.

I vividly remember lying in the hospital emergency room in August of 2020. Almost two years had lapsed since I was diagnosed with RA—I was terrified and alone. I was so sick that I could not get out of bed most days to even walk more than a few feet without my heart racing and my body giving out. I didn't even realize just how sick I was until I had some blood work completed about a month before. I drove myself to the ER. I arrived during the height of the COVID pandemic and immediately was put on every machine, monitor, and IV drip known to humankind. They took vials of blood. A few hours later, the attending doctor came in and said my blood work looked a mess (not in those words, of course) and asked if I had my affairs in order. *My affairs? In order?* Oh my god . . . I went black. My affairs? Like my end-of-life wishes? When he showed me my blood work, it became clear that yes, he was seriously asking if I had my affairs in order. My hemoglobin level teetered somewhere around seven. Just shy of needing a blood transfusion. My C-reactive protein levels had skyrocketed to over thirty-three, and if you aren't aware, that level is a sudden heart attack or stroke just waiting to send me to meet my maker. Every marker of bad health was evident in my lab work. It was the most alarming moment of my life. And I've had many alarming moments. This time was different. This time, I was no longer fighting for my career or my child's well-being. This time, I was fighting for me.

In all my life, I never thought I would face the end in such an in-my-face way. I thought I would die old in a hospice bed with my son by my side whispering that it's okay and I could go knowing that he loved me. Just like the way I said good-bye to my own mother. While I was in the hospital, I reflected on my life. I thought about my childhood. I thought about my mother falling down the stairs and my unlikely survival into the world. I thought about who I wanted to be. I reflected on being knocked down and getting right back up no matter what life threw in my face. I thought about my dreams. I thought about January 19, 2019, and how my father's death impacted my life choices and forced me to face reality and replace my old ideologies for new ones. I thought about the decisions I made and the sheer determination to be better and do better. I whispered forgiveness. I begged for mercy. I had dreamed at every step of my journey with or without intention. And I wasn't going to stop now.

When I was released from the hospital, it was God who intervened in my life story. I was no longer in control. The diagnosis was hemolytic anemia—a very rare blood disorder in which the body's immune system attacks red blood cells. I was directed to call an oncologist to care for me and prepare a plan for healing. I found the best oncologist in the area and was able to get in the next day, through miracles. This man was truly my hero. My health insurance sucked and covered *nothing*. This doctor was able to place me in a program that provided my medical treatments for free. This treatment was not cheap—$35K per treatment—and I was required to have six of them. I was scheduled for my first infusion mid-October of 2020. I went into the oncologist office, and they brought me back to a room with patients being treated for cancer. Under my mask and sunglasses, I was crying for them. I was crying for myself. I was crying for my inability to control my life anymore. After being seated in my recliner and getting set up with the infusion, I sat staring at the ceiling. The same feeling that I had when my dad died. The same glare. I wanted never for my life to end this way. And once again, I recanted that this was *not* how my story would end. I had begun a healing journey, and healing was it. No ifs, ands, or buts. Healing. Nothing but healing for me.

After a series of infusions and a newfound respect for the medical community, all of my health conditions are in full remission. I've lost 100 pounds. And I refocused my life to one of pure joy and embracing everything that is. I was able to redirect my life in a way that held my dreams within grasp. Through my dreams, I have learned that our dreams are not always about the big vision or how things might unfold. But our dreams are truly about the flame of happiness that we fan with joy, good intentions, and clear vision.

Dreams are born out of the internal strength required of healing—whether we are healing physically, financially, mentally, spiritually, or emotionally. Healing is the process in which we either create and envision our dreams or we fall into the darkest space and cannot get back up. We have the option to choose. I chose to believe that my story would not end there. My story will be one of power and resilience. One of courage and greatness. And one of passion and kindness. It will have an ending that dreams are made of. And I am not done dreaming and in this phase of my life, for me.

ABOUT CHRISTINA MACRO

Christina is a genuine leader, an intellectual, an authentic entrepreneur tapping into her own inspiration to lead others to greatness. As a servant leader, she has succeeded exponentially in her career in real estate, and also personally as a mentor, coach, mother, and friend. Through humor and compassion, she shares her stories in hopes that others discover ways to find and use their voices to dig deep to the core of their being to radiate from the inside out. Christina truly believes that beauty emanates from our souls and we have the ability to build dreams from a centered space using self-respect and self-awareness as the footing. We are all on this planet to support one another, and Christina inherently lives through her generosity of spirit which is unmatched in guiding others to excellence.

Connect with Christina

Email: hi@thebrainybroker.com
Facebook: @thebrainybroker
Instagram: @thebrainybroker
Twitter: @thebrainybroker

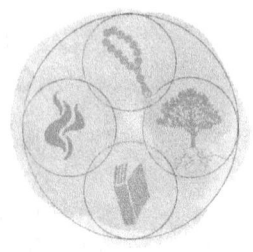

NO MORE HIDING

Melissa Malland

The clouded fog. The chaos of guilt running through my head. Keeping busy so I keep repressing the pain and sadness. I suffered in silence for so long. I knew I needed help two weeks after giving birth to my son after suffering postpartum depression with my youngest and realizing some major financial issues were going to hurt my family. My OB-GYN prescribed some anti-depressants and my internist advised me to see a therapist. I was on my way to recovery.

Or was I? Or am I still?

Depression is real. Mental illness is real. Those who say "Get over it" or "It's all in your head" have never suffered with mental illness and, quite honestly, are ignorant. Giving birth to my sons saved me, and going through postpartum after my third child was born saved me. I realized that I had suffered my entire life, but it was never addressed. Going through postpartum depression was a tumultuous time for me, in more ways than one, but it has taught me more about myself, and it finally brought things to light about what I had been suffering from and continue to suffer from even still to this day.

I remember through each of my three pregnancies and deliveries feeling sad and crying. My only solace was my kids. After giving birth to my third son weighing in at twelve pounds, three ounces, that's when it hit me. I was having some blood pressure issues while in the hospital and they kept a close eye on me. I was in the hospital for four days, which is customary after having a C-section. When I arrived home, I was so thrilled to have all of my boys with me under the same roof. I've always dreamed of having kids and a family. I now felt my family was complete, so I couldn't have been more ecstatic to finally be home with all of them.

The next morning I woke up and began taking care of my three sons. My mother lived right down the street from me and would come over to help me as I got "back on my feet." I remember that day she came over, and I just wasn't feeling like myself. She had told me I had this glazed-over look on my face. It was like someone else stepped into my body and I had disappeared. The best way to describe it was that I was functioning, I adored my baby, and I deeply craved spending time with all three of my boys, but *I* was gone. My body was working on robotic mode. I didn't have anything to say, and all I wanted to do was have my baby right next me as I slept.

Despite not having anything to say, I lost interest in things I once enjoyed doing, and I couldn't eat. I was just a body. Nothing more. The feeling of impending doom and the fear I was going to die loomed over me. Later that afternoon, I had ventured outside for the first time since giving birth to walk to the mailbox.

That same feeling started to come over me once again. I felt like I was going to pass out. It was as if God was on my side because my mother had been driving down the street at the same time. I waved her over frantically, and she pulled in my driveway.

My being sick was worrying all those close to me. She was a tad impatient as she was helping me every day since my husband went back to work and she was trying to run errands. I gulped down a glass of orange juice as she thought my blood sugar was low. That wasn't it. Paranoia along with severe anxiety plagued me as well as this postpartum depression. I felt some pain in my shin, and I was petrified it was a blood clot as a result of my C-section.

My mother gave me orange juice and her daily pep talk as she tried so desperately to get her daughter back. People were starting to get frustrated with me, and they didn't understand why my behavior was so drastic and had changed dramatically. The worst part was I couldn't explain it either. My elation over having a baby was shrouded by some out-of-body experience that had stolen Melissa from her family and friends. The pain in my leg wouldn't dissipate. As my mother burped my baby and my two older boys played in their playroom, I quickly took the phone into the hallway and dialed 911—even though those people who were closest to me thought I was going insane and my thoughts were completely irrational and off base. But they neglected to understand that what was happening to me, both physically and mentally, was real. And as I sat on the steps, I could hear the sirens nearing.

The ambulance had quickly pulled into the driveway with a loud screech and first-aid responders hustled to the door. At that point, my mother had the baby in her arms as she burped him. She thought she had just seen a ghost and was completely perplexed about what was happening, as I had not told her that I called 911. The responders popped up the stretcher as my baby stayed in my mother's arms and my other two babies continued to play in their playroom.

I couldn't stop shaking, I couldn't catch my breath, the last thing I wanted to do was to be away from my babies. They were my only happiness. They were my solace. But no one believed me, no one could handle that my feelings were *real*. I was trapped and I couldn't get out, and those around me held me prisoner as well.

I learned so many years later that if you do not suffer from a mental illness, you can't understand it. There are ignorant people out there, but I believe most people are simply not educated enough. The stigma centered around mental health/depression needs to be buried and never dug up again. It's ironic, but my husband who thought I was more of a hinderance, said, " I never would have believed anxiety and depression would be like this, but it is tough and it is real" after he had most recently gone through some events that caused his anxiety and depression.

I lay on the stretcher and looked back at my mother. My blood pressure continued to skyrocket as we headed to the hospital. When the ambulance doors opened, my father and husband were there. They looked like deer in headlights and didn't know what to expect. I went through a series of tests to check for the blood clot in my leg, and by the grace of God, I did not have one. Due to impatience, both my father and husband were itching to leave, and once again, I was viewed as a hinderance.

What no one understood was that I didn't feel like myself, but the feelings I did have were real. They were mine and I was almost made to feel humiliated for having any feelings whether they were mental or physical. That has always been the case, and it took almost fourteen years to finally recognize that my feelings are valid. That I don't have to, nor should I, continue to repress and suppress my feelings for the sake of others.

There were many dark days ahead. When I arrived home, my focus was on fixing myself. I began taking medication and seeing a therapist weekly. Thankfully, I was doing those things, because I was going to need the support. It was only two weeks after I had given birth when my husband lost his business. To make matters worse, I also found out that I was going to need major abdominal surgery. Due to having such large babies, my diastasis muscle split in half, and I had two hernias, which made me still look pregnant. I was grateful that I had some tools to use and help me cope with the major issues going on with me personally and my family.

My determination was to get better for me so I could be the best for my sons. Depression can make you question yourself and feel insecure, less confident, less valued. I felt so many things during this time period. They were so palpable, but I couldn't home in on anything because of that outsider that invaded my mind and body. My mind needed to heal, and I needed to find myself again—or quite possibly, the new me. Quitting was not in my vocabulary, and that invader was going to be kicked to the curb. I wasn't going to allow this to steal my joy or stop my dreams from coming true. I had my teaching career, I was in the middle of completing my master's degree, and most importantly, there were memories to be made with my babies.

Besides taking medication and seeking therapy weekly, there were other things I began doing to help myself. I started walking everywhere and anywhere. I would walk around my neighborhood or find scenic boardwalks and areas near the water. Sometimes I would walk alone and sometimes I'd walk with my sons. The benefits of walking were immeasurable to me on so many levels. I was able to have some mental clarity and peace, and focus on the present while also getting back in shape. There are many people I know who suffer from depression, and I always recommending walking. As of today, fourteen years later, walking is still part of my daily routine and I highly recommend it.

Yoga became a huge part of my life while going through postpartum depression too. It was my outlet; an hour to myself. Yoga helped me focus on the present, the here and now, and most importantly, myself. Let's not forget that I was also meeting new people and socializing. I had been out of work after giving birth, and I was going to remain out of work because I needed to have major abdominal surgery, so socializing with others was important to me. Little did I realize that as each day would pass, all of these things I was implementing into my life was slowly but surely pushing the invader out. It helped me cope with the fact that I was having major surgery, which I've never had before in my life.

Fast-forward to life today. I returned to my teaching career. I earned my master's degree and passed my state licensure exam to become a principal, all while going through postpartum depression. There was not just one contributing factor that led to my progress, but I can tell you that therapy was so huge for me that I still seek therapy today. The medications did help, along with walking and practicing yoga.

You are the only one who is going to take care of you. No matter how many times people will say they'll be there for you, unfortunately, I learned that during the most difficult time in my life, when I needed those closest to me, my best friend of thirteen years left my side. And I recently had to go through a traumatizing experience within my marriage that taught me so much.

And my sons have taught me so much. I will no longer feel embarrassed or suppress my feelings for the sake of others. I will continue to take care of myself and put myself first. Mental health is my passion, and I have become an advocate for new mothers and all who suffer from depression and anxiety. Don't hide. Don't be embarrassed or afraid. If I can push through and follow my dreams, so can you!

ABOUT MELISSA MALLAND

Melissa Malland has been a teacher for twenty-two years. She is a mom of three boys, ages nineteen, sixteen, and thirteen, and she has been married for twenty-two years. Melissa has a bachelor's degree in education and a master's degree in education administration. She is licensed by the state of New Jersey to serve as a principal in any school within the state. Melissa currently lives in Toms River, at the Jersey Shore, and has since the age of eight. Melissa loves spending her free time with her family, taking walks, spending time at the beach, and reading.

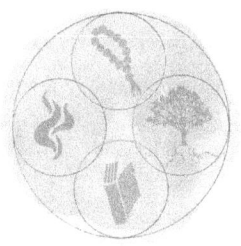

IT STARTS WITH TRUST

Sue Meitner

Beep, beep, beep, beep . . .

Is that my alarm? The noise keeps getting louder and louder. As I finally open my eyes, I realize it *is* my alarm—and it has been going off for the past thirty minutes! How is that possible?

I jump out of bed in a sheer panic. It's only 6:30 a.m., and I am already running behind. Those precious thirty minutes are lost—and as a single working mom, I would do anything to get them back.

I assess the situation and realize I still have enough time to shower and get dressed before waking up my daughter, Allyson. I take a speed shower, throw on my clothes, blow dry my hair, and slap on some makeup. It's days like these that I am grateful my other child is in college. That's one less schedule to juggle.

Okay . . . time to wake up Allyson. I open the door to her bedroom and am accosted by a smell that almost knocks me over. What on earth is that? Oh no. Did Allyson accidentally lock the dog in her room last night? I hit the light switch and Holy Christmas . . . the dog has literally pooped all over the bedroom floor. How is this happening to me, today of all days? I have a meeting first thing this morning. I close my eyes and think to myself: *Do not lose your mind. Take one thing at a time.*

I gently wake up Allyson, and she instantly notices the smell and then sees the dog mess all over her floor. Before she can freak out, I calmly ask her to go into the bathroom to get dressed. I run downstairs to let the dog outside, and then grab a roll of paper towels and some carpet cleaner. I sprint back upstairs and stare at all the piles of poop. Where do I even start?

I'm going to tackle this one step at a time, as I do everything else in my life. I take off my sweater and start cleaning the carpet. I do the best I can but quickly realize this is a job for professionals. I'll call the carpet cleaner when I get to work. I walk out of Allyson's bedroom sweating from head to toe, smelling a bit like dog poop. It's time to start all over again with another shower.

Allyson and I finally get in the car and off we go. I take a deep breath. It's only 8:00 a.m., and I feel as though I have just run a marathon. Is this how every working mom feels as she grabs her keys and heads off to work? I drop Allyson off at school and realize that I still have time to grab an iced tea from Starbucks. That should get my morning back on track.

On the drive to the office, I sip my iced tea and remind myself how lucky I am, crazy morning and all. I have a career I absolutely love that allows me to help others. I am raising two wonderful children, and I am surrounded by friends and family who love and support me.

When I graduated from college, unaware of what type of job I wanted, fate led me to the mortgage industry where I have spent three decades growing a fruitful career while raising a family at the same time. I've had the luxury of attending my children's basketball games and tennis matches, visiting college campuses and taking family vacations. Admittedly, there were times I worked during a game or two . . . but who doesn't multitask?

Getting to this point in my life has not come easy. There have been many pivots along the way, and I'm sure there will be more in the future. I am learning to embrace change and accept that it is part of my journey.

Juggling a career as a single mom is not easy . . . and simply not possible without *trust*. I must trust the people around me and my family and be willing to ask for help—whether it's with a load of laundry, preparing a meal, or going on a grocery store run. I can admit that I can't do it all by myself because it really does take a village. I am so lucky to have my parents living nearby and always willing to help. They have been wonderful stand-ins at school events and in times of mini-crises—like the time my son Drew totaled his car while I was in a board meeting.

I must also trust the people I work with. I have found that by surrounding yourself with people who are authentic and who genuinely want the best for you, you can't go wrong. Some of the best advice I've ever received was to identify your areas of weakness and hire people who are strong in those areas. Then trust them to do the job. When you give yourself permission to ask for and receive help at work, you tap into the true power of collaboration. And sometimes that leads you to discover even more about your business and yourself. I tend to be a big-picture person. I love to throw my all into every goal I set, but I sometimes need help determining the steps along the way. I know where I want to go, but I count on my team to help me get there and manage the details.

Admitting that you can't do it all can make you feel *vulnerable*. However, as I reflect on my career, I recognize that embracing my vulnerability is a strength. Being open and honest with others makes me authentic and a better leader. Accepting that I'm not always right and that I make mistakes allows me to pivot and change direction when necessary. It's so important to be open and honest with yourself—especially if you discover you aren't finding joy in achieving the goals you set for yourself. This doesn't make you a failure. It's merely an invitation to follow a new path so you can continue growing and achieving to your highest potential. The summer of 2018 was my time to be vulnerable and to grow.

It was a hot July afternoon, and as we walked across the University of Alabama campus, my son Drew asked me how I liked the campus. I told him I loved it, and he asked, "How would you know? You've been on the phone with work the entire time." That was my wake-up call. I could not be everything to everyone, and something had to give. I couldn't fake it anymore. I needed to learn how to really be present—especially with my family. It was difficult to admit to myself that I hadn't been present for years and I had lost the happy, fun version of myself. I needed to find her.

Why wasn't I happy? I was the CEO of a successful mortgage company that I started on my own in 2010. I was an award-winning leader in the mortgage industry surrounded by a curated team of talented professionals. I had reached the goals I set for myself. But I was stressed out, overworked, and exhausted—all the time. I still loved building and leading my team, but I wasn't sure I loved owning my own company. It was taking a toll on me, my health, my family, and my friends.

In the past, I had been approached by companies who were looking to join forces. But I always dismissed the idea. I was doing just fine on my own. Or was I? While speaking at a conference in the fall of 2018, a colleague asked if I had considered joining forces with the CEO of another lending company who just so happened to be attending the same conference. He noticed that I had lost my sparkle and thought perhaps this would be a way to get it back. I forced myself to take a closer look. I thought about how it would feel to lose total control of my own independent mortgage company. Would that make me feel like a failure? Would it make me look like a failure in others' eyes? Would I care?

I realized I needed to put aside my ego and be grateful for all the success I had achieved in my career. Now was the time to pivot. So, at the end of 2018, I trusted my instincts, allowed myself to be vulnerable, and merged with another company. The merger allowed me to continue leading my team of operations and salespeople and gave me the backing and support of a larger company. I gained more time with family and less stress over things like payroll and taxes. It was the best thing to do. We were stronger together and still are to this day. I no longer have my CEO title, and that is okay, although it wasn't easy at first.

I will never forget the day we finalized the company merge, going over each detail of what would stay and what would change going forward. All those years of hard work were being disassembled and rebuilt to work more cohesively with my new team. More than once I found myself choking back tears, needing to excuse myself from the meeting to regain my composure. Thankfully, my new leadership team is made up of truly wonderful, compassionate people who gave me the space and support I needed to take this huge step.

Being vulnerable allowed me to see what I had was not what I wanted anymore. By looking inward and opening myself to consider different opportunities, I gained strength and realized I didn't need a CEO title to be successful. I could find a new measure of success.

Trust and vulnerability have played a key role in my career, but they would be nothing without *confidence* and *determination.* I believe in myself and know that I am one of the hardest workers in the mortgage industry, which has allowed me to be confident in any role I take. I have also learned to be comfortable feeling uncomfortable. This can catapult you to another level of success.

Confidence led me to start my own company, and determination made that company a success. I remember writing my memoir *Crazy Lucky Girl* and feeling so grateful and proud of myself for the journey I have been on. My confidence allows me to speak at large meetings and conferences, run a team of operations and salespeople, and become a top loan originator in the industry. With confidence also comes the courage to try new things, whether it's filming TikToks, writing another book, or starting a podcast. If you believe in yourself, there is nothing you can't do.

As I look back on the last decade, I believe that having trust, vulnerability, and confidence has allowed me to soar in my career, while still being a role model and rock for my family. By pivoting and trusting myself, I have developed new ventures and friendships that I would have never had the opportunity to explore. The main objective has always been in pursuit of helping people—whether it be in purchasing their dream home or in building their business. I am able to be a confident and passionate leader in the mortgage industry because I trust in myself, and I believe that I am good enough to achieve whatever I want to achieve. I know it's okay to ask for help, and I know I can trust people enough to help me.

I finally pull into my parking spot at the office with just minutes to spare before my morning meeting begins. But before I can even get my car door open, my phone rings. It's the repair man I scheduled to come fix the dryer. He is sitting in my driveway with no access to the house. Are you kidding me? How did I forget about that? I close my eyes, take a deep breath, put my car in reverse, and back to the house I go. Looks like I will be taking yet another meeting in my car.

This is the life of a crazy lucky girl, but it's my life, and I wouldn't have it any other way.

ABOUT SUE MEITNER

Sue Meitner, CMB (certified mortgage banker), is a leader in her profession and community. Her passion is helping to enrich and empower people to identify their vision of success and plot their course to reach it. Sue is an award-winning author, entrepreneur, motivational speaker, mentor, and mortgage expert. She enjoys sharing the ups and downs of her life and career to help others gain a new perspective of their own growth strategies, as exemplified in her book *Crazy Lucky Girl: Do You Have the Keys to Success?*

Sue is a graduate of George Mason University with a degree in communications. She never expected to work with mortgages, but with just the right combination of business, sales, and relationship-building, she discovered this career was the perfect fit for her. She finds helping people buy a home to be extremely rewarding.

Active on social media, Sue offers information on home buying, the economy, mortgage programs, and business growth—plus never fails to applaud the success of colleagues. Sue was recently chosen as correspondent for suburban Philadelphia on the nationally broadcasted show *Financing The American Dream*, airing on CNBC, Bloomberg TV, and several streaming services. Her podcast, *Grab Your Keys,* is her latest initiative in motivating others by discussing keys to success with professionals in various industries.

Do you need help finding your keys to success?

Get started by using the exclusive QR code below to download Sue's free Business Success Game Plan workbook!

Visit SueMeitner.com to follow Sue or purchase her book.

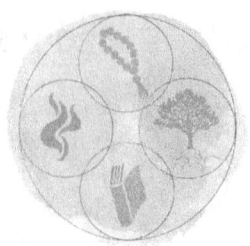

HARNESS THE POWER OF YOUR DREAMS AND LIVE FREE . . . BY DESIGN

Ellie D. Shefi

Have you ever looked around and thought to yourself, *How did I get here?*

Are you living your life on autopilot, doing your best just to get through each day? Is your life dictated by the never-ending items on your to-do list? Or by the demands and expectations of everyone else? Perhaps you are living a life that was determined long ago by someone else—one in which your dreams didn't matter and you never had a say?

I get it. I've lived that life. A life where I was chained to my past. A life where authenticity, abundance, and joy seemed out of reach. A life where I felt pulled along a path by a current beyond my control. A life where I dreamed things would be different but felt powerless to make them so. Then, slowly but surely, I learned the keys to freedom. Through almost five decades of getting back up every time life has knocked me down, I've developed tools to make my dreams come true and live life on my terms. And I'm here to help you do the same.

Who am I to guide you on your journey to living a life that's free by design? I'm Ellie. I'm typically introduced as an attorney, entrepreneur, #1 international best-selling and award-winning author, featured speaker, strategist, teacher, trainer, mentor, media host, consultant, coach, philanthropist, and publisher— but I haven't always lived a joyful abundant life on my own terms. I've escaped abuse and domestic violence. I've had thirteen major surgeries and survived cancer. I've struggled financially, lived in my car, and eaten the food restaurants were throwing away at the end of the night. And yet, despite those events and circumstances, I've learned to take back my power, dream my biggest dreams, and intentionally create a life I love! I may have been forged by fire, but I choose to live free by design.

And now it's your turn!

With these tools I share, you'll chart your new course and set your GPS toward a life that's free by design. First, you'll identify where you are, where you want to go, and what obstacles lie in between. Next, by learning how to create an impervious mind, embrace the power of gratitude, and master visualization, you'll close the gap to align your current and future lives. Then, you'll be ready to put it all together, intentionally design a life you love in all aspects, and, at last, live your dreams!

So, are you ready? Are you ready to make powerful and lasting changes to your life? Grab your favorite notebook and pen, and let's dive in!

Now . . .

Imagine living a life you love . . .

A life where your dreams come true . . .

A life where you live every aspect on your terms: wealth on your terms, health on your terms, relationships on your terms, courage on your terms . . .

A life of showing up as you want to be in all of your glory . . .

A life free by design!

Step One: Identify

The first step to living a life that is free by design is to identify where you are, where you want to be, and the obstacles in between.

Where Are You?

Let's begin by assessing where you are in your life right now. What's your current reality? Take inventory of your life in a deep and meaningful way so that you're clear about where you're starting. Dig into every aspect of your life: finance, health, relationships, self-care (are you even on your own to-do list?!). You might find some areas of your life are awesome while others need an overhaul. Be honest with yourself about the story of your life as it currently is.

Mirror, Mirror

Play along with an exercise that will help you dive deep into your life—you need a mirror and open mind. Ready?

Look at yourself in the mirror. What do you see? Describe your physical self.

Now, as you look deep into your eyes, describe in detail who and what you see.

Next, describe your life. If you're stuck, consider what you say when you talk to others about your life. How do you describe it to them? How might they describe it to you? Are there any life events that have shaped you; if so, what effect has each had?

Knowing your starting point is the first step in recalibrating your compass and programming the GPS for your new life. After all, when you want to go somewhere, what does your GPS need to know? Just two simple pieces of information: your starting point and your destination! Soon, you'll begin getting clear on your destination, but for now, focus on taking a raw, honest inventory of your life in its current form.

Where Do You Want to Be?

Now that you're super clear on your current reality, ask yourself: Is this what I want? Does my current wealth bring me joy? My health? My relationships with others? With myself?

If you answered no to any or all of these questions, then it's time to identify where you want to be. To approach this question, let your imagination run wild! It is time to recall and supercharge those past dreams or even create new ones! And now, don't just dream, but dream *big*, dream *free*! This is your chance to see infinite possibilities!

Let's have some fun . . . to dream the ultimate reality, think back to when you were a child and made birthday wishes. In that frame of mind, ask:

What do I want?
What does living life on my own terms look like?
What does my authentic, in-control, joyful life look like?
What does my dream life look like?

Go ahead and describe where you live, what you do, how you feel, who's in your life (and who's not). Describe what financial freedom looks like; what peak health looks like; what amazing relationships look like. Note observations, feelings, events, and accomplishments. Capture every wondrous detail!

Assess Your Obstacles

Now, what's getting in the way of living your dreams?

Identifying your obstacles can be tricky and emotionally taxing. Start by simply asking yourself: Where am I stuck? Finances? Career? Health? Relationships? A combination?

Don't focus on all of them at once. Pick one area and drill down. Be really honest with yourself, and you'll reveal limiting beliefs, bad habits, and disempowering narratives that stop you from living the life you want. Become clear on the obstacles you are creating for yourself.

Now, go even deeper and contemplate *why* you have been creating these obstacles—why you're self-sabotaging, getting in your own way, or limiting your potential. The answer may lie in events and circumstances from your past that have shaped who you are today. It's important to identify those pivotal moments that have created the beliefs and paradigms that brought you to this point of your journey. Later, I'll show you how to break through these patterns, but for now, simply identify them.

Pick another area of your life and repeat the exercise. Don't be surprised if you find similar obstacles popping up. But take heart. After you've learned to handle them in one area, you'll be set to tackle any other places they might arise.

Step Two: Align

You've reached the next step! This is where the rubber meets the road! It's where you close the gap by using my tools and resources—creating an impervious mind, embracing the power of gratitude, and mastering visualization—to get from where you are to where you want to be.

Create an Impervious Mind

Creating an impervious mind is *the* key to living a life free by design because—let's face it—life happens. And you need to be able to overcome old and new obstacles that stand between where you are and living your dreams. So, how do you create an impervious mind? You master the language that you use and then use those words to write a story that changes your perspective.

Master the Language You Use

Revisit your notes from the Mirror, Mirror exercise. What words did you use to describe yourself and your life when you looked in the mirror? Were they empowering? Or did you go straight to criticism—the wrinkles, the extra pounds, the stalled career, the failed marriage?

Let's try that exercise again. This time, focus on being nice to yourself and use only empowering words. Look at your eyes again, but this time, don't focus on the wrinkles; instead say, "Thank you, eyes . . . You're looking very sparkly today."

While it may seem awkward at first, with practice (yes, consistently using empowering language takes practice!), it'll become the norm, and you'll stop tearing yourself to bits.

Now that you've replaced your disempowering labels and

beliefs with empowering ones, it's time to claim who you are, see your dreams, and create your life that's free by design! Grab your notebook and pen and write down at least half a dozen affirmations (those magical "I AM" statements). Remember to write them in the present tense, as if you're already doing, feeling, seeing, believing, accomplishing, and embracing your dreams and a life lived on your terms!

Next, let's supercharge your affirmations with incantations. With what?!

Incantations are affirmations that get your physiology involved. Take the affirmation "I am strong" and picture someone putting some oomph behind it: saying it out loud, punching the air, beating their chest, whatever makes them actually experience and feel the words they're using. Get your senses involved. Go ahead . . . pick one of the affirmations from your list. Now, say it with power, with emotion, and with a corresponding movement. Really embody it! I bet your incantation let you physically experience your affirmation that time! Powerful, isn't it?!

Change Your Perspective

The words you use, and the meaning you ascribe to them, produce physiological responses and *become* your truth. Have you ever noticed that the more you tell people you're tired, the more tired you feel? The more you tell people you're stressed or overwhelmed, the more stressed and overwhelmed you feel? The words you use and the stories you create about a situation are more powerful than the situation itself! So, using your newfound empowering words to rewrite your stories to change your perspective is the next step in designing life on your terms!

What do I mean? Let me show you:

My friend is a blind woman who was born to a poor family in a village in rural India where it was common for daughters to be sold into marriage for a dowry. Her mother and father knew that she wouldn't attract a high dowry, but without one, feeding her meant that someone else would starve.

One day, her mother led her to a bus stop and left her there. Abandoned. Frightened. Alone.

For years, this was my friend's reality. She told herself the story of how her parents were embarrassed by her, how she brought shame to her family, and how she was such a burden they had to cast her aside in order to be free from the shame and financial burden she imposed upon them.

This story defined her until one day she made a powerful decision. She decided to change her story and change her life. She shifted her perspective and took control of her narrative.

Today, she will tell you that she was born to a loving mother and father in a poor village in rural India. She will tell you that her parents feared her mistreatment by a future husband even if he was willing to pay a dowry. They worried for her future. The only way they could help her have a better life was to let her go.

So one day her mother took her beloved daughter by the hand and led her to a well-lit bus stop near the police station, where she was sure to be found by a policeman. Not wanting to frighten her child or draw attention to what was happening, she sat her daughter on the bench and quietly walked away with tears in her eyes.

As her mother had hoped, a kind policeman found her and took her to the safety of an orphanage, where she was adopted by an incredible family in Canada. She has been more loved by her adopted family than she ever thought possible. She is thriving every single day—all because her loving mother selflessly released her to a better life. Her mother loved her enough to let her go, and for that she is eternally grateful.

My friend's story is a powerful example. Although the events of her life are what they are—her mother left her as a very young blind girl at a bus stop near a police station in rural India—her story reminds us of the power of the words we use and the meanings we give them. As my friend so poignantly demonstrates, you can use the story you tell yourself about events in your life to either keep yourself in an emotional prison, or you can take the key and set yourself free. Changing the meaning she attached to the events of her past set her free. Her shift in meaning didn't change the facts of what happened, but by changing her story, she found a new life, and a new future.

When you change your perspective, everything shifts. You replace chains of the past with gratitude, joy, forgiveness, compassion, and love, and you're empowered to take control, become the architect of your life, and fully live your dreams!

An "Attitude of Gratitude"

Now, let's talk about the power of gratitude. Yes, gratitude. Have you ever noticed that when you allow yourself to feel truly grateful about something, you cannot simultaneously feel angry, anxious, fearful, worried, or frustrated?

Go ahead, try it. Think of something for which you are truly and deeply grateful. Put yourself back in that beautiful moment. Notice how you feel. Notice the warmth. Notice the sense of peace. Notice the love. Notice the joy. Notice the appreciation. Of course, you can feel anger, worry, fear, or frustration before and after you feel grateful, but negative emotions are impossible to feel at the same time as gratitude.

Feeling grateful interrupts whatever negative emotion you're experiencing long enough to help you shift your perspective and fuel your strength to persevere.

I've spent the better part of two decades living in and out of hospitals, fighting for my life, abandoning my dreams. At one point, I grew tired of the pain, tired of the struggle, and tired of the constant fight to survive. I was giving up. I had had enough. I was done fighting the doctors' death deadlines. Then one day, everything changed. It was a day I had to go have another excruciating test. When it was time for me to go for testing, the porter came to get me from my room and wheeled my wheelchair down hallways that he had never taken me through before.

He wheeled me through the hallways of the area in the hospital where everyone was either paralyzed from the neck down and on a ventilator, or in a coma and on a ventilator. I looked into room after room and realized that any one of those patients would give *anything* to feel the pain I was feeling. In an instant, I realized that my pain was an incredible blessing, and that I was so lucky to be able to feel it travel around my body. In that moment, I made a choice to once again take control of my life. I thanked God that I still had nerves that were connected and synapses that were firing as they should. What a gift! I turned my pity party into gratitude and my weariness became resolve. I became flooded with gratitude for my body and all it provided me.

The ability to find and feel true gratitude is the ultimate mind hack. It is a powerful tool—one that can be learned. Just as you can train your mind to assign empowering meanings to life's events and you can train your mind to frame things in a positive, powerful perspective, you can also train your mind to operate from a place of gratitude. Changing your meaning takes practice. Changing your perspective takes practice. And living in gratitude takes practice. The more work you do in your gratitude practice, the stronger it will be. It's like any other skill you've honed in your life. You can do it!

See It, Achieve It

Earlier, when you dreamed of a life lived on your terms, you got clear on what it is that you want. So, how do you turn that into reality? Through the power of visualization.

Let me demonstrate:

I want you to envision that you are standing in front of a lemon tree. And in front of you is a beautiful, ripe, amazing lemon. Pull it off the tree. Feel it. Squeeze it. Now walk that lemon back into your kitchen and pull out a knife. Cut that lemon in half. Ooh, it's so juicy. Now, lift one half to your nose and smell the lemon. Squeeze some of the lemon juice into a cup and take a sip.

Did you pucker?! Yes, you did! Are you salivating? Yes, you are! But there's no lemon in your hand. You didn't actually smell a lemon. But your body reacted physiologically because your mind made the association. In your mind, all those steps—from picking to tasting the lemon—were real!

That's the power of visualization! Your mind cannot tell the difference between what's real and what's not. Pretty wild, right?

The same goes for designing your life. If your mind can see it, you can achieve it. Unlike the earlier dreaming exercise, in which you were an observer and you were imagining your future life from an objective point of view, visualization compels you to put yourself *into* the vision and feel it. You sit in it; you taste it; you smell it. You are not just objectively observing from afar. You move out of your head, into your heart.

If you want that Ferrari, smell the leather, feel the steering wheel under your hands, feel your foot hitting the accelerator. If you want to live in that beach house, sit on the balcony listening to the waves with a glass of wine.

So, what are your dreams?

Step Three: Design

This is it! This is your call to action! You took inventory of your life—you *identified* where you are; where you want to be; and what obstacles stand in the way.

Next, you *aligned* your life by learning how to close the gap. You understand the importance of empowering words. You're practicing affirmations and incantations to feel the power of your words. You're on the journey of changing your perspective—of taking ownership of your experiences and attaching empowering meanings to them. You're whole-heartedly embracing the power of gratitude and practicing it until it becomes the default way that you move through the world. And you're learning to master the art and science of visualization. You're dreaming your biggest dreams!

Look at that! You have all the building blocks you need for the final step. It's time to take charge and use these tools to grab hold of your dreams and intentionally *design* a life that you love in all aspects: life on your terms, wealth on your terms, health on your terms, a career on your terms, relationships with others and yourself on your terms.

You have everything you need to be the architect of your life! Everything you need to show up as the person you design! Everything you need to make your dreams come true!

Now go forward and live them! Live your best life—the joyful, authentic, abundant life you love!

Live a life that's free by design!

ABOUT ELLIE D. SHEFI

Ellie is an attorney, entrepreneur, #1 international best-selling and award-winning author and publisher, sought-after speaker, strategist, consultant, and coach who provides her clients with practical, easy-to-implement tools and strategies that generate results. She helps entrepreneurs to grow their companies; authors to write and publish their books; and speakers to amplify their message so they can scale their impact.

Host of the Free by Design™ television show and the You Are Not Your Scars™ podcast, Ellie is often interviewed in publications and on others' podcasts and television shows, including NBC, ABC, CBS, the New York Times, Forbes, Entrepreneur, Yahoo News, the LA Tribune, and TED Ed, to name a few.

Ellie is also the founder of the Made 2 Change the World™ Foundation (www.made2change.org), a nonprofit that equips and empowers the next generation with the tools, resources, and strategies they need to create the lives, communities, and world they envision.

A member of the National Academy of Best-Selling Authors, Ellie's books include *Unlocking Your Superpower: 8 Steps to Turn Your Existing Knowledge into Income; Sisters Rising: Stories of Remarkable Women Living Extraordinary Lives; The Authorities: Powerful Wisdom from Leaders in the Field; Women Who Shine* and *SuccessOnomics.*

To connect with Ellie and learn more about her work, including how you can get involved with the Made 2 Change the World™ Foundation, please visit ellieshefi.com.

https://www.facebook.com/ellieshefi
https://www.instagram.com/ellieshefi
https://www.twitter.com/ellieshefi
https://www.linkedin.com/in/ellie-shefi/

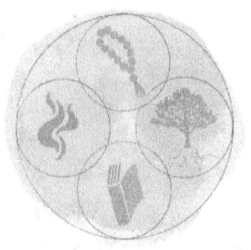

GOD-SIZED DREAM

Candice Shepard

Through my childhood, my bedroom was a bright, sunny yellow. When my parents switched it over from "little girl" to "big girl," my mom suggested yellow as something fun, positive, and uplifting to wake up in every day. It being the '70s, we had paneling on the walls, so we put up yellow paneling. My bedspread was yellow. We painted the bookcase yellow. Even the carpet was yellow. It was always sunny in my bedroom. It was my safe space. I listened to music, wrote in my journal, prayed, had sleepovers with girlfriends and giggled into the wee hours of the night, did homework, planned my future, and spent hours deep in thought in that bright, sunny room. That yellow tint over everything, akin to rose-colored glasses, shaped my mind in a way that is still very much imprinted in the fabric of who I am.

That was how my mom rolled too. She would never allow anything to keep her down for long. If she was sad, she didn't stay that way. If she was discouraged, she would find a way through. If there was trouble, she found a solution; she would always pick herself up and push through whatever she was facing. Things might get tough, but there was always room for the sun to shine, always a reason to have hope, always something to dream about, plan for, and work toward. In our house, dreaming was encouraged. But so was planning and working and doing the hard things.

As a little girl, I was headstrong. Okay, that's maybe an understatement. I was bullheaded, determined, tenacious, unstoppable. I would charge through any situation, full speed ahead, and nothing could stop me. In *Women Who Shine*, I shared a story that clearly embodies that full-steam-ahead way of life. I was probably seven or eight when someone tried to deny me the opportunity to play on the boys' baseball team. The main reason I wanted to play on that team—instead of the one I was "supposed" to play on—was solely because of my current abilities and my desire to grow. I was nearly denied because I didn't fit the profile for the players on that team. It was a boys' team, and I was not a boy. End of story. Enter my dad, my hero and champion, who stood strong and said, "She's as skilled at [this thing] as the other kids on this team, boy or girl, and this is where she belongs." I think that was the day I stepped into my potential. My perspective changed in that moment from "some things can't be done" to "anything is possible."

You also know from WHS that I am a high achiever. I've been blessed with a lot of great successes. None of it was luck. It was, and is, prayerful obedience to the will of God and really, really hard work. You also know that where I am now is most certainly not where I began. Sometimes it seems like where I am now is a completely different planet than where I began.

When I was living on the planet of pain and shame and heartache, where hurt and overwhelm was part of my daily life, it was almost impossible to believe there would ever be anything more. I used to lay in that sunny yellow room begging God for something different, something better, something more in line with the calling I knew he had on my life. The sun seemed so dim and out of reach. Some days it seemed impossible to believe the sun would ever come out again. And yet, that sunny yellow room again became my sanctuary, enabling me to dream again.

Confession time . . . I've never been a big "dreamer." I am

- a list maker
- a box checker
- a planner
- a doer
- an achiever (can anyone say Enneagram 3? High D on the DISC? Print 3/8? ENFJ?)
- an outside-the-box thinker
- a *big* thinker

But *dreamer*? Dreamer is not something that has ever been a title particularly fitting for me. That is, perhaps, troublesome from the perspective of writing a chapter in a book called *Women Who Dream*, but hold that thought.

When my parents were redecorating my baby bedroom to a sunny, yellow, big-girl bedroom, a wall hanging seemed to appear out of nowhere that read, "Dreams take time, patience, sustained effort, and a willingness to fail if they are ever to be anything more than dreams." That quote *makes* the title of dreamer fit me. I am very much a dreamer, from a perspective that makes sense to me.

My parents put skin on the idea of what it means to be a dreamer. My mom is very much a dreamer and big thinker, and my dad makes the idea of dreaming, that was still nebulous to me, very practical. My dad makes me laugh all the time; he is so funny. He can take a heavy situation and lighten it up with a joke that will inevitably elicit laughter. For years after I played on the boys' baseball team, my dad used to joke with me, "You can't do that, you're just a girl." Then he'd chuckle with his deep infectious laugh. I knew what it meant. I knew that the world would frequently say things like . . .

"Little girl, step back."

"You're just a girl."

"You can't."

"Stop trying."

"Stay in your lane."

"Who do you think you are?"

And on and on.

But I also knew from that moment on, those expectations would never stop me. I could be both a dreamer and a doer.

But then one day, something stopped me, pulled the rug right out from under me, knocked me flat on my back, and took the wind right out of me. I went from hanging out in the sunny yellow room because it was my safe space to dream, to hanging out in the sunny yellow room because it was my safe space to survive, hide, and escape the awful mess that was going on around me. I stopped dreaming. I stopped planning. I stopped thinking big. I started trying to determine how I could breathe for another day, get myself out of bed, and force myself out of the sun that was my safe haven and into the torrential rains—whether or not I wanted to do it.

Through it all, I prayed. I thought I was merely surviving, but in hindsight, God showed me another perspective. Through the surviving, through the praying, I was also becoming. I was allowing God to take a horrible situation and make it his. To take something unthinkable and make beauty from ashes. I was changing from who I was to who I am. I was allowing him to plant God-sized dreams into my life and my future. It was a time of rest and transformation, although I was too hurt at the time to see that. All I was asking God for was survival. And then I started asking for escape and deliverance from the situation. Eventually, I would ask him for deliverance from the stronghold. But in the middle, in the becoming, the God-sized dreams were evolving and growing and taking root.

Three dreams in particular were being planted into my soul at that time and have finally come to fruition—thirty years later! So often, we fail to ask God for his dream. We fail to recognize that the dream we're meant to chase will always come true if it comes from him. The dream we're meant to have will always come from him. And even more often, when we ask God for something, we give up before the dream he has planted comes to be reality.

In that time of becoming, God planted three dreams:

1. You will own a law firm one day. This law firm will be used to grow my kingdom and serve my people.

2. You will mother a motherless child.

3. And I will make all of the things you're going through right now . . . all this yuck . . . I will make something amazing from it, and you will help a lot of people with your story. And your story will bring me glory and bring healing to some of my dearly loved daughters.

I do now own that law firm, and we do use it to serve. A law firm that serves the kingdom sounds strange. But God is so good. I am now a mother to a child who was previously motherless. It is beautiful and it is hard. But God is so good. I do now use that horrific season of life to glorify God and help him heal his hurting daughters. I never, ever, ever, ever thought that particular dream was possible. But God is so good.

Y'all, nothing is impossible with God, and God-sized dreams are not only possible but the best dreams you can have. Because if it's from him, you can't stop it. If you're obedient to that God-sized dream, he can use it in a million beautiful and amazing ways.

One day, my family and I were having dinner at my parents' home, and my eleven-year-old daughter started talking about something that she wanted to do. I don't even remember now what it was that she said she was going to do. It was bold, audacious, and really cool. My dad looked at her and said, "You can't do that, you're just a girl." And then he chuckled with his deep, infectious laugh. My daughter had never heard this story, and I held my breath waiting to see how she would respond. In that split second, I prayed that I had poured enough into her that she wouldn't back down, that had her own internal strength and grit would allow her to stand firm. Under her breath, but just loud enough for the whole room to hear, she said, "Just watch me." The whole room exhaled. My dad said, "That's my girl," and we all went on with our day. I later told her the story and expressed to her how proud I was of this response and my desire that she never lose her determination.

In the waiting and the wondering, in the rising and the falling, in the healing and the hurting, in the becoming, there he is. Make room for your God-sized dream.

ABOUT CANDICE SHEPARD

Candice thrives in many arenas: Jesus-lover, mama, sister, daughter, orphan advocate, friend, attorney, business owner, creator, mentor, speaker, author, encourager, and servant leader, and the list goes on.

Originally from the Midwest, Candice proudly calls North Carolina home now, along with her four children and a bunch of other critters that she loves and cares for. That midwestern pragmatism is still very much present in her parenting style, daily living, and business endeavors.

As the CEO and managing attorney of Shepard Law, PLLC in the Charlotte, NC, metro area; founder and president of the Board of Directors of Tribe 14:18 Ministries, a nonprofit that seeks to care for orphans and the families who love them; and a certified coach, best-selling author, and international speaker with The Athena Tribe, Candice seeks to empower others in all aspects of life, from home to work and everything in between. She is also a legacy author for the Inspired Impact series. You can find out more about her in *Women Who Shine,* and connect with her on the websites below, if you want to work with her or get involved.

Let's connect!

Web: www.ShepardLawPLLC.com
www.Tribe1418.com
www.TheAthenaTribe.com

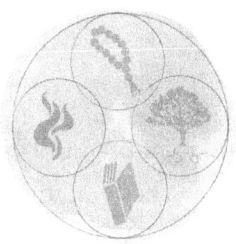

DREAMS FOR GENERATIONS

Linda Yang

Why does dreaming about the future come so easily for some people but not for others? The opportunity to dream is free, but for some people, like my parents, the imagination required to dream of something better is only unleashed by significant life-changing events.

Survival

Explosions of beautiful fireworks decorate the night sky, accompanied by the usual loud whooshes, whistles, and bangs. As far back as I can remember, our family has watched America's Independence Day fireworks every year. However, the flashes of light and loud booms sound exactly like bombs exploding during wartime. It's ironic that the way the United States celebrates its freedom and independence reminds my parents of the war they experienced in Laos.

For my parents, war meant death, and survival was the only priority. As refugees of the Vietnam War, my parents and grandparents did not take survival for granted. The Vietnam War created chaos, as did several other wars in the area. During that time, Laos, a small country in Southeast Asia where my grandparents and parents lived, was the most heavily bombed country in the world.

My parents would often tell me stories of their escape from Laos in the middle of the night, amid heavy gunfire and bombs exploding all around them. They would tell of how they ran from one village to the next, hoping to find some measure of peace and relief from war. Thankfully, my parents made their way to a refugee camp in Thailand and had the opportunity to relocate to America in the late 1970s. Although they did not have any money and were unable to speak English, America gave them an opportunity to dream about a new future—something they did not have the luxury to do in Laos.

Perseverance

When my parents arrived in America, they did not take their opportunity to dream for granted. They held firm to an important, timeless value—perseverance—which helped them achieve their dreams in the face of new challenges in a new country. Perseverance required putting forth constant and relentless effort, despite difficulties and resistance. Determination helped them escape war-torn Laos, and once they arrived in America, persistence helped them learn English and build a life for our family.

Soon after they arrived in America, my parents worked in the farming industry. Farming meant starting the day at 4:00 a.m. every morning to beat the blazing California sun, but they were willing to work hard to support our family. The work provided an income, but it didn't afford proper healthcare for a family with children. My parents' constant and relentless efforts to provide for our family led them to pack everything we had into our car and drive across the country from California to North Carolina in search of better opportunities.

They followed their dreams and were able to secure full-time jobs that provided healthcare coverage. My father worked in a plastic packaging factory, and my mother worked for a textile factory, sewing seams on socks, and was paid according to her production. The jobs were labor intensive and required long hours. My parents worked relentlessly and saved enough money to purchase two sewing machines, which allowed my mother to sew at home. Their tireless and constant work ethic soon carried over to me. Every weekend throughout our high school years, my twin sister and I sewed seams on socks to help provide for our family and save for our college educations.

Through their actions, my parents taught me that perseverance is vital in accomplishing my dreams. They worked constantly and never gave up despite many difficulties—just so I would have opportunities to realize my own dreams. Perseverance often requires a tremendous amount of sacrifice, but no sacrifice was too great for my parents when it came to their dreams or mine.

Imagination

I believe imagination stretches dreams and inspires one's vision for the future. Especially for those with humble beginnings, the future can be transformational.

From the beginning, my parents did their best to protect me from seeing the harsh realities associated with starting a new life in a new country. At first, I didn't understand the physical and mental toll of working long hours on a farm day after day. I didn't know that my parents' laborious jobs translated to little economic and financial wealth, and I didn't comprehend that my family had to rely on government assistance to help put food on the table.

I do remember clearly that during my early childhood years, I had fun dreaming, imagining, and pretend-playing. I remember daydreaming and wanting to be like my favorite movie stars, musicians, and professional athletes. It didn't matter if the actresses looked different from me. It didn't matter whether I understood what the musicians were singing about or that I didn't have a musical instrument. I didn't care that I couldn't run very fast or that I hadn't found a sport I enjoyed. The only thing that did matter was my imagination, propelling me forward with a belief that I could achieve anything and be anything I wanted. Only my imagination limited what I could achieve. My twin sister and I shared dreams of all shapes and sizes with each other. My big dreams allowed me to see so many possibilities—nothing seemed out of reach. All I had to do was close my eyes and imagine it.

As I got older, I reached a point when I started to comprehend my parents' struggles. I still recall like it was yesterday when I had to share one egg with my twin sister because my family needed to make a carton of one dozen eggs last the entire week. I started to gain a perspective and understanding of life's harshness, which my parents had tried to keep from me. I gained an appreciation for their sacrifices. Around that time, my dreams also started to evolve and grow bigger. Slowly, my dreams started to not only encompass my own desires; my dreams began to cast a wider net that also embraced my family.

As a first-generation immigrant born in America, my aspirations often reflected achievements I desired as the first in my family. I dreamed of being the first to graduate from college. I dreamed of being the first to own a business and have multiple sources of income. I dreamed of having a high-profile and well-paid professional career in order to provide for my own family and for my aging parents.

Challenges

Accomplishing dreams is an adventure filled with many challenges. My journey has taught me that setting goals and taking measurable actions stretches my capabilities and enables me to realize my dreams.

When I set goals, I set realistic and measurable action steps toward making my dreams reality. I've recognized through my own experiences just how difficult it is to persevere and keep pushing onward in the face of resistance. Even when working smart, it's hard work and there are still challenges to overcome. Taking action requires diligent work, extra effort, sacrifice, and never-ending commitment.

In college, I studied longer hours than most of my peers at

the library because it took me longer to read and understand concepts. Quite often, I had to reread the text and find additional resources to fully understand the materials. After several years of working a full-time job, I decided to go back to school for my master's degree in healthcare administration. At that point in my life, I was married. We were struggling with bills, and I could not return to school full-time. I made the choice to work eight-hour days and attend school part-time in the evenings. Some days I felt exhausted. I often chose to skip social gatherings, and my weekends were filled with reading textbooks and writing essays. Other personal choices I made throughout the years were limiting travels for vacations, emphasizing quality time with my family instead of quantity, sacrificing taking a honeymoon right after my wedding, and saying no to great opportunities that did not align with my dreams. In each circumstance, I chose a path and stuck to a plan that was realistic and measurable.

During challenging times, I reminded myself why I could not take my opportunity to dream for granted. This mindfulness helped me refocus and served as a constant motivator. I've learned that the hardest part of taking measurable action happens internally; sometimes the battle inside my mind made it seem like my dreams were out of reach. Like all of humanity, I also had limiting beliefs about myself. Although I had goals and aspirations, I still doubted my capabilities, and I feared the unknown. However, in the face of that self-doubt and those limiting beliefs, I chose to invest in myself. Throughout the years, I also chose to build upon my strengths, acquire new skills, and confront my weaknesses.

Investing in myself allowed me to overcome challenges, and it stretched my capabilities in ways I could not have anticipated. Investing in myself connected me with other like-minded people, and we cheered each other forward. Working toward any dream takes perseverance, but the wonderful thing is that you get to choose your dreams, and they're only limited by the stretch of your imagination.

Impact

My dreams continue to change, and they're shaped by my perspective of the world and my life. Nothing has impacted my life more than becoming a mother. My children have inspired me and stretched my capabilities in ways I could never have imagined.

My dream for my children is that I'll be able to inspire them to have amazing dreams of their own—without bounds or limits. I hope my children's dreams are filled with visionary goals and aspirations. Just like how I was inspired by my parents, I hope my children will know that they could achieve anything and be anything they want. I remind myself and my children every day to appreciate our opportunity to dream. With this appreciation, I've come to recognize that the impact of achieving my dreams extends beyond me. When I achieve my dreams, it can inspire others to make a difference in their own lives, and it leads to a positive impact in families for generations to come.

ABOUT LINDA YANG

Linda Yang is an experienced, innovative leader specializing in healthcare information technology and analytics. With over fourteen years of experience within many reputable healthcare organizations, Linda also holds a master of health administration in healthcare informatics and comprehensive technical certifications.

Linda continues to lead by example as one of the top experts in the industry. As a mentor, speaker, and author, Linda shares her experience as a first-generation Asian American woman in hopes of inspiring others to pursue their own dreams and passions. Linda enjoys imparting tools that have helped her overcome challenges, gain self-awareness, and find meaningful purpose. She is also an advocate for encouraging women to explore a career in information technology.

Linda lives in North Carolina with her supportive husband, Bee, and their energetic children, Madeline, Meredith, and Jeremiah.

To secure Linda as a speaker or to learn more about mentoring opportunities and inspiring resources, contact her here:

Web: www.PositiveScope.org
Email: LindaYang@PositiveScope.org
LinkedIn: www.linkedin.com/in/lindayang-mha

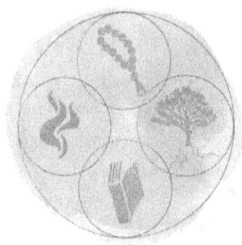

THE MAGIC OF YOUR INNER TEMPLE

Amalai

Who would have thought that falling, showing my nude body in front of an audience, and getting my home listed in a short sale by the bank would liberate profound and rich meaning into my life?

It was during the month of December in 2016 that I decided to take a tour of Turkey and visit the city of Cappadocia.

I was not used to the cold weather after living in Costa Rica for so many years, so I covered nearly all my body and head in clothing. I remember that only my eyes could be seen.

It was later in the day, as I was coming out from a hand-made-ceramic store and starting to walk into the next adventure for my day, when suddenly I felt a bolt of high-voltage lightning shoot through my whole body. The shock in my body started in my coccyx and rose to my crown; my entire spine was shuddering!

Ouch! I said in my mind as my head started spinning uncontrollably and my sense of equilibrium disappeared.

What could have caused this traumatic event? Well, as I stepped onto the sidewalk, I had slipped on the icy pavement in front of the shop. I found myself sitting down upon that cold and unforgiving winterly place, looking up at the skies—again!

I started laughing. It was the nervous laugh. You know the one where you laugh at a terrible joke that simply isn't funny or when you're feeling anxious.

A hero came to my rescue. The tour guide. His look was one of deep concern. He gently offered me his hand and helped me stand up, returning to the normal world of being vertical.

I said, "Everything is okay." I took his arm and added, "I will walk holding onto you from now on."

That was my second fall that day.

A couple of years later, toward the end of November 2018, I decided to close the door to a successful career in the corporate world and start my journey into entrepreneurship. I enjoyed many years as a leader at IBM, Thomson Reuters, and Cargill, but I could not refuse the continual call of my heart to venture into new freedoms to support others.

I chose to become nomadic and enjoy the freedom to go anywhere in our world. My first destination was Bali, the capital of yoga in Indonesia. This was an easy choice. I had been on a spiritual journey for several years, and Bali seemed like a great place to be again and to start this new chapter in my life.

However, during my last days in Costa Rica as I was preparing to head toward yoga central, disaster hit! Intense pain in my waist and hips started to become unbearable. This was the last thing I wanted to experience in my new life of freedom. Prior to this *incident*, I had visited the doctor several times, and his only suggestion was to inject drugs to help relax my muscles.

As the pain kept appearing and intensifying, the remembrance of *the fall* came to me, and I knew it! I ignored my body, believing I was superwoman, and now I was facing the consequences.

Damn! I said to myself.

Immediately, I headed to the hospital and asked them to take an X-ray to confirm my fears, with the expectation to have an accurate diagnosis and guidance on how to get better. However, the answer was devastating, and I felt totally frustrated. It felt like I had been given a life sentence.

"Well," said the doctor. "Your coccyx was broken and healed in the wrong way, which is causing the pain. There are many nerve terminations there, and it is impacting some of your main nerves."

I was expecting the hospital to provide a solution to my pain. After all, isn't that what doctors are for? My racing mind kicked in, asking, "Why now? What should I do to get better?" I kept calm and decided not the let panic take over.

The doctor then added, "You need to learn to live with the pain. This is an area of the body that we are not operating on anymore, so just understand that this is part of your life."

As you can imagine, within that moment, I felt abandoned and helpless. I wanted to cry. I was yelling at him in my mind: *Who are you to dictate that life sentence?* His statements were so damning and final! My heart sank.

I was starting to cry. Finally, he added, "Right now, you must go to the physiotherapist to try and control the inflammation. That will reduce the pain. You just must accept in your mind that pain will be an everyday part of your life."

FUCK! FUCK! FUCK! Do you really need to say that? I was yelling at him in my mind.

After beating Hodgkin's lymph cancer at the age of thirteen, I decided that *I* get to decide what to believe. And I decided that I know, from an inner knowing, miracles are possible. But in the medical examination office, I was unable to avoid the power of every word the doctor had said. They had penetrated my body. The spell was thrown. My whole human system just believed it. My understanding that he, and no one else, had power over my life did not feel enough. I felt utterly defeated.

I was less than two weeks from starting my great adventure. My soul was yearning for new freedoms. I was looking forward to the trip, and I had decided that nothing and no one was going to delay it! So, I carried on as planned.

I did follow the doctor's orders and received some physio-therapist sessions. These did help to reduce the pain. I was able to move better, but the pain was there, lingering on. An ever-present ghost that could not be exorcised.

With all that, I arrived in Ubud, Bali. As I landed, it felt like a huge weight had left my body. The thrill and excitement of being on my adventure filled me completely, encouraging me to keep handling the level of pain and following the complicated instructions I received about the ergonomics and protocol to make life bearable.

I arrived during the rainy season in Bali. My first stop was to stay at a beautiful retreat center located in nature called Yoga Barn. I had decided to enjoy a ten-day immersion-shamanic breathwork and a 200-hours yoga teacher training.

During my stay, there were horrifying moments as I was walking across the wet and slippery floor: thoughts and visions of falling again kept appearing. The ever-present ghost nudging at my confidence.

It felt that I was becoming a car or house uncontrollably swirling in a tornado, subject to its will. But I was able to see the calm within the eye of the tornado. Something was there. It felt like an old memory. But it was too difficult to see clearly, too difficult to get myself there as I had done on other occasions.

Gradually, the memory returned. Yes! I used to meditate and shift energy within my body. I know how to do this! Then the memory was pulled away. It felt it was impossible to return onto that stage. And as if I wanted proof that I could not trust my feet, I slipped once again as I was going down the stairs. It seems that I didn't know how to walk.

Then, I finally made a decision that would change my life.

I was going to freely fall into the whirlwind of the tornado. I was ready to see what it was showing me, so I started to go inside and observe. I was discovering the act of surrendering to an invitation to heal. As I was swirling, I became aware of three gifts that were going to expand my consciousness:

The Fear of Failing

I was starting to be an entrepreneur. My life/emotional coaching practice (at that time) was up and running. I was doing this in parallel with my corporate job. Self-reflection and natural observation of my life problem helped me to realize that perfection within myself was still there. It had never left and was ever present. A gift. The questions I asked myself were, *What will others say if I fail? What if I am just lying about all this, that I am dreaming to create and share with the world? What if everything I told myself is just bullshit and false promises?* As I was considering these thoughts, I was also encouraging myself by saying, *So what?! It is my life, not other people's lives. And if I fail or fall, well, I will get back up and keep tweaking and creating my dream. I have the gift of persistence, so I will always get up regardless of how many times I fail or fall!*

The Fear of Dying

Nightmares persisted of seeing myself many times a day, slipping and hitting my head on the unforgiving hard ground and dying. I remember there was a point that I told myself, *And if I died, what's wrong with that? I am going to die at some point.*

Am I too attached to my body and this life? I asked myself. Then I responded, *If I die, I die. I will die doing what my heart desires and with no regrets!* "I ACCEPT TO DIE," I shouted to myself, with a new mandate to my ego mind to know *my* decision.

The Lack of Trusting My Feet and Feeling Paralyzed

At the age of nineteen, I had started my career in the corporate world, always having a job, always enjoying the regular paycheck each month. Who doesn't enjoy a regular income! But now, I realized that I was afraid. Yes, I was in Bali, which appeared to everyone on the outside that I had a wonderful new direction in life and that I knew what I was doing. At some level, probably mentally, I was telling myself that liberating story, but my emotional body and my physical body had yet to catch up and were totally freaked out. The life I knew, keeping me safe and secure, had gone. I was entering into a new life of the unknown. A new charter and destination. I started to realize that I was outsourcing my inner authority. This was the most powerful revelation to understanding self-empowerment, freedom, and consciousness itself.

Revelations were gradually unfolding, as if orchestrated by a benevolent intelligence. Thoughts, energy within my body, behaviors, and confidence started to improve little by little, day by day. I started feeling good, with a new sense of freedom, self-awareness, and a start of evolving into my new self. I finished the 200-hour yoga teacher training. What you might be interested to know is that it was right after my fall in Turkey that I felt directed by the Spirit to study in Bali! Of course, I didn't know the reasons until two years later. "Trust your magic" is a saying that comes to mind.

Of course, while I was in Bali, self-care had become a daily priority. Regular massages helped to heal pain and trauma from my body, and at the same time I was growing stronger—emotionally and energetically. The beauty of my inner world, my inner temple, was introducing itself and aligning with its *human being*. I was becoming whole.

The falling experience taught me how to listen to my body and understand its language. The doctor's spell had been exorcised and the veil to wellness removed. A new world was opening up. The new knowledge and understanding, from past experiences, were beyond the mental or intellectual; rather, it had been embodied within every cell—fully accepting who I am, my potential, victorious over my fears. Miraculously, the pain was almost gone after a few months.

Following the Bali adventure and adding another qualification to my portfolio, I returned to Costa Rica and then went to Peru to attend a retreat in Puno I was organizing, and to participate in a sexual shamanic immersion. On this retreat, I had the opportunity to focus on activating the second chakra: the sacral chakra and the key to flourishing sexual relationships.

As part of my healing process and personal liberation, it felt important to examine and explore my relationship with sexuality and nudity. A sensitive subject for women.

Being the perfect woman, as Western civilization programs us to be, puts immense pressure on women, a mandate that can become intolerable. Of course, this burden of perfection was programming that I allowed to enter my being, both consciously and unconsciously. I was conforming to people's expectations, or what I thought those expectations were, hoping I could be accepted and do the right thing to receive love.

As I prepared for the retreat, I started to realize how much I feared people would see all the faults that I was feeling within myself, all my imperfections, all my naughty thoughts, all my weaknesses, all my flaws!

You have probably heard of ecstatic dancing: a free experience, where people move their bodies to the rhythm that they are feeling in the moment. During the retreat, I was enjoying an ecstatic dance—with a twist that everyone is naked! *Yikes, I* thought. *This is going to reveal my insecurities!*

So, I mustered as much courage as possible and onto the dance floor I went, joining other naked beings. During this ecstatic dance, I allowed my body to feel the music and to move my body in harmony with those frequencies and sounds. I felt a total connection. I started to relax. Men were dancing. Women were dancing. People were dancing with each other, enjoying the sense of harmony and freedom. So, I decided to be open to dance with another person, vulnerable and showing all my flaws. *No hiding now, Amalai,* I told myself. Someone passed by with whom I connected. We danced together for a bit, not touching but enjoying each other's presence. *Okay, that went well,* I said to myself. I moved onto another person, and then another person. I felt great. *It's okay to be naked,* I told myself. Then *wham!* I started to dance with this particular guy. Nice looking with a gentle smile. We stared at each other's eyes, feeling the music and dancing rhythmically, in tune, as if we had practiced choreography together since we were children. Then it happened! I felt a sudden shock, I started feeling sick, and my face burned.

I felt I merged energetically with him. We became one. I was able to feel everything he was feeling. He was feeling and seeing everything about myself, beyond my *nudity.* I felt so transparent. I was exposed. I started to feel afraid of this type of profound connection of acceptance and union with another.

Once again, fear started to rise and overwhelmed every part of my body. I backtracked and cut the connection with the man. It was a beautiful experience; one my soul was searching for, and I cut it!

Why? Why? Why? I asked myself. *Why didn't I allow myself to explore this connection of acceptance and union with another?*

I started to realize that another healing of unknown inner trauma was inviting me in regarding my nudity and connection with a man. *Here we go again, Amalai.* I started to ask questions and observe the tornado again from the calm. This is how I started navigating the waters of my sexuality, of my nudity itself, of allowing pleasure in my life. Tons of questions started to arise:

- What is it that I fear about being accepted and connected with another?
- Do I like men or women or both?
- What do I fear the most about being nude?
- What gives me pleasure?
- How can I touch myself with love?
- How do I really want to be fucked?
- How do I want to fuck others?

Questions came thick and fast, like a consuming tidal wave of impending inescapable doom. *Hold on,* I told my brain. *Slow down. Let's take this step by step.* From the tidal wave, tons of questions were uncontrollably washing over me. Some of them were too frightening to even consider.

Memories from my childhood returned. It was time to revisit those locked away and painful moments when I was sexually touched as a child. I felt guilty. But I knew that it was not my fault and that it was not right to be touched and violated by another human being, especially as a child. So, I asked myself, *How can I deal with this conflicted feeling of guilt and pleasure at the same time?*

There were so many emotions. Yet, little by little I faced them head-on. I confronted those memories, the people involved. I made the decision to forgive them, accept that I was *not* guilty, and I forgave myself for holding onto that guilt. *Time to move on,* I told myself. *I am a vibrant sexual being! I deserve pleasure, acceptance, and connection with another!*

Within this raw state, fully exposing myself to myself, I started to feel the rise of love from my heart. My inner being was healing me. I started to feel whole again. It became clear after doing a full immersion in this spiritual sexual shamanism I was liberated. I felt free. I felt myself opening to the world, ready to be seen as I was, embracing myself in all ways and listening to my inner being.

And this is how I understood the role of sexuality in my life, how it reflects in the intimacy of relationships. I kept diving deeper and deeper, experiencing, feeling scintillating sensations that my body wanted to reveal, becoming freer and freer, choice by choice, moment by moment.

An incredible inner transfiguration was underway. A new resurrection was emerging. A new me! Connecting with my body and sexuality was elevating my intuition, my inner knowing. A connection was forming with my inner being, my connection with the subtle world, my connection with nature—for we came from nature, and we are beings of nature.

And as I was enjoying this connection and dancing with the trees and singing and being myself and daring to become more authentic each day, life was bringing another experience to learn to trust my intuition deeply, not only from the mouth out, but from every atom of my body.

It was early April 2021. I received the news that my dear Uncle Saul passed away. It had been a challenging year as so many other beloved ones left this earth already.

Regardless of knowing that our spirit is eternal and infinite, the pain my human body felt was exhausting. The last couple of months I was receiving messages of so many departures of dear family members that I was still processing. I was continually sighing, knowing that I was still mourning them. I know this last uncle, though, was the last.

Saul was like a father figure, so my foundation of security was crumbling. And two days later, I received a call from my neighbor letting me know that a bank letter arrived saying that my house was going to a short sale for lack of payment.

"What? How so if I have the money in the bank account?!"

A memory from six months back came to me. During the month of June while I was in Costa Rica, I had this intuition to visit my bank where I have my house loan. I put it on my list to go. And of course, just thinking of the queues and all, I kept postponing. My intuition was telling me to go, and I decided to ignore it and prioritize other things.

And now, I was here. The automatic payments stopped working.

From one side, this was for not listening to myself and acting; and on the other side, I felt that another foundation of security, my home, was going away.

I felt insecure, unsafe, abandoned, left behind, ignored, lonely.

I walked the darkest night. And the only light that was coming to me was that the only safe place left, my root, my anchor, my stone, was within.

I realized the material things like my house, the material beings like my beloved uncle and family members were visitors, not permanent. And nothing is permanent; therefore, my foundation can only be what is infinite and eternal in truth, and that was my source.

Learning this lesson of not listening to my intuition, on not paying attention to the small things cost me almost $10K, which was the cost of the bank withdrawing the short sale.

From then on, I listened and acted accordingly, and from then on, my intuition was my best friend.

As you may realize already, life wisdom is always there, creating the opportunities our souls are yearning to free themselves from, the illusion that many times we fall into.

Now let me tell you this: I had the tools, I was ready to see the rawness in myself, I was inviting this rawness and authenticity every day. I believe it was this desire of communion with my inner temple and inner source that allowed me to understand the spiritual meaning of each experience and to embody its wisdom.

And I believe that that journey to the inner temple is waiting for each of you who are ready to meet with your radical authentic self and reclaim your inner authority, your inner goddess, access to the magic of your soul, and feel the radiant love of your inner source.

Remember this:

1. Your body holds an infinite intelligence waiting to emerge if you connect with it. Its power is for you to access and listen to.

2. Only you can choose what to believe about your body.

3. If you fall, it is okay! You always have the capacity

to get up again and again; you did it when you were a child, and many times you laughed when you fell. Other times you cried, but immediately after, you'd get up again. Always!

4. Your sexuality could reconnect you with your wildness within, with the rawness within you, the freedom, and with the permission to be seen, to shine, to be nude, and to be radically untamed and unapologetically yourself.

5. Your intuition has been communicating with you always, and many times you have followed it unconsciously. Your intuition becomes more real and accurate as you start recognizing it. It might be trial and error at the beginning until you recognize with absolute certainty which is your intuition and which your ego.

6. Following your intuition does not mean everything will be rainbows and flowers. It might be difficult sometimes, but it will keep you in full coherence with your soul.

7. And the most important: remember who you are. You are source manifested in a body! You are infinite and radiant love! That is your truth, that is your foundation, and that is the flame living within you, even though you might not be able to see it now. It is there, always, permanently, unconditionally, and lovingly.

I am so grateful that now I facilitate sacred programs for women to reconnect with the magic of their Inner Temple, based on the pillars of body, sexuality, and intuition. As a teacher of mine said to me, "My healing is the training, and the training is the healing." So, my own healing has become the training that I share from my heart with the world.

Again, you are source manifested in a body, and everything you do is source experiencing itself through you. There is no separation. Separation is only the illusion we are breaking ourselves free from.

Honor your life, as it is the sacred path of remembering who you truly are.

ABOUT AMALAI

Amalai is the founder of Escuela Amalai and Joyful Live Academy and creator of the Dance of Freedom and The Magic of Your Inner Temple.

Amalai accompanies women leaders, entrepreneurs, healers, and lightworkers in their journey of self-exploration, self-healing, and self-mastery so they can live in authenticity, freedom, joy, and fulfillment as well as support others.

She also lives and teaches in Costa Rica, and the USA (Crestone).

Her students said, "Amalai has created a life-changing experience with the program to activate your magic." Amalai is a certified coach by the ICF, NLP, and Timeline Therapy® instructor, HeartMath trainer, yoga teacher, PSYCH-K facilitator, meditation instructor, Angelic Reiki Master, Akashic Records Trainer, a channeler, and past-life regression facilitator. She has worked in the corporate world for twenty years leading regional teams.

To learn more about how you can connect and work with Amalai, please visit her website at www.Amalai.Love, where you can find information about her programs, events, and services.

Download your free five days of self-love from her website today. And if you want to accelerate your self-healing and self-mastery, join her advance programs.

Facebook: YoSoyAmalaiLove
Instagram: Amalai.Love
Instagram: Joyfullife.Academy
YouTube: Amalai Love
Web: www.amalai.love

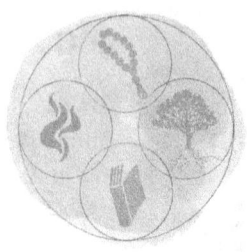

SELF-DESIGNED DREAMS

Teri P. Cox, MBA

What an amazing and spiritual journey *life* is!
As I embrace this next major chapter in my life, reflecting on the past decades, it feels like a dream. I'm humbled and grateful for it all:

- For the ability to channel my energy and combine my strengths, strategic thinking, and creativity.
- For my family, friendships, and business and personal connections.
- For the deep, loving marriage and soul partnership I shared with my husband Bill for so many years.
- For overcoming challenges and evolving through loss and grief.
- For my power with words, authentically from the heart, and actions for inspiring, engaging, and connecting the golden dots for problem-solving and positive impact.
- For invaluable life lessons worth sharing.

I'm so grateful for those blessings that embody my soul and the woman I am today. Those experiences—the magical breakthrough moments, the love, the wisdom—are collectively woven together, like golden threads into my life tapestry, protecting and carrying me forward.

The best of those—the golden nuggets—are all about change.

My first critical lesson came from a challenging family situation during my youth in Pittsburgh, PA. I was raised in a middle-class neighborhood in the 1950s by my loving parents who both worked. My father had a hardware store, while my mother worked for the City of Pittsburgh. Education was a priority for my family, so they made sure I was committed to my daily classwork. I excelled as a student, was supported by my great teachers, progressed to an accelerated program, and had lots of friends and fun social activities. All good, right? Except I was emotionally abused by my maternal grandmother who lived on our first floor. An ultrareligious Hungarian woman, bitter from losing most of her family during WWII, she was racist and sexist, felt cursed because she had five daughters and no sons. She took it out on us, except for my older brother, Jack, whom she favored. Her dominant bullying presence was constant with criticism and negativity. I tried to avoid and ignore her as much as I could, but her hurtful messages got to me, damaging my self-esteem and confidence. Some of those messages, now internalized, still haunt me today.

We put up with her for years, excusing her because she was the elder matriarch. Then, during my junior year in high school, she was so offensive to me and my two friends that I finally reached my limit. Overcoming fear to take a stand, given our family pattern, I chose to confront my parents. After serious discussion, we all agreed it was time for a change. My mother and aunts got together and rented an apartment for grandma. She moved out. Such a relief! What an empowering lesson for me and dramatic shift for my family to restore peace and harmony throughout our home!

Yet, what if I hadn't spoken up? Nothing would've changed. It's so important to act beyond fear, against abuse of any kind, and seek positive solutions, especially during times of emotional upheaval and political divisiveness on a global scale. Since then, I've continued to push beyond fear and self-esteem issues and developed keen protective antennae against abuse of any kind.

I'm a team player, but I learned to be an independent thinker about most things. I don't accept the status quo when innovation is better. It's good practice to think *outside the box* to consider better options. It's wise to be proactive about designing the changes you want for your life, then take action to make them happen.

I recall a conversation I had during a lunch meeting with a dean of the University of Pittsburgh, College of Arts and Sciences. I was his guest during the thirtieth anniversary of the founding of the Women's Studies Program. While at Pitt in the 1970s, I minored in that program. I had a self-designed major in communications and speech, with some of my courses taken at another university near Pitt campus. Knowing much of my story, the dean offered this perceptive insight: "You had a self-designed major and success as a student, then, from what I can tell, you've had a successful self-designed career, marriage—a self-designed life." I hadn't thought about it that way before, but he was right!

While a student, I also led an independent study research project, managing twelve students to gather needed information. Then after graduating, I was hired as editor to produce *HELP YOURSELF: A Women's (People's) Resource Directory for Pittsburgh,* published by the University of Pittsburgh, sold in local bookstores. I handled the PR and media interviews, which launched my career. I became PR director of the local Mental Health Association and hosted an issues-oriented radio talk show, *Impact,* on two local stations as a side gig.

Those experiences and opportunities during and after college built the foundation for a positive, independent, entrepreneurial mindset, igniting my passion for connecting the golden dots to creative solutions, with projects that make a difference.

A defining life-changing event was my interview with a spokesperson for a major oil company headquartered in Pittsburgh. He was on my show to discuss an Arab oil embargo making the news. Afterward, I recruited him to chair my media committee at the Mental Health Association. He also served on our board of directors. We both worked on local United Way campaigns, alongside the Steelers and Pirates of that era. Bill Cox became my mentor and trusted friend. Always encouraging and respectful, he said I was talented and special, but could tell I sometimes doubted myself. I shared the story about my grandmother and how I changed the situation. He applauded my action, but explained that, because of her abusive messages, "my mirror was cracked": I couldn't see the light that others saw in me. His supportive comments bolstered my confidence.

With new courage, two years later, I moved to Atlanta for a new position as the PR director of the Atlanta Merchandise Mart, loaded with demanding, nonstop responsibilities and challenges. I promoted rotating weekly regional markets amid special events and local southern politics. That stretched my skill set at times, requiring me to adapt and learn quickly. I kept in touch with Bill for his advice, as needed. Less than two years later, I moved back to Pittsburgh for a higher-paying marketing job. I reconnected with Bill, and our special friendship evolved into something deeper.

On New Year's Day in 1982, Bill became my beloved husband, soulmate, and partner in all things—and my biggest cheerleader! We were married in Denver and later moved to San Diego because of two transfers by his company. Ultimately, we settled in central NJ, where we both were employed by, then served as strategic communications consultants to, the healthcare and life sciences industry.

We found the perfect center hall colonial house near Princeton and loved sharing it with a family of cuddly fun-loving felines. We worked long hours with great clients, often commuting into New

York City. We also served in leadership positions, volunteering for several organizations with missions that mattered. We enjoyed discovering the great social and cultural activities in the tri-state area—concerts, Broadway plays, fine dining, and dancing. We attended formal events and engaged in PR and advocacy campaigns, sometimes working with celebrities and political leaders, and some became friends. We took long weekend trips and wonderful vacations as often as possible to explore most of the world. Everything meshed perfectly together. We were living the dream!

One of our most memorable vacations was a business trip and visit to Japan when we met Bill's family and saw the key sites in the country. Bill's father was part Japanese, growing up in Yokohama before he moved to the US, and he married and settled in Ohio. He arranged most of our visit with family connections—a personalized way to enjoy the country and its culture. We learned about traditions, such as *kintsugi,* the unique way the Japanese repaired cracks and gouges in broken dishes and pottery by filling them in with gold, transforming them into works of art rather than discards. What a beautiful idea! In many ways, Bill's *golden* messages of love and support over the years helped to repair those old cracks in my self-esteem.

As time went on, my work with corporate clients expanded. I needed to deepen my knowledge about business operations, finance, and marketing. We both were working in New York City, so I began coursework toward an MBA at New York University. That's when our dream life began to unravel.

Keeping up with work and my courses, I also had to take on the responsibility of managing my parents' healthcare. I rearranged my schedule and made regular weekend trips to Pittsburgh for several years to help my mother care for my beloved dad who had Alzheimer's disease. After his passing, the trips continued for years, as I became my mother's support caregiver while she was dealing with congestive heart failure.

During that period, Bill partnered with me in my *virtual*

strategic communications consultancy. We set up offices in our home, working mostly by email and phone with other like-minded, seasoned colleagues across the US, in Japan, and in the EU to help with our healthcare clients. Given my personal experience, and understanding the burdens on family caregivers, I was blessed with the opportunity to recruit organizations such as AARP, National Council on the Aging, Alzheimer's Association, Interfaith Caregivers Alliance, and others on behalf of a client company sponsor. Then, I partnered with them to create *CARING TO HELP OTHERS*, an award-winning user-friendly training program manual to help organizations train volunteers to assist caregivers of older adults. That program helped over 13,000 community organizations across the US and in Japan. It also had a website until 2018, utilized by millions of community agencies and caregivers, setting a new gold standard for programs serving the needs of family caregivers.

My mother passed away from a stroke in 1998. With little time to grieve, three months later, Bill was diagnosed with prostate cancer and other complicated illnesses. That's when we began our convoluted, arduous journey through his challenging eleven-year battle with cancer and more before he lost.

I managed his care and kept it all going in our lives until Bill was gone. Then I still tried to keep going, numb and in denial about how dramatically my life had changed. I resisted the truth until I couldn't any longer. I entered a period of darkness and fear about my unknown future and how to move forward.

With support from caring friends, I took time for quiet contemplation and meditation, a spiritual practice I've used since learning about it at Pitt. Closing my eyes, breathing deeply and going inward, I asked questions of my intuitive wisdom, a deep power we all have within us if we take time to listen. I found the answers I needed to take the first steps. The driven quintessential caregiver, always helping others, I gave myself permission to finally let go. I found the right resources to start learning how to keep going. With compassion and grace, I began to heal by focusing loving care and attention on *myself*. Stepping out of darkness into the new light of life, I was transformed.

It's been over a decade. I've been on this amazing metamorphic journey through loss, change, and personal growth. I've been enjoying life again with new friends and social groups, dancing to the music of local bands, dating, and traveling to favorite spots to visit special friends and loved ones. I've taken on new consulting projects and partnerships, books to write and coauthor, new courses, public speaking opportunities, and more. I've found new ways to pamper myself and fill my cup with gold.

Since 2020, the entire world has been rocked to the core by the COVID-19 pandemic, growing anger, violence, and divisiveness. Millions of lives have been dramatically impacted. Yet, I remain full of gratitude and hope for the future from the collective good and positive developments I've seen in the world.

I've had some setbacks, felt isolated and fearful at times, postponed projects, and needed much quiet time. Yet, I also seized the opportunity to sell my house of thirty-four-plus years during a rare hot sellers' market. As an agent of change, I've felt blessed, more prepared because of my journey and the powerful lessons I've learned while navigating through change to keep making progress. Here's some of that wisdom for connecting the golden dots that's worth sharing:

1. Change is inevitable. Nothing in life remains the same. You can't control or stop it, and resistance is futile.

2. The more you embrace change, the easier it is to navigate through it. How you respond makes *all* the difference!

3. Be patient and compassionate with *yourself*; give *self-love* during the process.

4. What doesn't kill you, transforms you. *Never give up!*

5. Work through fear by meditating, creating a vision and goals for the future, and continuing to take action.

6. Keep a positive mindset and express gratitude for all of the blessings in your life.

As I embrace a *major* milestone decade this year, I'm focused on maintaining my health, staying positive and connected, and achieving new goals, no matter what is happening in our world. My dreams are about reinvention, new companionship, new experiences, and opportunities for greater abundance, growth, peace, and joy. My vision is about carrying forward the best of my story, and all I bring to the table—my strengths, my gifts as a change agent, and the wisdom I gained from my life journey to inspire and help others navigate through change. With my brand, Teri P. Cox, MBA, I'm building a platform for sharing my story and key messages on social media, writing and publishing new content, public speaking, and consulting with new partners on products and services that support my passion for making a difference both for companies and individuals. Age is just a number! It's *my* time. I've earned my wings. I'm ready to fly!

The two greatest gifts God has given to us are this profound, beautiful journey called *life* and an amazing, resilient human spirit that can transcend beyond any obstacle or darkness, keep shining brightly, and soar to new heights.

Stay positive and keep dreaming! Find golden opportunities to make an impact! Now more than ever, our world needs your special gifts.

ABOUT TERI P. COX, MBA

With passion and creativity, Teri P. Cox has dedicated her life and career to challenging the status quo, connecting the golden dots to better solutions, and transforming through change and loss. An award-winning consultant, strategist, author, and speaker, Teri's provided leadership and expertise serving companies, professional women, those with cancer, and organizations supporting family caregivers across the country. Her projects have made a difference for millions.

Since 1992, Teri has led her firm, Cox Communications Partners, LLC, to position clients for results, helping them build win-win partnerships with aligned stakeholder groups. In 2005, Teri was named one of the *PharmaVoice 100* most inspiring people in the life sciences industry.

Teri is a past-president of the Healthcare Businesswomen's Association and served on the American Cancer Society (ACS) regional board. As advocacy leader, she received the national ACS St. George Medal award.

Teri has an MBA in marketing from New York University's Stern School of Business and a BA in communications/speech from the University of Pittsburgh.

Teri has been featured as a coauthor with Jack Canfield in the best-selling book, *The Recipe for Success*, and guest on podcasts, including *Ordinary People Doing Extraordinary Things* with Keri Roberts.

To learn more, you can connect with Teri P. Cox, MBA at:

Email: tcox@coxcommpartners.com
Linkedin: www.linkedin.com/in/teri-p-cox-mba
Facebook: www.facebook.com/teri.p.cox
www.teripcoxmba.com *(under construction)*

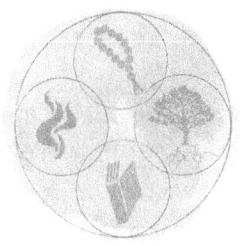

TWO CHOICES

Lori Anne De Iulio Casdia

L ife is about choices. It's actually rather simple. There are truly only two choices: yes or no, up or down, do it or don't do it, right or left, forward or backward . . . stuck or unstuck . . . you see what I mean?

Well I was stuck. So stuck that I lost myself. I got completely swallowed up. There were signs all along the way warning me that I completely ignored.

I had allowed myself to be "justed" to death. Just do this and just do that. It resulted in the greatest loss in my life of myself. I was willingly giving pieces of myself away. One tiny piece at a time until I couldn't even recognize who I was.

It was kind of like gaining weight. You gain a pound here a pound there then one day you look in the mirror or see a picture and wonder what the heck happened. It sneaks up on you, but it was always a choice.

You see, I was in love—truly thought I had a partner. The partner I had always dreamed of, a partnership that would last the ages. I would see myself walking silently down the beach in my eighties holding hands with my man. Like my parents. We were going to be together forever. We were great together.

Complemented each other. We made such a good team, or so I thought.

Little by little, he was telling me, "Don't act this way," "Don't dress that way," "Think this," "Think that."

I would fight myself thinking, *This isn't right. This doesn't feel right. This shouldn't be this way. Life is supposed to be joyous.*

I'd do whatever he said. When I didn't agree, I'd push back, and he'd push back harder. Call me names. Punish me by not speaking to me or just ignoring me. He would refuse to call or text me during the day or communicate in any way like he normally would have. And the ultimate slap of disapproval was that he would become magically too busy and unavailable.

I was stuck. I lost who I was trying to be, what others around me wanted and needed me to be. I didn't like this version of me—what I had become. There were signs all along the way, a nudge here, a sign there from the Universe, God, source (whatever you refer to as your higher power). We are given nudges, signals that tell us something isn't right. Like a flag on the field in football.

When I was growing up, I was taught, similar to the Jack Canfield Success Principles, to take 100% responsibility. Anytime something occurred that was uncomfortable or caused a disagreement or discourse, I looked at it and assessed what I did wrong. *How did I contribute to this event? What action or words did I say or do that created this discourse between us?* I would choose to take it all on . . . 100% responsibility for the discourse. It hadn't even crossed my mind that sometimes it wasn't my issue or responsibility at all. I don't believe he ever said he was sorry or took responsibility at all . . . ever!

So when he was having issues, suddenly I would feel—literally feel—the pain, the heartache, and the depth of his issues. It would feel like a cloud over me. I felt the heaviness from the weight of the issue or event. Even though it wasn't my issue at all, I would take it on as if it were mine to solve. I couldn't separate their issue from my responsibility. I needed to find a way to separate their "stuff" from mine. But I didn't know this yet. I was still sleeping—walking through life like I was in a dream.

And then one day I looked up and saw this huge pile of hay in front of me. That pile of stuff was everything I was holding here—in my heart and in my head. Each straw of hay represented a different issue. It was staggering, overwhelming, and seemingly something that one person couldn't overcome.

I decided that I must get out from under this huge mountain of hay. If it was all mine, then I would fix or repair each and every straw. But I could see some of the issues and I knew deep down intuitively they weren't really mine, but I owned them anyway. Sometimes just because I was in the room or someone shared their story with me, I would own it.

I had a choice to make. I had an opportunity. I didn't want to be stuck anymore. I wanted to make my own choices. I wanted to *get* to do things, not *have* to do things, and I wanted to find that eighteen-year-old girl who was strong, intelligent, and unstoppable. Where had she gone? Why did I allow her to fade away, get swallowed up?

I was in search of answers. I wanted to get unstuck. I didn't want to feel fearful, helpless, lost, scared.

And then one day, something happened.

I went to an event for work. It was a beautiful ceremony, I was in a peaceful place within myself, and as I surveyed the room, I saw this woman staring at me with sad eyes. As if she were there specifically to speak to me. I had to walk in her direction to leave the auditorium. As I passed her, she stopped me and apologized for disrespecting me. I had no idea what she was talking about. She proceeded to tell me a story, show me pictures, detail every step, move, and maneuver. Yes, he had been cheating on me with her.

I went numb. No emotions. I didn't get upset. I felt nothing. As if I already knew. I asked questions to gauge whether she was telling the truth. She happily proved it with pictures, emails, and texts. She had it all. It was almost as if she were enjoying telling me her tale. I did and said nothing. I came home and crumbled. I couldn't get the images out of my head. The words she spewed. It was simply awful.

After weeks of weeping and running scenarios over and over in my head, I decided no more! No more tears, no more walls, no more of this nonsense. It no longer served me. I tired of having my grand pity party. I chose to find a way to become unstuck. Whatever that meant.

I searched and searched for answers. I read self-help books, I went to psychics, mediums, had tarot card readings, and watched YouTube videos of astrologists, tarot cards, horoscopes. All in search of the inner peace I was seeking.

I eventually found myself in therapy, trying to figure my way out of this fog of disconnection, of why this was happening. What did I do? Was I not enough? Pretty enough? Smart enough? Didn't I matter? Wasn't I enough to love? Therapy offered help and guidance, but one day something my therapist shared resonated so deeply that I started to read everything I could on the subject.

She said it sounds like these people are all narcissists. I hadn't heard this word before.

Narcissists have an inflated sense of their own importance. They have a need for excessive attention or admiration, always have troubled relationships, and lack empathy for others. They are typically extremely magnetic and charming. They are looking for obedient admirers. A good time. They don't like conflict or dissension. Your sole role is to prop up their insatiable ego. They even tell you what to think and how to feel. They are unapologetic about all of it.

They lie about themselves and others. They are entitled and manipulative, and they take zero responsibility. They are experts at deflection and blame; they blame you for what they are doing and accuse you of it. It is a mind game that doesn't end well for the receiver.

I found myself making excuses for his bad behavior or minimizing myself for the hurt that I was feeling. I found myself trying to reason and use logic to help him understand the painful effect his behavior had on me. I thought if he understood how much he hurt me, what was hurting me, and why, he'd change. I found out with a narcissist it doesn't matter. He wasn't getting what he wanted or what he needed. That is all that mattered to him, and sadly that is all that will *ever* matter to him. So he moved on.

Months later, I found myself at a friend's spiritual weekend event. My friend, Paul Saladino, a psychic medium, intuitive counselor life coach, certified hypnotherapist, and energy healer located on Long Island, had this event every year. I remember this day so clearly. Little did I know it would change the trajectory of my life.

Paul had hundreds in attendance. I sat in the back alone, sad and weepy as I had been for months, trying to sort out what had happened. I was a little nervous to be there, feeling anxious about being there alone but a little empowered.

Then this speaker came up. Her name, Debi Silber. The words coming out of her mouth spoke directly to me. Truly, at some points, as if in a movie, everyone else blurred and she was looking directly into my eyes and into my heart, talking directly to me. Her confidence was unshakable. Her knowing was innate. She knew me . . . she saw me . . . *Yes, yes, yes, this is what I am feeling, saying, hearing, and thinking.*

I bought her book, the #1 international bestseller, *The Unshakable Woman.* I devoured the words, her stories, and felt compelled to reach out to her. I needed to figure this out. Through working with her, I found out yes indeed, he and others in my life are narcissists. I was calling them into my life and had to learn to stop that. But how?

With Debi's help, I discovered I was suffering from post-betrayal trauma. You see, Debi Silber is the founder of the PBT (Post-Betrayal Transformation) Institute, author of *Trust Again (I am one of the fab 14 - part of my story is referenced as Julianna, p.45) and* is a holistic psychologist and a health, mindset, and personal development expert. Through our work, it was so clear to her and now me I had severe trauma from betrayal.

I would take the physical abuse I received years back over the emotional abuse—because wounds heal. Black and blues disappear, but owning all the bad in someone else's life, questioning your every decision, choice, breath, step, questioning one's self-worth predicated on what could not be described as anything less than a selfish narcissistic predator is unquestionably the cruelest, most devastating experience. Not only is your heart breaking, but your mind, body, and soul are too.

In life, there are always only two choices (pulling emotions and ego out): yes or no, go or stay, right or wrong. You can do something or not do something. It sounds so simple, but when you throw the heart in, the game seems to change. The mind almost goes into a drugged state.

Life shouldn't be an emotional roller coaster. It should and will be challenging and a ride but not a daily emotional roller coaster—walking on eggshells, never knowing if Jekyll or Hyde is going to appear.

The betrayal puts every minute of every day of the past with them in question. Healing from the pain caused by another person involves healing our self esteem, self-worth, trust issues, and more.

Now we have identified what was keeping me stuck and what I was allowing to imprison me. How do I find myself again?

I knew at this point it was time to move on. I never played the victim. Actually I didn't feel like a victim. Okay, maybe when I was having my pity party. Instead, I took responsibility for my actions, and apparently, I was taking responsibility for others as well. I needed to find a way to take this pile of hay—issues, challenges, unfinished feelings, situations, and interactions—and figure out how much of it was actually mine.

I started the process of taking each straw of hay off the pile and discerning whether it was a *me issue* or a *them* issue.

You may be asking why the delineation. It's about being able to unravel what we need to take responsibility for and what we don't. Sometimes it is partially our responsibility, and sometimes it isn't our responsibility at all. By looking at the issues as they come and being able to identify them, you take the amount of time we dwell on an issue down to seconds. Many times others want us to solve their problem—own their problem merely so they don't have to own it themselves. That's not okay! Say it to yourself, "That's not okay."

That *me issue–you issue* switch is a really important toggle that we all need to learn how to use. I found by being able to recognize what was mine and what was others' enabled me to stay genuine to myself. When you do this, you won't find yourself doing things that don't or no longer resonate with you. You will be a better friend, partner, lover, mother, aunt, teacher, coach, mentor, whatever you are to the people in your life.

You can only imagine what I found on this journey. I had to actually process each piece of hay. It was arduous. It was sometimes painful, regretful, but it had to be done. I was not going to be swallowed up any longer. I had to face my past if I wanted to be free and have a future. I had to learn to trust, in myself and then in others.

Through this process, I found that I had rediscovered myself. I found that I had tried to accommodate so many people that I lost who I was. I was swallowed up and trying to be somebody to everyone as opposed to just being genuinely myself.

I went through a huge transformation between the betrayal and today. Now I seek and find joy every day. I do my power hour of meditation, reading, gratitude journaling, exercise, and affirmations. I get to serve others and help them achieve their vision and dreams and Soar to Success. I only own what is mine. I know what I want and what I don't want.

After my journey of transformation, I do what I want, when I want. I am completely myself. I have no walls. I allow people to see my vulnerabilities. I embrace my friends, loved ones, colleagues, and clients for all they genuinely are and encourage them to embrace themselves, as they are perfect in every way. I endeavor to always be the best me I can be. Some days I am better at it than others.

Now I know it is all right to be vulnerable. It is human to make mistakes. Before, when I made a mistake, I would beat myself up for days and weeks on end. I would bring it back up years later and be unrelenting to myself. No one could possibly say harsher things to me than I did to myself.

So I practiced differentiating between issues that were mine and others'. Every day I would get better at taking that learning curve down from two weeks to within seconds. I would be able in any circumstance to look at the situation, assess it, and determine what was my responsibility, if any. Now it's just natural and I can make this determination within seconds. Might I even say now it is a habit. A better, healthier habit.

I am so grateful for all of my experiences because it made me who I am today. It made me a better coach. It drove me to learn more about how I could assist and coach others to Soar to Success. I started to study and get certified under Jack Canfield, Tony Robbins, Patty Aubery, Mary Morrisey, Bob Proctor, Brené Brown, Byron Katie, Dr. Joe Dispenza, Dr. Joe Vitale, Ray Higdon, Esther Hicks, Simon Sinek, and many more. My goal was to learn from the best in the industry to serve my clients as best I could—to bring multiple styles and tools to my clients. It morphed into the Lori Anne method of Soaring to Success.

I added to those tools affirmations, gratitude journaling, meditation, essential oils, healing sound bowls, AFT reset, mindset, power hours, and more. I was introduced and certified as a Ho'oponopono practitioner and Kundalini Meditative Yoga practitioner.

I felt alive. Everything was clearer. I couldn't absorb enough from these experts in the craft.

I am sharing my story to let you know if I can do it, if I can transform into a beautiful butterfly serving others, then you can too. This is to let you know there are tools out there and coaches out in the world ready to guide you through the journey. Be it this simple tool of a *you issue–me issue* or other ones to help you gain clarity and to get you from where you are to where you want to be. To help you navigate the journey so you don't lose yourself but actually grow yourself. To remind you that all of our Success Codes are already within us when we are born. We merely need to look inward to achieve our fullest potential and be able to discern what we will own. To help you get unstuck if you choose to be unstuck. Whatever you choose is the right choice for you.

My final words are yes, it is scary. Yes, it's work. Yes, you will have to jump some hurdles and have some challenges. But aren't you worth it? If you even paused for a second at that question, allow me the liberty of helping you: most definitely you are worth it. I encourage you to try to see the signs at the nudge. I can promise you that transformation will leave you feeling happiness again; you will find joy again. You will reconnect with your higher power and find your purpose. You will be in alignment with who you really are, and you will not have to do it alone. Look inward and follow your dreams. There is a reason why you are here. So you can choose to play a higher role, serve a higher purpose, show up for you, and show up BIG. It might just lead you to your happy ending.

ABOUT LORI ANNE DE IULIO CASDIA

Lori Anne is a life and business transformational success coach, high-performance coach, business and marketing positioner and strategist helping entrepreneurs and business owners who are just starting out or who feel stuck in their life and business to create the business that will sustain the life they desire.

She is the radio host of Healthy Lifestyle with Lori Anne and has been seen on Fox, News 12, Jack Canfield Success TV, and more. With thirty-five-plus years' experience in business and marketing, adding tools as a master mindset mentor, and becoming a life coach, Law of Attraction practitioner, and more, Lori Anne has spent thousands of hours learning from the best in her field to bring you the best tools. Lori Anne is an award-winning coach and speaker, and she believes her life's work is to bring positive creative energy into the world.

Her purpose is to use her love and compassion to illuminate, inspire, educate, and empower people to fulfill their fullest potential, find and embrace their life purpose, live their highest vision, forge a strong foundation, guide them to achieve their vision and dreams, and Soar to Success.

To connect with Lori Anne for speaking engagements; to learn more about her programs, events, retreats, free resources, and coaching services, you can contact her directly:

Web: www.LDCStrategies.com
Email: lacasdia@ldcstrategies.com
FB/IG: LDC Strategies

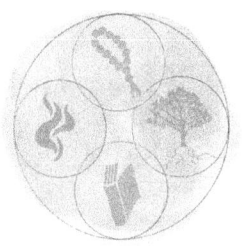

TRUST YOUR TRUTH

Keri Gavin

My fingers were tightly wrapped around my mom's hand for balance as I hopped from one grocery store tile to the other in the checkout line. A grocery store checkout is the perfect place for a seven-year-old to get fidgety.

I misstepped on one of the orange squares and bumped into the elderly woman behind me. As my eyes glanced up, I was met with a cheery smile from a well-dressed, silver-haired, rosy-cheeked, beautiful blue-eyed elderly woman. In hindsight, she was like a real-life Mrs. Doubtfire. "Oh, no problem, dear," she said as she gently helped me stand upright again.

After a few moments of small talk between her and my mom, the elderly woman leaned forward toward me. Her hat was perfectly placed on her head, and her blue eyes began to widen with wonder. She leaned in closer toward me and asked, "What do you want to be when you grow up, sweetie?"

Hopping back and forth, swinging my skirt behind me with each turn of the squares, I didn't even look up, but I proudly announced without hesitation, "A mom!"

Out of the corner of my eye, I could see her stand tall again, and she giggled a bit as she responded, "Ohhhh, how cute, but that's not a job, sweetie! What do you really want to be?"

I remember a feeling of confusion. It was as if someone had told me the sky wasn't blue. Being a mom isn't a job? It isn't a thing? My little brain was having a hard time computing what she said.

It was in that split second—with a stranger, who asked a simple conversational question—I quickly learned there were rules of life according to the outside world. Just like that, my own self-trust started to wobble.

Confused, but wanting to respond, I glanced up as she towered over me, my pigtails swinging with each turn of my head as I was trying to make sense of that new information. I politely responded, "Um, well, I think I will be a teacher then!" I replied with a smile beaming across my face!

"Oh, how wonderful!" she answered as her hands clasped in front of her with approval. I felt a sense of confused acceptance. My sweet seven-year-old heart was struggling to reconcile what I truly desired with what the world was telling me was acceptable.

It was the first time I felt a disconnect between what I knew to be true for me and what others wanted for me.

It was technically our senior year at Keene State College, but logistically my best friend Erin and I had one extra semester in the fall after our graduation in May. We had taken our sophomore year off together while the rest of our friends stayed the course. We returned to Keene State the following year, which put us behind the rest of our friends by only a semester since we both had taken some classes at community colleges in that time. Since we were together for that bonus semester, it wasn't a problem—we were actually excited to have one extra semester together before the "real world"! Because we had one extra semester, I made the decision (with her guidance and support!) to do an exchange semester at North Carolina State University for the spring semester so I could live with my then boyfriend.

While I didn't want to leave our off-campus house, we both agreed it was a great opportunity and adventure, and since we'd have a whole extra semester together, just us, why not! We agreed January 1, I would move to North Carolina and return to New Hampshire for the fall. We would live together in the fall to finish the credits needed for our psychology degrees and then be out in the big world with the rest of them.

It was midday on a Wednesday as I was doing some schoolwork on my computer. An AOL instant message popped up on my computer from one of my closest friends Mikey. "Can you talk?" he asked. My heart skipped a beat, and my stomach felt like it dropped through twenty-seven stories in an instant. It was unlike him to message me like that—I intuitively knew something happened. "Of course," I replied. "Call my cell.'"

I stood up and began pacing the bedroom, looking outside to the parking lot of the apartment as I waited for his call. It couldn't have been more than two minutes, but it felt like one hundred years. Barely hearing a full ring, I answered the phone. "Hey, what's wrong?" I asked in a panic. With a deep sigh and hesitation in his voice he responded, "I don't even know how to tell you this . . . Erin died." The room felt wobbly. My body started to tingle, my eyes were darting back and forth outside looking into the parking lot. My body was processing what he said before my brain could even recognize it.

"What?" I said, "Erin who?"

"Our Erin," he responded.

"What do you mean? Not possible. Wait, what? How? I don't understand?" I choked out.

"We don't know much," he said. "She passed away in her sleep, and we don't know anything else yet."

It couldn't be real. She was twenty-one. Nobody at twenty-one just goes to sleep and doesn't wake up.

"There has to be a mistake," I said. My brain was racing. It had to be someone else. Maybe he was confused.

He wasn't confused. It was real. The poor guy had to keep repeating it to me over and over. My brain would not accept it.

After a whirlwind of flying home, going to our apartment, finally being back with my college framily (friend/family) as well as somehow navigating a funeral I never thought I'd experience, life was moving on. I was angry, I was sad, I couldn't understand how the world was existing without her.

Days turned to weeks, and weeks turned to months, but the heaviness, pain, and sadness stayed. As the end of the summer came, I made one of the most difficult decisions of my life. I knew I couldn't live in our college town without her, without any of our friends, alone. I knew for my mental health and my own well-being, that wasn't an option. But I also knew I was just a few credits away from my degree.

I prayed, I asked for guidance, and I asked for signs, but it wasn't until I turned into my own heart that I got my answer.

I knew I had to finish my semester, but I also knew I had to do it in a way that worked for me. I journaled and asked myself some questions to access clarity. I talked with my therapist and my parents and ultimately decided that the best way for me to do this was to commute the two hours to college, stack my classes back-to-back, sit through six hours of classes, and commute two hours home three days a week. The other two days I nannied full-time 7 a.m. to 7 p.m., and I would manage to keep myself busy.

As I wiped my tears sitting at the beach one afternoon, I knew I didn't go that far to only go that far. I knew she would be so mad at me if I didn't finish! I vowed to her in the moment that I would create a life of memories and moments full of life enough for the both of us.

I also knew it wasn't as simple as everyone was telling me to just "go back and finish it out." I had to do this my way. I had to create a path that worked for me and still got me to the result. That was one of the first monumental moments when I leaned into my self-trust rather than outside approval.

I finished my psychology degree and just a few months later started toward my master's in education in an intensive accelerated program. A few months into that, I got pregnant and three months later got married! Just as I graduated from Lesley University with my masters in Elementary Education in May, my sweet baby boy arrived June first.

This was it. This was what I had been dreaming of all my life. After ten years of nannying for other families and being an elementary school teacher, camp counselor, and babysitter since the age of nine, my dream of becoming a mom was finally real.

From the moment I held him in my arms in the middle of the night, to the sleepless days and weeks to follow, it was everything I dreamed of and more. Sleep deprived for sure, but I was never bothered by the middle-of-the-night feedings, countless hours in the rocking chair, and many nights in the moonlight cuddling this fresh, sweet, new baby boy. I actually quite enjoyed the stillness of these moments while the rest of the world was asleep and it was just me and him.

About three to four weeks into this new role as mom, I sat in the glider chair for a late-night feeding in his room. I found myself staring at his little soft cheeks, his fluttering eyes as he was slowly closing them back to sleep, his tiny arm tucked under my side and his other arm across his chest as his little fingers gripped onto my pointer finger. The full moon poured light into his bedroom so bright it was as if it was daytime. As I sat gliding in the chair studying all his features, tears began streaming down my face. He already looked bigger, fuller, stronger. He was changing so fast, and it was already going so quickly. Even if I didn't know what day it was, every day was spent with him, and yet, I felt like I was already forgetting things.

It was at that very moment I decided I was not going to go back to teaching, and I was going to find a way to work and be with my kid(s). I didn't want to miss anything. I wanted to see it all. I had dreamed about this my entire life, and I knew there was no way I could not spend my days witnessing this little human explore and discover the world.

I decided I would go back to nannying where my son could come with me. I found an amazing family that welcomed me and my sweet baby Monday through Fridays. At the same time, I had discovered a passion for documenting all these memories I didn't want to miss through photography. Photography had always been a passion of mine, and through all my childhood years you could always find me with a camera. I just wanted to document memories, even from a young age. I was always the one taking pictures with friends, family, and especially if we ever went on trips or adventures.

As I was documenting my own life, my own family, my own memories, I started taking my camera everywhere I went. I started a personal blog that documented our adventures. That quickly turned into taking photos of the neighborhood kids as we all played in the backyards, then friends and family Christmas cards, and before I knew it, people started asking if they could hire me! It was so surprising to me because I never set out to be a professional photographer! I simply didn't want to miss moments from my own life, and I began documenting things through the lens of a mother's love. Being present in the little moments and freezing them in time.

If I'm completely honest, I didn't know that could be a full-time profession! I did have one friend, Melissa, who was a professional photographer, so with these increased inquiries, I reached out to her for some insight. I told her people were asking me to take photographs of their families and she squealed with excitement. "You have an eye for this in a way that can't be taught, Keri. Trust that! You can learn business as you go, but the creative eye is so natural for you!"

In the months and years to follow, I spent late nights and early mornings reading, studying, and learning photography as a craft in online forums and websites as a business. (Pre-Facebook and online education as it is today!) I began attending workshops and hiring mentors, and before long, I was officially a professional photographer documenting real-life memories for families in the Boston area. Things were really picking up, and I was able to do meaningful work and be with my kids. It felt like a dream come true.

Just a few short years later, I found myself divorced at thirty years old with two small children under the age of four and with a creative business. By identifying something that I loved to create and share with people and making money doing it, I had created an accidental successful business! If you had asked me years before if I could imagine that as my future, I would have said you're crazy.

But despite things going well, as I was newly divorced, I couldn't help but feel like everyone in my world started planting the seeds of doubt in my head. While it may have been coming from a good place and wanting me and my kids to have safety, it was difficult to hear people telling me to go back to teaching because it was "safer." It was difficult to hear that I was "just taking pictures" and it was time to get serious. I was serious. I had been serious for a few years! I had created a business that brought me and others so much joy. While it was amazing, I found myself noticing other people's opinions in my head; just as my business was beginning to grow, doubt was also beginning to creep in.

I decided against all odds and approval to dig deep down into the essence of who I am and remember that even when it's difficult to hear other people's opinions, I trust myself and I know what's best for me. So I continued my photography business and did not get a nine-to-five. The truth is, I never dreamed of being an entrepreneur; I didn't have lemonade stands on the sidewalks or make bracelets to sell in school like many others did. I did always dream of being with my kids as they grew up in the world. I had mostly found my groove of doing work that felt so meaningful and also served my clients!

My business began to grow and expand. With the amazing support of my fiancé, close friends, and family, I was named Best of Boston photographer as well as a few other awards. I was 99 percent referral based; I had created incredible relationships with my clients and colleagues. It was working! The more successful I became, the more questions I started to receive from other creatives asking how I created this successful business. The more I started sharing with them, the more they started creating their own success.

As I continued to grow with photography, I realized I was a great teacher when it came to helping others do the same with their creative work. I was using my (formal) education skills but in a different lens. I was leveraging my psychology background and education skill sets around teaching success to creatives, coaches, and other service-based entrepreneurs.

Once this really started to pick up, I noticed a new fear pop up: What if I don't really know what I'm doing helping other people? I somehow started to believe that I wasn't as good as I should be at the mentoring side of business and I needed to know the real secrets I was somehow missing, despite having created my own success firsthand. I had fallen in love with helping other people create their own success by doing things their own way, but I somehow felt like I was missing a big secret to this next level of success for myself in this new arena outside of photography.

This fear got so big I began going outside of myself and hiring other business focused teachers and mentors who I thought knew all the answers.

I started implementing and doing things they were suggesting, even though I knew they were against my own beliefs—against what I knew to be true—and before long, my business started to go the other way, the opposite of thriving. Things started feeling more difficult and frustrating, and I wasn't helping and serving as many people as I wanted to. It wasn't true that I wasn't good at business at all. It was that I was doing things that I didn't believe and didn't feel good about!

The brutal truth is, I spent a few years using various crutches as to why I couldn't fully get back in the game and go after my dreams of fully supporting people to create their own version of success for themselves. I let myself off the hook for a long time, until one day I realized all the excuses I was telling myself were simply just excuses and not the truth. I had been putting myself, my dreams, and my goals on hold simply because my confidence got rocked a bit. And rather than question if it was true, I allowed it to control my dreams.

I had to take an honest look at myself and ask the hard questions.

Was it true I wasn't good at business?

No. I had already created a very successful business. I didn't struggle until I started implementing things I didn't actually feel good about, that were against my grain, that were against what I know for myself.

This is what I know to be true:
Every path to success works. It's choosing the path of getting there in a way that we want to do that creates success. If the destination is the same, it can be as simple as asking, Would you like to take a train or would you like to take a car? You'll end up in the same place, it's just a preference.

This is what has helped me and other people:
Your heart is your compass. What brings you joy and lights you up is not an accident. Remembering that and being reminded of that consistently is one of the most essential parts of reaching your goals.

This is my brilliance:
Navigating the currents of success through a framework that allows you to access your desires and what you naturally enjoy is what allows you to create your own version of success with your

values and priorities. You don't have to choose between making memories with your loved ones and making money—it's an *and*, not *either-or*.

This is my genius:

I help people turn down the volume of self-doubt and turn up the volume of self-trust by changing the way they think about things so they can make the impact and income desired by sharing their heart with the world. Supporting people to go from being a success seeker to a self-trusted CEO (clear empowered operator) of their life and business unlocks anything and everything they desire. I have a unique, simple, and powerful ability to reframe and offer an alternate perspective that allows people to access more relief, more freedom, more grace within themselves.

This is what I believe to be true:

We must tell ourselves the truth about what we actually want for our lives—not what our parents want, not what our children want, what we want. Then, and only then, can we start to take the microsteps toward that becoming our reality.

- I am here to hold the space and the vision for creatives, coaches, and service-based entrepreneurs, to say that you absolutely can go for this!
- It's okay to pause.
- It's okay to pivot.
- It's okay to lose your confidence.
- It's okay to burn it down and start again.
- It's okay to start over.
- It's okay, and I would assert even essential, to get the right kind of support for the journey. We aren't meant to go it alone.

The most important piece, above all else, is to know how to access what is true for you and then surrounding yourself with people who align with that.

That is the very thing I help people access: the confidence and power within themselves to create their own version of success. Full Stop.

Once I was able to quiet the outside noise and come back to my own self-trust, my own self, my own voice, my own intuition, my mentoring and coaching practice began to grow again. I absolutely love to help people discover it's all part of the human experience, and that it is 100% possible to create whatever is important to you in a way that brings you joy and lights you up.

When we can train our brain and regulate our nervous system and learn the rules to the game, whatever we want to create in this world is available to us.

I knew from a very young age I wanted to be a mom, and I briefly let a stranger question that dream. I started a photography business and almost allowed people to talk me out of it for the illusion of safety. I did allow other people to tell me there are only certain ways to create success even if it compromised what I knew to be true for a little bit. This is the journey of what I call the great remembering and forgetting. This human experience is a roller coaster of emotions—and sometimes we forget what we know to be true for ourselves, and we need to be reminded.

There is no one roadmap to success, but rather a compass that is calibrated to your own heart. Cultivating a practice and the emotional intelligence to come back to self-trust above anything else is our way to success. When we navigate the currents of success, we must always start with the desires in our heart first.

We can chart our own course, align our inner compass, and launch ourselves into the life we imagine when we trust ourselves to know the way. That is my brilliance. That is the magic I help people create for themselves. Remember, your success is inevitable. I believe in you.

ABOUT KERI GAVIN

Keri Gavin is a success and business mentor for creatives, coaches, and service-based entrepreneurs. Keri empowers and educates success seekers to become self-trusted CEOs (clear empowered operators). Self-trusted CEOs create businesses that are centered around their passions, values, and priorities first so they can make the income and impact they desire while actually living the life they used to dream of!

Keri is a former teacher turned successful professional photographer for fifteen years, turned professional success and business mentor. By combining her love of teaching, personal business success, and passion for helping others, Keri supports others to create their success their own way.

Keri is the founder of Rebel Hearts Business Academy and The Heart of Money Experience. These programs are centered around empowering and educating Creatives, Coaches, and Entrepreneurs to make money doing what they love, so they can do more of what they love to do! She is also the host of The Confident Creative Podcast—*Daring for the Dreams*, where you will hear insights and conversations that take lived experiences and turn them into beneficial life lessons for all of us.

Keri's clients and students achieved massive success in their own life and business because the magic is found in creating and sustaining a successful mindset, which leads to a successful life and business. As a mindset expert, Keri has a unique approach to shifting perspectives and helping people access insights for themselves in everything she teaches.

To learn more about how you can connect and work with Keri, please visit her website at www.focusingontheheart.com where you can find her programs, sign up for her weekly newsletter, and purchase her self-study powerful programs.

You can find her on social media here:

Facebook: Keri Gavin Rebel Heart Entrepreneur
Instagram: @keri.gavin
TikTok: @keri_gavin
The Confident Creative Podcast, *Daring for the Dreams*

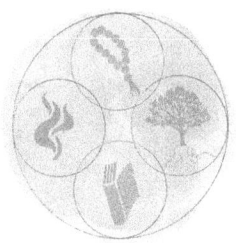

YOUR HEART KNOWS THE WAY

Mary Gervais

Follow your heart. It knows the way. Follow your heart and open the door to amazing adventures, surprising self-discoveries, and exciting levels of personal empowerment.

When we listen to our inner voice, when we believe in our intuition and innate wisdom, we create new pathways for our heart that can lead to greater peace and joy in our lives.

My own follow-your-heart spirit began when I was very young with treasured childhood books like *Patrick Muldoon and His Magic Balloon* and *The Story of Heidi.* These books opened the door to a world of wonder: the Swiss Alps, Buckingham Palace, the Sphinx, Italy, and Japan. The stories also created the first "pull"—a tug that fed my natural curiosity about the world and where I might fit into it.

When I was ten, I received a gift subscription to *National Geographic Kids* magazine. Every month I devoured the "Go on Safari" and "What in the World" sections. Around the same time, I met a Belgian foreign-exchange student who was staying with family friends. I thought this was super cool, and it ultimately inspired me to apply to Rotary International's Student Exchange program.

I was fifteen when Rotary selected me to go to Johannesburg, South Africa, on behalf of our local club, my community, and the US. I spent a year training for the trip and was excited about my destination. But as the departure date neared, it became increasingly clear that internal resistance to apartheid made travel there unsafe. When Rotary International called to explain this, I had only one question: "Where can I go instead?"

The one country with an opening was Bolivia. I said yes, hung up the phone, and grabbed *The World Book Encyclopedia*. Visions of ancient civilizations, lush jungle vegetation, and soaring Andean mountains swirled around me. I was enthralled; my parents, less so. My mom was more than a bit worried. But *my heart knew* that I was meant to go, and I did.

In Bolivia, I learned to think and converse fluently in Spanish. I developed confidence in speaking before groups. I learned to manage my own finances and make decisions, and gained a greater sense of who I was as a person. I also learned to appreciate and accept other people and cultures.

I was gone for a year. When I returned home and began my senior year of high school, I struggled with reconciling my newfound independence with once again being looked upon as a seemingly "ordinary" teenager in a beautiful but ordinary small town in western New York. Luckily, I had some incredible friends, and our Rotary Club's Swedish exchange student, Helene, and I also became fast friends. We instantly bonded as international travelers with a passion for dreaming big dreams.

In addition to traveling, two early passions that always gave me pleasure were baking and cooking. So when I applied for college, hospitality management and culinary programs were high on my list. On the way home from one college visit, my mom suggested we make an impromptu stop at her alma mater, an all-women's college near Albany, NY. I loved the feel of the school and ended up having an incredible conversation with the admissions team. The school didn't offer hospitality management or culinary arts, but they did have an international studies program. Eureka! I knew instantly that I would be my best self at this college.

Nearing our high school graduation, Helene said she wished I could go home with her. We looked at each other and said, "Why not?" So, we hatched a plan and presented it to our parents. Everyone was on board and, although gap years didn't exist in 1983, my college agreed to defer my entrance for a year because studying in Sweden fit in with my major. As things fell into place, my dad reminded me that "Where there's a will, there's a way." His advice was important, and such affirmations have always encouraged me.

I also remember my exhilaration when my flight departed JFK in late August. That excitement lasted throughout that year abroad. I studied Swedish in the mornings and attended school in the afternoons. I traveled to Denmark, England, Russia, Finland, and Norway during school breaks, and my best friend from high school joined me for four weeks of backpacking around Europe in the summer. When we couldn't find accommodations in Venice or Pisa, we went with the flow and slept in a Venetian convent and under the Leaning Tower in sleeping bags. Everything aligned that year: friendships, love, self-development.

Meanwhile, things were not so well-aligned at home. My parents had divorced and my childhood home was sold. Mom moved to a nearby city, and Dad moved out of state. Neither was very open to speaking about the family dynamic. It was painful, and although there was a good sense of community and support-ive mentors at my college in New York, it took almost two years since returning before I felt back in the flow.

My college coursework included a junior year semester in Spain, which I extended to a year with an internship at a Seville law firm.

While there, I bumped into a group of fellow American stu-dents on the street who needed directions. I asked them about their travels and discovered they were visiting Spain as part of a program called Semester at Sea. It's a floating university that travels the world, and it was wonderful hearing about their adventures.

School vacations gave me a chance to explore Morocco and the Iberian Peninsula, which includes Spain and Portugal—countries with a vibrant, alluring, and culturally rich balance of history, culture, food, and incredible people. These trips also forced me to step out of my comfort zone, discover new passions, find my natural rhythm again, and create lifelong friendships.

From the moment I met the students on the street in Seville, the allure of a Semester at Sea beckoned. I called the university that hosted the program and discovered that it included multiple-country study, interdisciplinary coursework, and hands-on field experience. The fall voyage itinerary included stops in Japan, Taiwan, Hong Kong, the Philippines, Malaysia, India, Russia, Turkey, Yugoslavia, and Spain. Serendipitously, they had one spot open because of a last-minute cancelation. There was only one problem. The program cost about $11,000. How could I ever afford this? Would my college even allow me another semester abroad? But the pull was there to keep asking questions. Yes, there was a $2,000 grant still available; yes, I could apply for a $2,000 loan; yes, there was still time to apply; yes, yes, yes.

I was living with my dad that summer, and he said, "If you can pay for it, go for it." Challenge accepted! I called my college and after numerous appointments with the school's administrators, I obtained permission to go.

I worked three jobs from 7 a.m. to midnight, but at summer's end, I was still $550 short. My dad said he'd never seen me work so hard and funded me for the balance. Determination, hard work, and a belief that this could be done allowed me with the voyage of a lifetime.

After graduation, the bright lights beckoned and I moved to Manhattan. As the song *New York, New York* goes, "If I can make it there, I'll make it anywhere."

Naturally, my heart led me to the travel industry. My first job as an assistant manager in a travel company was a good experience, but after nine months, I knew I wanted more than a desk job. Soon after that, I spotted an ad for a sales and marketing position with a Chilean airline that was set to begin flying into JFK. The job description was written for me! I applied, was hired within three weeks, and began pitching Latin America as a destination. I worked with tour operators and travel agencies to create cultural experiences such as winter skiing in July, wine tours, visits to the Chilean fjords, and adventure tours in Patagonia. When the company transferred me to Washington, DC, I built partnerships with the South American embassies, World Bank, International Monetary Fund, and International Development Bank. I traveled for work, and in my free time took trips to Paris, Los Angeles, Iceland, Thailand, Jamaica, and Egypt.

A trip to Puerto Rico added a new trajectory to my life. I fell in love with the island's beauty and its unique culture—a mix of Taíno, Spanish, African, and North American influences. The ocean, the island life, and the people beckoned; I left my job and moved there.

I also fell in love with Bobby. We became friends immediately, but the energy between us was electric, and within three months we were engaged. He made me laugh all the time, and together we found joy in the simple things such as going for walks, seeing foreign films, or exploring new towns on the island. When you know, you know—and it's true, you do.

I insisted on having our wedding in San Juan so my family and friends could experience some of what I loved about the island and its culture.

From the start, Bobby and I supported each other's careers, so when his company offered him a position in Florida, we weighed the pros and cons. The opportunity for his professional growth made it impossible to refuse this offer.

In Florida, I became a sales manager for a cruise line. My

territory spanned the East Coast from Florida to Savannah. A favorite part of my job was my weekly drive to the port and along the coast. It always made me feel alive and grounded.

Our daughter was born in Orlando, and shortly after her first birthday, we made another career move and settled in the Washington, DC area. But after our son was born, I no longer wanted to travel for work, so I took a job in pharmaceutical sales. Life was busy, but I managed to maintain my daily routine of a run or workout. This personal "time out" has always given me the ability to notice when my intuition pings me.

And my intuition was once again pinging me, this time in the direction of that love for baking. I find great joy and relaxation in the process and have many priceless memories of going to my grandmother's house and licking the beaters, enjoying her famous sponge birthday cakes, or coming home after school to my mom's freshly baked cookies. I'm sure those happy moments fed my dream of opening a bakery.

After two years in pharmaceutical sales, Bobby and I talked about making that dream come true. In the evenings after the kids were asleep, I researched franchises and local Maryland bakeries, and began writing a business plan.

When I took my plan to a banker, I realized that it's impossible to get a business loan without solid collateral. My small business adviser also suggested that Bobby and I complete an assessment to determine our tolerance for risk. This was a good exercise, and I definitely won out as the family risk-taker. That being said, we both agreed to use our house as collateral. We felt confident in our professional abilities and believed that if the business didn't work, we would sell the house, cover the loan, and I'd return to corporate America.

The grueling underwriting process at various banks took months, and I still didn't have the money to begin. The turndowns were disheartening. The major stumbling blocks: a lack of sufficient collateral and the perceived high risk as first-time business owners.

"Where there's a will, there's a way" kept running through my mind, so after rejection number eight, I called my dad. He was an entrepreneur and reminded me that I just needed to find a banker who believed in me and my vision. I kept going. By the time I arrived at bank number twelve, I had my story down, knew all the questions that would be asked and could easily rattle off the projections, use of money, and repayment timeline. The banker and I clicked. He loved my vision and gave me the money I needed.

Finding the balance between being an entrepreneur, mother, and wife took some effort. It was challenging to juggle family, a staff, and the marketing and profitability while also producing a high-quality product at a reasonable price. Bobby helped with the kids and ran the business on Sundays until we could afford a full-time manager.

The sense of pride I felt innovating with new ideas, watching team members grow, and supporting the community was also recognized by the Frederick County Entrepreneur Council as start-up entrepreneur of the year. It was, in short, the best job in the world. Baked goods make everyone happy, and spreading joy is immensely powerful.

Seven years flew by. Bobby was again offered an incredible job, this time in Massachusetts. I was excited for him but I mourned my loss—the idea that I might have to sell my business made me extremely unhappy. But I also recognized that whatever decision I made would have to support our family vision. Family was my priority and I knew that I could always rebuild. The business went on the market. Within two months we had a buyer, but in the midst of moving, the deal fell through. We moved as planned, my assistant manager took charge, and I commuted for six months.

The business did finally sell, but getting to that point was fraught with unpredictable highs and lows. One of the most important lessons from that experience: Remember to trust and take care of yourself.

Our Massachusetts home in the Holyoke mountain range put us close to nature, which was wonderful for the family's well-being. I was present for my family and felt fulfilled as a mom, but I missed the passion that came from running my business.

How would I find my way back? Informational interviews with community leaders to learn more about the area and their organizations was a start. I read self-development books and met a soul friend and mentor who introduced me to StrengthFinders. This self-development assessment tool helped me identify my natural talents. It lifted my spirits, put me back on track, and guided me to the next leg of my journey—taking me in some positive new directions.

I taught a university class module called "Reinventing Yourself." If you really want to master something, teach it. I became a mentor to young women at a local college and became the annual fund director at a local university. I loved being able to give back to others.

Three years later, we moved again when Bobby was offered a job in Rhode Island. Part of my move-again pact was that I would start work on my MBA since I was interested in teaching at the university level.

Growth comes from change. Reinvention takes planning, and as a family unit, we were getting pretty good at that. Bobby settled into his new job, the kids settled into school, and I networked with local organizations while also enrolled in a full-time online MBA program. In 2013, online education was still in its infancy and when I opted in, it was with the goal of interacting with a global community and engaging with new technologies. I loved the challenge.

When I received my degree, the university hired me as a course evaluator for its MBA program. I also started doing informational interviews with female leaders, community advocates, and entrepreneurial organizations, and was hired as the director of the Rhode Island Women's Business Center (WBC). The WBC trains and mentors women in business and provides them with many opportunities for growing their businesses. This was soul work!

A brilliant digital designer and former editor from *Better Homes & Gardens* came in with an incredible idea for an e-commerce platform for people who loved old homes. After a few mentoring sessions, she came back with a plan for how the business should be structured. She also explained that she had ADHD and needed a partner to handle the operational and business side of things. When I asked if she had anyone in mind, she said, "What about you?" I was surprised and genuinely flattered and said I'd think about it.

Having been part of renovating my family's cobblestone house for ten years while growing up, the idea fascinated me. But the strongest pull centered on my ongoing desire to start another business. I meditated on this and asked Bobby for his thoughts. Always supportive, he said that it sounded interesting and if I could acquire the start-up funding, I should go for it. Honoring the pull, I wrote the business plan, resigned at WBC, and took the next step in my entrepreneurial journey.

An angel investor provided our initial funding. Creating an e-commerce platform with high-quality content was exciting. But I knew we needed outside mentoring for such essentials as branding, social media development, data collection and metrics, and load time and mobile responsiveness to monitor the first twelve months. So we applied and were accepted in a five-month program at Mass Challenge, a New England start-up accelerator.

The program provided top-notch mentorship in designing ways to produce avenues of growth, funding, and collaboration with strategic partners. We started to scale rapidly, launched our online service directory and marketplace, and built an excellent working relationship with one of our Mass Challenge mentors who came onboard as our CEO. I pivoted to head of sales and brand partnerships.

That autumn, we pitched to venture capital investors and received a commitment. However, negotiations between them and our angel investor did not go smoothly, and a controlling-interest struggle ensued. Ultimately, after a somewhat-tortured gut check, the CEO and I walked away from the company. Peace, clear boundaries, happiness, and ethical standards are never up for negotiation—even after three years of hard work.

I believe there are no failures, only lessons learned. Challenged and pushed forward, I came away with countless nuggets of knowledge, experience, and wisdom.

A few months into COVID, opportunity again knocked for Bobby's career: an offer in Cincinnati would return him to his love of diversity and inclusion. The timing was good. Our daughter had just graduated as an RN, and our son was humming along in his university studies. I started networking with the entrepreneurial community, connected with a wonderful women's service organization, and began co-hosting a weekly Heart-Centered Entrepreneurs Clubhouse room.

COVID quarantine gave me the gift of time to become more spiritually connected with myself. I practiced yoga at home; the mind, body, spirit energy was just what I needed. I also read numerous spiritual enlightenment books, and daily meditation opened my heart.

I began to acknowledge an accumulation of feelings that I didn't know existed: present fears, early childhood pain, even past-life trauma. Inner child work, forgiveness, and heart connection conversations ensued. I learned that I could not fix others or be a people pleaser, which led me to set new boundaries and speak with more clarity.

Forgiveness is freedom, and the heart presents itself for natural healing. By adding mindfulness and gratitude, and letting everything be a renewal of love, joy, and peace, beneficial energy begins to flow.

Honoring my adventures and intuition, saying yes, showing up for my family and others, and realizing there was more that I needed to explore within myself to be all that I was meant to be has been wild, fun, messy, and marvelous.

We are here to grow, not to be complacent. Trust the adventure and let your dreams guide and inspire you to embrace, express, and embody all that you are. You don't need to know the *how*. It doesn't matter whether the circumstances are perfect or if you are perfect in the circumstances. Just keep moving forward, always follow your heart, and get ready for an unforgettable journey.

ABOUT MARY GERVAIS

Serial entrepreneur and innovator Mary Gervais has helped thousands of women fulfill their dreams of starting, building, and growing their own companies.

Driven by a desire to create more meaningful connections between people and to make the world a more honest and open place, she has also established herself as a leader and guide in co-creation—a form of collaborative innovation where ideas are shared and improved together.

Thriving on new experiences, Mary's love of world travel has led her to live and work in Bolivia, Sweden, Spain, Chile, and Puerto Rico. She has used her marketing savvy and business acumen to create both retail and online enterprises, and she is the former head of Rhode Island's Women's Business Center.

Mary is also a firm believer in the idea that when life hands you a grand idea, embrace it, even if you don't know how to make it happen. Dream big and be bold. Leading by example, Mary continues to show others how to live an abundant, healthy, and joy-filled life.

To learn more about Mary Gervais, you can visit her website at www.maryhelengervais.com.

To connect with Mary, please contact her directly at:

Email: mary@maryhelengervais.com

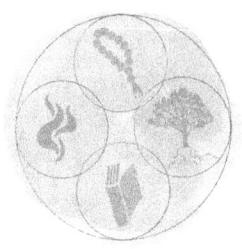

ONCE UPON A TIME

Tiffany Donovan Green

Once upon a time there was a young woman who dreamed about a life full of potential and adventure. She was creative, curious, full of youthful charm and vigor. She formulated goals, educated herself, and committed to achieving her dreams. She was confident, determined, and comfortable in her power. Anything was possible.

Then one day, this woman woke up to find herself adrift. She was exhausted, having expended herself in tedium for many years, for she had generously donated her body, mind, and spirit to the needs of others. Suddenly, the benefactors of her labor no longer required her assistance, and she discovered herself bereft of passion and purpose.

Sound familiar? Not all but many women find themselves in this predicament when their children leave the nest. I am one of these women. In my youth, I studied, I traveled, I took full advantage of life. I worked hard and had the good fortune to attend a highly rated law school where I met my prince charming and embarked on what I believed would be a fairytale life.

I was (and still am) a notorious dreamer. But the reality of a demanding career, complicated pregnancies, and the needs of my family dented my original aspirations. With my husband's career on the rise, I made the decision to leave the workforce. I enjoyed motherhood, but I was surprised by how quickly my confidence and self-worth faded. I panicked and attempted a return to office but did not have the physical, emotional, or mental ability to sustain a professional comeback. I gave up on the pursuit and doubled down on the duties of the devoted mother.

Don't get me wrong—I *loved* raising my boys, and if I could do it all over again, I would make the same (or many of the same) choices. But the experience came at a high cost, a cost that our society does not always recognize or reward. If you give yourself in entirety to another, whether that person is a spouse, a child, or other person of significance, it is often a challenge to find yourself again. And if you do, you might not even recognize yourself. I have casually observed that individuals who give up their careers to take on the full-time at-home parent role are taught to undervalue themselves, surrender their dreams, and sacrifice their power.

And I'm here to say, screw that!

We need to remember who we are, be honored for our service and sacrifice, and be given the chance to fulfill our passions and purpose. But first, we must learn to dream again—without restraint, without judgment, and with the extravagant imagination of a child. Only then can we rediscover ourselves, our youth, and our vitality. And for me, that's where it all began . . . Once Upon a Time.

It was an innocent inquiry: "You're turning fifty this year, what should we do to celebrate?" my husband asked. My expression and demeanor revealed that I was not thrilled. Fifty years. How did that happen? Give birth, blink, and you're fifty. That's how I felt. It didn't seem fair. As a young woman I was going places: I earned a position at a top law firm on Capitol Hill; I was offered a fellowship to study German law at the University of Heidelberg; I had plans . . . BIG plans. But I couldn't do it all. Did I fail? Sometimes it felt that way.

He tried to cheer me up. "We could go on a trip?"

"Meh . . . " I sighed. "Who would watch the kids?"

Silence.

Reluctantly, he suggested, "What about a party?"

"Party?" I perked up.

Providing Tiffany an opportunity to host a party was like offering bloody remains to a piranha: devoured and digested before the last syllable.

As a creative, nothing gets me going like a themed event. But I had to be original given that many in our community had already celebrated their fiftieth and most of the popular themes had been used previously. Pressure on.

My oldest child, a sophomore in high school at the time, had the opportunity to participate in an educational trip to Europe with his history class. Concerned about his severe nut allergy, my husband and I decided to trail him. We traveled separately to Europe, kept our distance, and did our own thing. We toured Versailles and various castles and palaces in and around Munich. It was regal, it was romantic, almost make-believe, and . . . then it came to me:

An immersive experience that dares imagination, distant in time and tradition, an illusion of artful indulgence, a fiction, a fantasy: a *Royal Fairytale Ball.*

The event was magic—the room twinkled with glittering tiaras and elegant satin gowns, which swirled and swayed to the delicate cadence of the orchestral waltzes. Participants were spellbound and starry eyed. There was laughter, there was awe, there was wonderment. The fairytale theme provided guests with a sort of freedom, an opportunity to transcend the ordinary, to make believe and become a brilliant star in their own story. It was more than a night to remember—it was an *opportunity* to remember, to rediscover youth and inspiration, to stretch the mind and wander in the world of the inner child.

That is when things began to change both for me and for many of my guests. A few who had unsuccessful relationships found companionship, some went back to school or started new careers, some packed up and moved on to entirely new adventures, and some, like me, retooled, reinvested, and reinvented themselves.

Since then, every year on my birthday I gather with friends for coffee, lunch, or drinks to celebrate and reminisce about the Royal Fairytale Ball. Naturally, we wore our tiaras. Many of my friends commented on how the tiara made them feel: Pretty. Powerful. Important. Buoyant. Young. There was something magical about these fancy little crowns that seemed to transform the mind and bolster confidence.

A tiara is an ornamental headpiece typically reserved for formal occasions. It's a symbol of power and beauty. Tiaras denote distinguished status and thus could imply elitism. In this light, the tiara might embody a negative connotation since aristocrats and elites are seen throughout history as undemocratic, securing undue privileges at the expense of the majority. But what if the tiara was democratized and rebranded as a symbol of self-love and used to lift individuals up so that they could perceive their unique worth and beauty? I can envision women, and all genders, using this symbol to come together to support each other, to celebrate their strength and potential, and to remember who they are and what they are capable of—at any age.

When my youngest child readied to leave nest and I approached the end of my tenure as a stay-at-home mom, my first thought was *game over*. I was spent, disconnected, and afraid. I didn't recognize myself; I didn't feel like I had an identity outside of the children. When I looked back toward my youthful ambitions, they seemed foreign and unattainable. I had forgotten my passion and my power. But that tiny tin tiara taught me to dream again. I went back to school to study design and founded my own design firm specializing in green interiors. I started an environmental nonprofit with my children to teach them the values of environmental stewardship and activism like my mother taught me. And most recently, I created a tribute to the tiara, a social and philanthropic society dedicated to self-empowerment: The Tiara Club.

Anything is game, because anything is possible when you reconnect with an unfettered imagination and let yourself dream.

ABOUT TIFFANY DONOVAN GREEN

Tiffany Donovan Green is an entrepreneur, event organizer, and interior designer in Fairfield County, Connecticut. She is the founder of The Green House Interiors, specializing in healthy sustainable design, and a co-founder of The Global Preservation Society, a 501(c)(3) organization dedicated to environmental stewardship and sustainability. Most recently, Tiffany founded The Tiara Club, a social and philanthropic organization dedicated to self-empowerment.

Born and raised in southeastern Michigan, Tiffany earned a BA in history and political science from Albion College; an MA in history at Oakland University in Rochester, Michigan; and a JD/LLM from Cornell Law School in international and comparative law. She lived abroad in Scotland, Germany, and France, and worked at the law firm Jones Day in Washington, DC until she retired to raise her children. She is currently pursuing an MA in interior design from Fairfield University in Fairfield, Connecticut.

Tiffany lives with her prince charming in southwestern Connecticut.

Web:
tiffanydonovangreen.com
tiaraclub.org
the-green-house.com

Instagram:
@tiffany.donovan.green/
@the.tiara.club/
@the.green.house.interiors

Facebook: https://www.facebook.com/tiffany.donovan.10

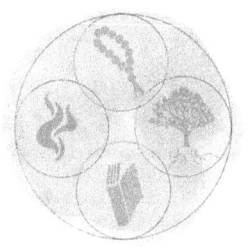

RECLAIMING WONDER

Linda Gonzalez

I n the summer of 2021, a dear friend called me to share a children's book author program offered by Kate Butler Books. She heard me talk about writing a children's book as a gift for my granddaughters and thought I might be interested. While I had talked about writing a children's book for many years, I had never really thought of it as a dream to one day come true. In fact, at this point in my life, I was not sure I had any dreams that I planned to pursue. If I did, they were focused on the life I wanted for my children and, more recently, my grandchildren—not for me. Even my work in higher education, for twenty-five years, revolved around the dreams of my students. This was not intentional. Like so many women, my early adult life focused on a list of to-dos prioritized around children, family, and what society often refers to as work-life balance where there is little *life* and even less *balance*—as if there is a magic script that determines our capacity for knowing how to foster such a balance. When speaking with other women approaching sixty, I learned that we had many commonalities. There was one in particular that started to haunt me. The idea of self-care and how to find it or, in some cases, rediscover it, in a world where so many of our boundaries get blurred. This thought gave me pause and a reason to dig deeper into the life I am living.

When my friend reached out to share the opportunity of writing a children's book, we were still working our way through the storms of a global pandemic. During some very dark moments, the negative voices in my head told me that there was no way I could do this. At that time, my goal was to do my best to overcome this difficult time so I could enjoy time with family and friends again, continue to support my students working toward earning their college degrees, and start planning for retirement at the traditional age of sixty-five. This was all very important to me. But was there something more? Where was the beautiful sense of wonder about life that often gets lost along the way for so many women? And what is the role of wonder, if any, in my self-care plan that I was encouraged to make part of my fiscal goals this year? Sitting still in a space of reflection about the possibility of writing a children's book for my granddaughters, I became more uncomfortable and scared. Hanging out in this place of uncertainty is what disrupted my life and encouraged me to take the first step. When I dug deeper into my root system, I started to discover that not only was this something that I could do, but it was also something that I had to do. Through these still moments, the words of my favorite author, Parker J. Palmer spoke wonder into my heart: "the God whom I know dwells quietly in the root system of the very nature of things."[1] And this is where my story begins.

When I turned fifty-five, I was very mindful that age sixty was a mere five years away. It was unavoidable. Direct marketing to me about the senior years accelerated at what felt like an exponential pace: emails about planning my financial security for retirement were filling my inbox, and I needed an Excel spreadsheet to keep track of the various "screenings and tests" advised by my healthcare professionals as part of my preventive medicine.

1—Parker Palmer, Let Your Life Speak (San Francisco, CA: Jossey-Bass, 1999).

My positive inner voice recognized the relevance of all of this but knew that for me to truly live out my purpose, the one planted in my root system, I needed to answer a very powerful question: "What else?"

"What else?" became like a broken record in my soul that renewed my sense of wonder. I felt inspired to focus on the *life* part of the equation in that work-life balance that I either lost or never had. Not the bucket list of items that are one and done, although these are important too. Rather, the discovery of dreams that I had either buried or never knew existed in the roots of my soul because I was too busy jamming up my brain trying to multi-task to get stuff done. The conscious and intentional wish list that I ask my granddaughters and students about when we explore their dreams together. The ones that give me an image of a life of victory and purpose. With great determination and practice, I learned to sit in silence, listening to the voice in my root system. The idea of writing a children's book as a gift for my granddaughters became an unwavering thought that bloomed from this daily exercise. With abundant gratitude for this discovery, I signed up for the journey and promised to enjoy the ride.

If Acorns Could Talk is a story that spoke to me during long walks with my granddaughters. They all love to collect bits of nature when we are outside. It is not unusual for us to take home a pocketful of branches, weeds, and rocks to spread around in our rooms as new home décor imagined by young girls with a natural wonder, uninhibited by the grip of perfection. What always struck me most was their fascination with acorns in the beautiful season of autumn. Or was it my fascination with acorns? Giving this question some attention, I discovered that I was not certain. Learning to dig deeper into my root system, I let myself explore the deeper meaning of our conversations on our walks together and began to wonder about the "acorn" and "mighty oak" moments of my life. I noticed that these special moments are not defined by age or experience, not even by ability or knowledge, but rather by my willingness to try new things that help me to continue to grow into my purpose.

To highlight this point, I think about the joy and gratitude I feel when my granddaughters talk about who they want to become when they grow older. They say it with great purpose and assurance because they completely believe everything is possible. There are no inhibitions or voices of self-doubt—no fears of failing or thoughts about being less than perfect—and the idea of who they want to become is like a mighty oak, growing new branches fed by hopes and dreams. One of my granddaughters at one point wanted to become a superhero. When I asked her how she would become a superhero, she leaped into the air, shouted that she would practice her flying, and fell flat on the floor. What I remember most about this experience is what happened next. She jumped up showing me her muscles, and with the same enthusiasm yelled, "I'm okay!" She was leaning into her purpose. Another granddaughter wants to become a farmer. So last summer she started practicing growing and harvesting her crops. Recently we saw a photo of her lying with a new litter of puppies, like a cultural anthropologist, practicing participant observation among the animals, fully living in her purpose. These acorn and mighty oak moments are in their root systems, and they find them with such ease. They are not stuck by the control of any negative voices. Instead, they keep their sense of wonder that allows them to keep growing into their purpose.

Learning from their approach to fulfilling their dreams about who they want to become, I started to write *If Acorns Could Talk* as a gift to them. It was a sunny summer afternoon in the Northeast when I wrote my first draft. In full joy and wonder, I was overcome by an uncontrollable urge to pour out the words and expressions shared with me through their beautiful voices and little faces on our nature walks together. Leaning into my purpose, I felt a great desire to evoke wonder in others, at every age. The journey of writing this book has reclaimed my sense of wonder about dreams that I'm yet to discover and eager to explore.

Next year, I will turn sixty. Rather than lean into sixty as if it is a difficult wave to navigate through, I will *dream* into sixty like Lily, the young girl in *If Acorns Could Talk,* and my beautiful granddaughters: Strong! Powerful! Confident! and Resilient! While I am unsure about what lies ahead for me, I am no longer confused about my self-care and work-life balance. The process of becoming an author pushed me to dig into my root system and rediscover the wonder of life that keeps me excited and yearning to explore at every age for as long as I am capable.

Acorns are not a metaphor for age. They are a metaphor for early learners on a journey filled with beautiful dreams. When cared for and loved, they grow into mighty oaks. I am very much an acorn when it comes to playing golf, a sport I started last year as an opportunity to spend time with my husband outdoors. And it is very possible I will remain an acorn in this space for the rest of my life. That still excites me because I know I will meet other acorns and mighty oaks along the journey of playing golf. I am also very much an acorn when it comes to being an author. In less than one year though, I am inspired by the mighty oaks who so freely share their time and talents to help me grow into a mighty oak in this space. When I remain in wonder, I am no longer fearful of mistakes or in search of perfection in the things I want to say and do. Instead, wonder inspires me to pause and listen for the guidance of the voice buried in my root system to teach me more about my purpose. It paves a path and provides a compass for me to lean into my purpose with great passion and enthusiasm. It is a great gift that I have begun to cherish. And I am excited about the learning and discovery, and about the people I am meeting along the way. Perhaps reclaiming wonder is one of the liberating benefits that comes with age—and one we should talk about more often when we contemplate self-care, balance, and purpose.

When I dream ahead, I envision a space where acorns and mighty oaks share life together, teaching and learning from each other. Whether the subject is history, technology, or art, intergenerational acorns and mighty oaks can form communities where learnings and teachings are generously exchanged. In these communities, diversity is valued, and kindness abundantly abounds. Everyone is living in harmony with each other and with nature. The acorns are caring for the mighty oaks and vice versa. There are no preferences and no privileges; just love. If you are reading this, I hope you pause and create the wonder of this image in your mind. What does this vision look like for you?

The journey of becoming an author is in its fledgling phase for me yet has already impacted my life in countless positive ways. For certain, it has stirred up dreams for my senior years that never existed until now. Fueled by wonder, it continues to serve my commitment to my journey of lifelong learning and living with enthusiasm. It is helping me to grow into the purpose destined for me.

Aging with wonder has become something I behold. Now, when I am floundering and in search of clarity about my purpose, I sit in the silence and dig into my root system where the vision of God dwells. What I discover here is infinite possibilities that are unencumbered and ready to be nurtured.

ABOUT LINDA GONZALEZ

There is an entire world community of acorns and mighty oaks with whom I would love to meet and collaborate. If you wonder about the acorn and mighty oak moments in life, please reach out to me on Instagram at @ lindamgonz or send me an email at lindamgonzalez3@gmail.com and let's discover "what else?" together.

Linda Gonzalez is a mentor and coach in higher education. Her passion is working with adult learners working toward fulfilling their dreams of earning their first college degrees. Her twenty-five-year career spans from universities in New Jersey, Arizona, and Utah. She holds a BS in marketing and management and an MA in cultural anthropology. In March of 2022, she became a best-selling author of a children's book, *If Acorns Could Talk* and is enjoying opportunities to read aloud with children. She has recently fulfilled the course requirements for the International Coaching Federation's (ICF) Leadership Coaching certification program through the Doerr Institute at Rice University and is currently completing her practicum as part of this program.

Linda lives in the Pocono Mountains in Pennsylvania with her husband. She is the very proud "Nanny" to five granddaughters ages one to six years old, and she never passes up an opportunity to play a family board game, plan an Easter egg hunt, and engage in healthy competition.

Linda Gonzalez would be thrilled to meet you!

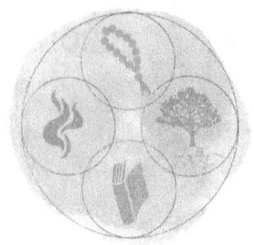

THERE IS MONEY IN YOUR CLOSET

Erin Bonner Hudyma

I wasn't exactly sure how or where to begin my story. Do you know how difficult it is for a Philly girl who loves to talk to try and summarize her life in just a few pages? Well, doll, here I go, trying to fit it all in, including the ups and downs and in-betweens.

When things are going well in our life, those feel-good vibes put a little extra pep in our step, am I right? In those moments, we want to put on our prettiest shoes, get out in the world, and conquer it. But no matter how hard we work on having a positive attitude, sometimes, we just get on the hot mess express and it's beyond our control. And we might cry, scream, curse, or lounge around in sweatpants when it does. Other times, we close our eyes, breathe, and count our blessings—because worse things can happen. And guess what—when we least expect it, they will. At any given moment, our worlds can flip upside down, and we might desperately long to be in a different time, craving bigger and better things.

Think about any moment when you may have felt this way. Did it ever stop you from wishing for more? If anything, I bet it intensified it, right? Even when life seems completely unmanageable, somewhere inside, tucked underneath all the puffy eyes, empty ice cream containers, and lipstick-stained wine glasses, remain our hopes, visions, and dreams. They might be forced on the back burner for a while as we come up for air, but they really are what keep us going during times of despair.

I want you to know that I see you. I was you. And I am here to tell you, if you look close enough, there are open doors waiting for you to walk through. You will find them because guess what— they are everywhere. They might be disguised or entirely hidden. But even the most damaged entryways can lead us to brighter paths. Just wait until you hear about mine! Our lives are constant peaks and valleys, and it's not about being at the top that matters. It's knowing what to say to yourself during all the in-between moments to shape what happens next.

My life started in southwest Philadelphia. The Bonner family, my family, had eight children. I was number six out of eight. Philip E. "Knute" Bonner, my father, was a World War II veteran, a Philadelphia police offer, and a Pennsylvania state auditor, and my mother, Pat Noone Bonner was a homemaker.

Since I was a child, I was my father's sidekick. He nicknamed me Bedbug. Our personalities, temperament, and the way we talked were so similar. To give you an idea of who my father was, let's just say one of his business cards had, "Teller of Jokes," underneath his name. But what I am most proud of in our likeness was helping others. To this day, I continue his charity, Knute's Angels, and adopt families during the holidays with the help from many people who make donations to, but especially from, Veronica.

In 2003, when I was in my early twenties, I purchased my own home. I was working as a clinical staff member for The Gift of Life donor program, which manages the recovery of organs and tissues for transplant (please register to be an organ donor!). Oddly, my father had become ill with heart issues a few years before, but he aged out as a candidate for a transplant. This never surprised me, though, because no one in the world had a better heart—his was ageless. Although I was quite young for such a huge responsibility, my mother thought it was best for me to become my father's medical power of attorney. She trusted me since I worked in the medical field, knew the best doctors, and was well informed when it came to such intimidating decision-making.

For the next several years, I continued to help my mother care for my father, scheduling my work and life around his needs. It was in the car, driving my father to appointments, where I would have some of the most important talks of my life. I loved breaking his chops and watching his old-school reaction to everything. He made me laugh so much.

In 2006, I met my future husband, Joe, at the Jersey Shore. I continued to work in the donor program until 2008, when I attempted a career in medical device sales. This was the same time as the stock market and housing crash. Not only was I one of many layoffs almost immediately after I started but my mortgage doubled!

After being unemployed for about a year and a half, I saw a commercial advertising jobs for a local casino. I was never a gambler, but the one thing I was always willing to bet on was myself. I decided to roll the dice and go for an interview. What could I lose? I came back with a job as a table game dealer. Though it wasn't my dream job, it allowed me to earn some well-needed money fast, and although I didn't know it at the time, it happened to be one of the biggest entryways to my future.

At the casino, I met many other unemployed people from all sorts of professional backgrounds and levels in the same situation. I developed a close friendship with another dealer, Margaret, and we shared our stories and pipe dreams in between games. To this day, she continues to be my greatest mentor.

In 2011, Joe and I were married. Six months after we tied the knot, I was diagnosed by our first fertility doctor with stage four endometriosis and had a tumor on one ovary. I come from the most fertile family in the world (each of my parents were one of seven), and go figure, I have fertility issues! Having a baby was one of my biggest challenges. How was this fair? All my sisters got pregnant when they sneezed! Of course, the problem was me. For being Irish, it sure felt like I was short on luck.

I endured four unsuccessful intrauterine inseminations (IUI) fertility treatments with three different fertility doctors. In between these treatments, I had to have two laparoscopic surgeries to treat the tumors and endometriosis. Though each surgery made the process more painful, it also made my determination to become a mother that much stronger.

On September 25, 2012, as my body was healing, we suddenly lost my forty-seven-year-old brother, Patrick. He passed away from diabetic heart disease. My younger sister, Bridget, then suffered a miscarriage in December. Shortly after, our father died in February 2013. I couldn't help but feel like my entire family was being sucker-punched and that normal life was out of our reach.

A week before my father died, I was taking him to a new doctor when he leaned over in the car and said, "Erin, my time is coming to end. When I get up to heaven, I am going to send you that baby."

One of the first signs my father was watching over me was in February 2013, when the Gift of Life program called me back full-time. My father always loved that I worked for this program, so it was quite fitting. But then on Labor Day weekend 2013, I was rushed to the emergency room with another ovarian tumor. Another laparoscopic surgery had to be scheduled in October.

When I was a bit back to myself, despite recommendations for a hysterectomy, I started the exhausting clinical and financial processes of in vitro fertilization (IVF). On September 25, 2013, exactly one year after my brother Patrick's death, my mother was at his grave site. She looked down and prayed to her son, "Patrick, if you are up there in heaven with your father, please push for Erin to get pregnant, and I'll know that the two of you are together."

Two weeks after my October surgery, I went back to work. On October 24, 2013, a rainy cold fall Thursday afternoon, I was running errands in my typical Philly tuxedo—a velour jump-suit—and felt the need to take a pregnancy test. *Positive?* For real? Later, no lie, Dr. Heinzel told me I got pregnant on September 25, 2013—that day my mother prayed.

Of course, I had a high-risk pregnancy. Did you really expect any different? But nothing else mattered other than becoming parents to our beautiful daughter, Svea, in 2014.

When Svea was nine months old, I had a hysterectomy. I was out of work for about eight weeks and returned to work with a very hectic schedule. I then realized I did not want Svea to be bounced around to my in-laws and sisters, so we made the decision for me to become a stay-at-home mom.

This is when all my experiences sort of bundled into one big vision. I remember sitting in the same spot on my couch, day in and day out, like the movie *Groundhog's Day*. Though I was grateful for the time with my daughter, I would find myself staring at the living room walls while she napped. With twenty-year-old reruns on the TV as background noise, I started to think about all I wanted in life and knew I had to step up my game.

When a great job opportunity was presented to me in 2016 by a well-known local hospital, I was honored. It called for either a master's degree or over ten years of organ transplant experience, and I had the latter. Unfortunately, I was not hired. Though I was let down, I never let it discourage me. I told myself God just had other plans.

The spark I needed came from a close friend, also a stay-at-home mom, asking if I was interested in going into business together cleaning construction sites. I liked the idea of having our own gig, but I knew with being in our forties and getting this off the ground, our bodies wouldn't allow us to keep up with the physical labor for a long time. But it certainly got me thinking about owning a business. The idea that stood out to me was an adult day care center, after everything I went through with my father. My vision now developed into a goal.

Every day, I sat in the same spot on my couch doing countless Google searches. It's funny how I am now able to value this, because back then, I remember feeling like a bum who did nothing all day. But little did I know with every search on my phone, I was one step closer to the new me.

In 2018, I attended an aunt's funeral. This event was a significant one. While there, I struck up a conversation with her adult caregiver, a local woman who had both a toddler and a newborn. She told me how she worked in the evenings after being with her little ones all day. During the mass, I kept thinking about this impressive woman's spirit, drive, and energy. As the church song, "On Eagle's Wings" played during the procession, what were my fears? Yeah, financial burdens always caused me to worry. But I never once doubted this dream. It never scared me. I always knew I would see the bigger picture, and that day, I did.

I went home and Googled "Homecare Companions—Eagles Wings." No other business had this name! I was off to a good start and felt a sense of inspiration. I held on to every little sign. The next thing I did was shadow my mentor/friend for a day in the life of a business owner. She educated me on capital needs and how to get more experience. The feeling was somewhat overwhelming, but I never once let it intimidate me. I knew I had to get creative financially, especially with concerns from my husband, since he is a "numbers guy." He never expressed doubt, but with a toddler, he naturally wanted to make smart choices for our family. I was reminded of my IVF days when I would stand in the shower and cry, praying for the baby I so longed to have. I took deep breaths and gave myself the same advice I did back then: "Take it one day at a time, Erin." And that's exactly what I did.

Money is probably the number one barrier when it comes to people following their dreams. But remember, this is where you really need to hunt for those secret doors and find opportunities.

The key is to never stop strategizing. My tactic was, "There's money in your closet." So, I began to clean out my unused clothes, home goods, and daughter's toys. And I saved every damn penny, especially the ones from heaven. I cut coupons in the local flyers, digital apps, and online. I had my car payment lowered and tucked the extra money under my makeup tray. Shh! Don't tell my husband. He still thinks the payment was $400 a month.

And here's a shocker. Now before I share this, I'm not trying to tell you to go out and trust this. But always keep the mindset that things are at least worth an inquiry, even just for a lesson learned. You know how you get those email scams about large amounts of unclaimed cash in your name? Well, I figured, let me just check it out. Turns out, I had overpaid on an electric bill years before in my first home and the money was owed to me. I kid you not, my makeup tray was starting to tilt from all the cash I was shoving underneath it.

I quickly learned that besides just equity, you also need countless services to start a business. There's so much paperwork, analysis, and countless hours of computer time involved. And let me tell you, girl, I'm no tech-savvy chick! It was agony for me. Believe it or not, up to this point, I did everything from my phone. I also needed a Tax ID, registration as a Limited Liability Company (LLC), and professional photography for a brochure.

How did I get what I needed without major funds to support it all? I used good old-fashioned bartering just like in the colonial days! Now Instead of trading deer skins for muskets, I exchanged fifteen meals for legal services from a close friend's boyfriend Scott. My rock, Margaret, came to my rescue with endless knowledge, and another friend, Kim, was beginning a photography business and offered to take all my pictures. Reaching out to your resources goes a long way. And any time I felt like I was hitting plateaus, for quick reassurance, I would take a trip to a good dollar store for office supplies, even if I was "putting the cart before the horse"— one of my dad's favorite sayings.

I was blessed to have a very large support system, not only with my husband, but with my mother's financial help, my fabulous sisters, and my mother-in-law, Joann, to help with Svea. My mother-in-law retired during this time and I remember her looking me straight in the eyes and saying, "You go ahead and do what you got to do. I got the baby." With that, she took Svea whenever I needed her to and became a full-time MomMom to our little girl and continues to enjoy every second of it.

Before I knew it, I became licensed in June 2019, accepting my first client that August. I went out myself and worked "in the field," with my first employee starting a few weeks later. My goal was now a reality.

Trust me, there were struggles. When COVID hit, I was forced to put the business temporarily on hold, and shift to mainly administrator work. Though the whole world seemed to be in an uproar, I never stopped focusing on my dream. I kept my eye on the prize. On top of the pandemic, my mother became extremely sick, and my sisters, Mary Beth, Bridget, and Deirdre, along with my niece, Tara, had to act as her hospital for weeks. Since I am one to put my money where my mouth is, especially when it comes to caring for my family, we got her through it. We also sold our family home and got our mom settled in a new apartment.

My business started to pick back up in January 2021 and slowly brought my employees back. Shortly after, I got credentialed with Medicaid, thanks to Linda, my office manager, which allowed me to accept other types of insurance. I am proud to say that right now Eagles Wings is now a team with several diverse team members, and we're expanding our client listing.

There's great value and appreciation in taking the smaller steps on the ladder of life, instead of the big ones. We learn from every stage. I feel that my pace allowed me to hold on tight and grasp everything I want to give back to this world.

There's still a lot more stairs for me to climb. I don't even think

I'm halfway there. My chapter in this book might be closing, but it's only the beginning of my story. In addition to physically caring for others, I want to guide others on how to find their path when life goes in, what we believe to be, the wrong way. And who's to say we haven't been upside down the entire time? It's all about perspective and the ability to see things from every angle. Be sure to know and trust there are better things to come, you just got to keep showing up. To that woman who is staring at her walls wondering what her next step is in regard to her next chapter in life, I *see* you, I *was* you, and I *feel* you. Every journey begins with one step, one email, and one phone call toward your dreams. To be continued . . .

ABOUT ERIN BONNER HUDYMA

Erin Bonner Hudyma is the president and founder of Eagles Wings Homecare, LLC. She has a clinical organ recovery transplant background, all while caring for her WWII veteran father, which inspired her to pursue her dream of becoming a business owner in home care. Eagles Wings Homecare helps people remain in their homes and continue to live life independently. She helps them with running errands, watering plants, or attending appointments. Having a heart of gold has always been her one main characteristic.

When she isn't busy tending to her clients and building her dream business, Erin loves being a dedicated mother, wife, family member, and friend. Any free time Erin has, you can find her in the shoe aisle seeking fabulous prices.

If you are interested and ready to become a business owner and eager to start your own homecare business, please reach out to Erin at Eagles Wings about franchising with a start-up homecare company. No special certifications needed, just a heart of gold and compassion. She has staff ready to help you build your new future!

Web: www.eagleswingshomecare.com
Email: erin.hudyma@eagleswingshomecare.com
Phone: 484-540-7586

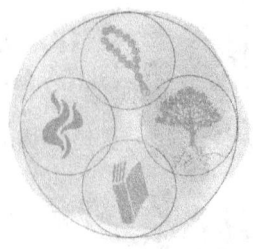

LISTEN TO THE LIFEGUARD

Erin McCahill

I loved to watch Nanny crochet the most beautiful blankets and could spend hours watching her quickly create masterpieces in single or multiple colors. Each one done with love to be graciously given to someone, expecting nothing in return. As an adult, I think back to those times and the way the yarn created intricate designs with a twist of the needle and different counts. And if it were not right, Nanny would unravel the yarn and start again . This is how my life journey has been. It's been a journey creating a masterpiece with many twists of life and finding the right count that works. It's been an amazing one that has been filled with the most incredible experiences, most devastating experiences, and everything in between.

It has not been easy. So many lessons given were not learned! So many times, I've ignored the universe and its large, red warning flags.

"Why?" you may ask.

It has taken me a while to figure this out.

Just as a blanket starts from a single piece of yarn, so does one's life. Along life's journey, these pieces of yarn will come together creating your crocheted blanket. You may not realize until later how important that single piece of yarn is in your life.

I am a daughter, sister, niece, aunt, cousin, friend, mentor, leader, innovator, and a personal and professional culture creator. This is what makes me unique and more. My life's design has taken on many different patterns that have been both easy and hard; it is a beautiful, intricate blanket that I've been putting together for years, and I will continue to do so.

I remember the day as if it were yesterday, I was four years old wearing my stylish corduroy pants, blue wind jacket, and of course pigtails with bows, and my favorite saddle shoes. I stood strong at the big sliding glass doors of our townhome in Missouri with my Snoopy suitcase all packed up with my most important possessions. I opened the door, headed out to the big, open field, "that wide-open space," with my parents behind asking, "Where are you going?" I turned around with the utmost confidence and said, "Colorado." And off I went walking into the wide-open field. Never had I been to Colorado before, but somehow, I knew I needed to go there. I have found that this piece of my life has become an integral part of my blanket.

In grade school, we were fortunate and took a family ski trip to Snowmass Mountain in Colorado. I had been skiing since I could walk, but this was different and harder. The fresh-fallen snow each morning was light, fluffy, and deep, which required a new skiing technique. I remember ski school and the challenges it gave me; this yarn was building upon my competitiveness and desire to be the best. As we spent the week there, I fell in love with all the snow, sparkly white lights, and fresh air. It started something in me: it energized me, gave me confidence, let me dream, and felt like home.

Little did I know I would eventually be accepted and attend Colorado State University. Mom and I flew out to tour the campus. I was excited and nervous, not knowing what to expect. We rented a big red Buick, and as we approached campus, we found out it was College Days, a holiday weekend for the school. My mom stopped at a payphone and called home and said, "We just arrived, and she is coming here. Remember Yankton's College Days?" and she laughed with Dad. This was the start of some of the most incredible and most difficult days of my life. It is also when some of the most important pieces of yarn were brought into my life.

In junior high, my friends and I would assist my neighbor by serving the summer lunch she held for the battered women's association. As a freshman in high school, we catered another battered women association meeting and I vividly remember wearing my white top, black skirt, and red apron, standing in the kitchen with the plantation shutters open, listening to courageous women speak about their situations. I could not understand or comprehend why anyone would put themselves in a situation like they described. I turned and asked her, "Why would they not just leave if someone hit them?" and "How could someone truly lose their self-identity. No one can be brainwashed." She looked at me and she said, "Yes, it happens."

I was taught to always work hard, play hard, and not let anyone see you down. My parents were strong. They instilled strong core values in us, which I'm so thankful for. I am a dreamer, have wildly big goals, and believe in myself and that perfect fairy tale. I look for the best in others, always trying to help others first. These are great attributes until they hurt you.

My parents and brother said good-bye at the end of the summer, and I headed to Colorado early for sorority prep week for my junior year. I'm thankful my dad was persistent and convinced me to rush freshman year and encouraged me to enjoy these four years to the fullest. Many more pieces of yarn started to be entwined into my design. A few days later, in the middle of the afternoon, I got a phone call from my parents to tell me my dad had pancreatic cancer. Immediately I said, "I am coming home," but they said no. They didn't tell me until I was at school because they needed to keep me living my life, not stopping on the road to my dreams and purpose. I was so lucky and grateful for the network of sisters that were there for me and held me as I cried. At the time, I didn't realize how important this sorority experience would be to me in my blanket's creation. This experience taught me so much, prepared me for my professional career, and introduced me to some of the most important and best friendships of my life.

Dad passed away my senior year. I had gone home in October, as it was time, we were told. I stood outside Dad's hospital room while he was speaking to our priest. He said, "Father, I know it's almost time for me to go home, I want you to do my mass."

I couldn't believe what I heard. I froze, silently cried, and never shared this with anyone. Dad stabilized; I went back to school. I got the call again during our Monday night formal sorority meeting that I needed to come home immediately. Everyone jumped into action to get me home. I was waiting for my late evening flight so there were not many people in the airport. It was lonely and I was scared. I had a layover, and each leg, the crew and passengers were so kind talking me through all the flights and allowing me to make phone calls to make sure Dad was okay. I was taken aback by the generosity of those around me and those giving up a first-class seat for me to be comfortable and make those calls. I called Dad several times along the way—him always asking if I was home yet.

At the layover, coming from all different locations, one of my uncles and some very close neighbors that we considered family ended up boarding that final leg of the flight with me because they too were called home. We had conversations with doctors on next steps and had to decide when it was time to help him be more comfortable on his journey. A decision that was one of the most difficult decisions a family must make. Family and friends were called to say good-bye; he held on until he spoke to everyone. Early in the morning of November 14, 1991, we were all sleeping best we could, me in the chair by Dad's bed, my mom, brother, uncles, and various neighbors in different places of the hospital. Then we all got a nudge, and everybody came running into the room. I woke up and knew he was going home. I still see his face and how strong he was being, but how scared he was too. I miss him so much!

The universe put me there that October day on purpose—it had more yarn for me. While planning the service, I insisted that our previous priest do mass because that is what I heard. My family and friends kept writing my idea off, but I was persistent and never gave up. It was the longest wake and most beautiful, packed church and celebration. Because I listened to the universe, our previous priest spoke about Dad, and as he described him, his voice cracked, and he became emotional as he thanked me for making sure Dad's wishes of him doing his ceremony came to fruition. Several people turned and looked at me and gave me confirmation and a sign of gratefulness.

I can still hear my dad's final father-daughter talk at the airport. It was a scene from a movie! I had spent the better half of the summer healing from a fractured vertebrae from slipping on cement stairs at my summer job. One of my best friends came to visit, and I'm so thankful she was there to fly back with me. It was difficult. I still see this movie playing out in my head all the time.

Dad's final talk:

"Live life to the fullest. Don't wait go grab your dreams. You can do anything!"

"Take care of your psoriasis, keep it under control."

"Finish school and get your master's."

"Stay healthy and let go of the weight."

I got my MBA, pretty much have my psoriasis under control when I am not stressed, and wow, have I lived life to its fullest!

I know he and Mom are very proud of what I have accomplished. It's been an amazing journey, but I have not let go of all the weight, and life has been tough at times. I had to become an adult immediately. I met my first husband, who I thought was the love of my life. Though we were from vastly different backgrounds, he turned out to be the start of the unraveling of the yarn.

I could not find the right stitch for my yarn. I was grieving Dad, and the pain was so hard to overcome. I suppressed it all. I wasn't looking at all the signs from the universe—those red flags. While growing up and giving back and servicing those who needed more (remember that piece of yarn from the battered women's association events), I was able to survive a mentally and physically abusive , and non-intimate marriage. I am a survivor of domestic violence. If I didn't service those or hear those women talk at that dinner meeting and ask those questions, I don't think I would have been strong enough to get out. I wouldn't have realized I lost my self-identity and was going through abuse. I'm thankful for the most incredible network of friends in Colorado and Connecticut to help get me out. I was rescued and started my career in sales, but I had to move as it was too close for comfort to my ex. So, everything went into storage. I packed up my Jeep and headed east, confident I would be back in a few months.

As I built my identity and life again, I met so many people, and I'm thankful for them all crossing my path, taking me in as part of their family, helping me grow into the person I am today, and being so supportive.

I put all my energy into my career. I worked hard, played hard, and what resulted were experiences I would never have dreamed of in both the corporate world and my personal life. I was asked to take on positions that challenged me, that helped me grow. Still suppressing the deep hurt of losing my father, I was determined to be the best, and I still held onto that weight. Incredible mentors taught me how to be human, be an innovator, be an influencer, take risks, motivate others, and build the best performing cultures. I built a reputation of taking calculated risks, failing fast while providing a superior customer experience and building high-performing organizations.

I learned many lessons along the way. Most importantly, I learned how to be who you are, to stand up for yourself and your goals. I realize now looking back that I did what others asked me to do, which might not have been the best for me. Advice from others and mentorship is so important, but what is more important is that you take pieces of yarn from that experience and that advice, and you put it into your blanket of life. Your life blanket is not the same as someone else's, and someone else's yarn and stitch will not fit into your design. I threw myself into my career for so many years and made so many great friendships, but I always put other people first, even if it would hurt me or put me at a disadvantage. I always found the good in others and always will, but there must be a limit. One of the most important life lessons I have learned is that you must take care of yourself first.

I thought I had all the right stitches and pieces of yarn together. A few failed relationships, another failed marriage, toxic relationships, a major career change, and an aging parent my life's journey stretched further than I expected—a crocheted blanket with stiches and yarn in one big, tangled mess.

I went out on my own but missed the corporate world; it's in my DNA. While looking for the right opportunity, I was able to serve others by sharing my story with the world during one of the most historic times, the COVID-19 pandemic. It was there that I finally realized after twenty-nine years that my pain for the loss of my father was so magnificent that I avoided every red flag, literally. The universe gave me so many warnings in so many situations, but the grief was too deep to endure, so I ignored it and didn't want to let go that one last ask from Dad.

But I finally got it! While at the beach setting my goals for the upcoming year and reflecting on the past, I realized the universe is like a lifeguard. If the lifeguard blew the whistle, raised the red flag to get everyone out of the water because of sharks, I would run away from the water quickly—because I always listen to the lifeguard. Well, I have been running right into dangerous waters, ignoring the red flags from the universe (lifeguard) and not listening at all.

I am a survivor and am excited about the crocheted blanket being built now. There may be some yarn that unravels along the way but not like before. Not focusing on self-worth and confidence will lead to greater pain. So, self-reflect and take care of yourself and serve others. This is where all those pieces of yarn early on in life came back around to help me. Giving back is so important. First, for showing up to serve and help someone else. And second, for your personal self-worth. It builds stronger character, and it puts you on the path of your passion and your journey. It is that next piece of yarn to be crocheted!

So, what does this mean? Focus on the signs the universe gives you, and if it is a red flag, pay attention. That red flag could be anything like seeing messages that unveil the truth, a sign or strong feeling to go left versus right and take a different road to your destination, even actions/reactions of others in situations— these are just a few I have encountered. It has taken me fifty-two years to understand the universe's most important lessons for me:

1. The universe will give you the same lesson over and over until you learn it. Understand it and do something about it.

2. Pay attention! If there is a red flag, back far far away from it. Don't run head-on into it!

If only, I listened earlier!

I have realized it comes down to avoiding the pain of a significant loss. I ignored these warnings both in my personal and professional life in different ways. It has put me in situations I really should not have had to go through.

I always show up to serve for others and now I also show up for myself. This is where I have been able to take my innate ability in leadership and build things greater than I could ever imagine. I have a greater purpose on this journey in life. I have had so many dreams come true, and having conversations with college friends, acquaintances, and new connections made me take a step back and go, "Wow, I am just getting started!" Everything has come full circle, and it is time to serve more by being a personal and professional culture creator. Amazing things will come along. Marrying together both my personal and professional experiences is how I achieve bigger and bigger dreams in life. This will let me leave a legacy.

I have never taken the easy road to get to where I am today. It has been a journey filled with making different choices than others would, standing strong along the way and never giving up. My favorite quote by Robert Frost says it all, "Two roads diverged into a wood and I—I took the less traveled by, And that has made all the difference."[1]

Though some choices may have been right, some wrong, taking the less traveled road has made all the difference in my life's crocheted blanket.

Are you ready to take the road less traveled by?

Come join me and create your personal or professional culture by taking the road less traveled by and making a difference.

1—Robert Frost, "The Road Not Taken," in Mountain Interval (New York: Henry Holt, 1916).

ABOUT ERIN MCCAHILL

Erin McCahill is a corporate leader, entrepreneur, mentor, innovator, a personal and professional culture creator. As a sales and customer experience leader in the telecom, technology, and financial industry, she has built a strong reputation in building new organizations and revitalizing low-performing organizations while providing a superior customer experience. Erin has received numerous awards in recognition of her success. She has found her passion that drives her: helping others build personal and professional cultures. Erin possesses a bachelor of science in business management and an MBA.

Raised in Connecticut and now residing in southern New Jersey, Erin enjoys sports, spending time with friends and family, travel, entertaining, and planning events. She takes you along her journey in life and shows us that when you serve others, life's pieces of crocheted yarn will connect other pieces to help when needed. Enduring tremendous loss as a young adult and as a domestic violence survivor, Erin shares some of the lessons learned in her personal and professional life. She is just getting started, and by putting both experiences together, she is working on bigger dreams!

Web: www.themccahillgroup.com
Facebook: @erinamccahillmba
Instagram: @erinamccahillmba
LinkedIn: @erinamccahillmba
Email: em@themccahillgroup.com

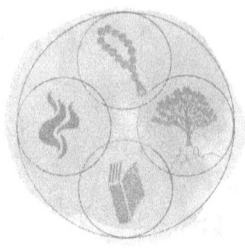

FROM FEAR TO LOVE

Laura Mount

I spent years trying to have children. It was a very dark time in my life. All my young-adult life, I lived under the assumption that one "accident," and you could get pregnant. Well, jokes on me, because that was not true for me. I wanted nothing more than to be a mother. I felt it was my birthright, and my body was deceiving me. I allowed myself to become overwhelmed with the grief and frustration of it. I was trying to control everything in my environment. I was eating only the best of the best. I was taking my temperature every day and trying to find my ovulation—which didn't always come. We were timing sex as best we could. I was on hyper alert, and every time we got a negative test I was devastated. I started acupuncture and Clomid, and doctors and I were holding so tight to the controls. This was the only thing that could make me happy. None of it worked.

At last, we came to the big guns. I said I would never do in vitro fertilization (IVF). I felt this was controlling things too much. It was too sciencey and "unnatural." But here we were, the last stop, the big kahuna. At this point I was desperate. I wanted just one baby, God, just one. I made a vision board, and I put a picture from a magazine of two babies. One girl and one boy to communicate that I didn't care which one I had. I got my schedule of injections, and I released control. I stopped fighting so hard for it and just did what I was told.

Fast-forward. My egg harvest was ridiculous! Forty-one eggs from one retrieval. We still got four good embryos. Tom had moved to Madison, Wisconsin, from Seattle to start a new job while I stayed back to go through the last stage of the IVF. On the way into the embryo transfer appointment, I called Tom to ask what I should do if the doctor recommended we put two embryos back. He said to do whatever the doctor said. I said, "Are you sure?" He said yes. The doctor recommended we put the two strongest embryos back, so that's what I did. Giddy with the idea of possibly having twins, I went back to my in-laws where I was staying, and every night I spoke to those babies. I put my hand on my stomach, and I told them how much I loved them and how long I had been waiting for them.

I never saw a positive pregnancy test. Never in my whole life. I was too scared to test. I waited for the blood test. When I finally went in a week later, my numbers were through the roof. They called Tom to give him the result because I couldn't bear to hear a negative result from anyone but him. He told me the high HCG number and said, "I bet we are having twins."

Sure enough, a boy and a girl. The perfect mix. One and done. Pink and blue. They came screaming into the world, and our little girl was the girliest of girls and our little boy was the sweetest boy a mom could ever ask for. I was so happy to have a boy and a girl. I would have the best of both worlds. The dirty knees and high energy of the boy and the sweet little girl that would give me grandbabies. I'm not saying these were the right thoughts to have—to put my kids in a box based on their gender assigned at birth—but it is a very natural thing for the mind to do. We start to daydream about our future as a parent the moment we find out we are pregnant, and these dreams contain preconceived ideas based on our lived experience and social cues. My little girl was surprisingly girlie. I had never been into girlie things even as a small child. She loved princess dresses and anything frilly. Princesses and My Little Pony were the thing of the time. While Lily's outward appearance changed over the years, I never lost the image of the future of her being a mother like me someday.

In March of 2021, we were in the middle of a pandemic, and I was sitting at my makeshift desk in the kitchen in the middle of a workday. My kids were both doing school from home in our tiny bungalow in west Seattle. One of the kids was sitting in the living room about ten feet from me, and I got a text, "Mom, when can we talk about me starting testosterone?"

Um, what? I walked over to the couch and said, "I love you, and we will talk about this, but not over text." I then walked back to my desk, sat down, and dove back into my email and worked the rest of the day to avoid thinking about the conversation we were to have later that day. *What does this mean for the future? Surely this is not real. It's just a phase.* My image of the future was still holding on strong.

That evening, my daughter sat across the table from my husband and I and announced that she wanted to be our son and asked if we would let her go to the doctor to get a prescription for testosterone. She was nervous and struggled to make eye contact with us. I was in such denial. This was a phase, it would pass.

Seven years prior to this conversation at the age of seven, she asked to cut her hair like her brother's—a.k.a. the number 2 guard on the clippers. I questioned her as to why, and she reported that the boys had a book at school that they wouldn't let her look at because she was a girl. She was in the second grade. I told her they would still know she was a girl. At the time I cut the kids' hair. I asked my husband what to do. What if I cut her long hair off and she hated it and was mad at me? Why was I suddenly so attached to her hair? He counseled me to take her to the hair salon and have her tell them what she wanted, and then it wasn't on me. What a genius. She ended up with a short pixie cut at the hair salon, and when they turned her around to see it, she was so happy. I still have a photo of that big grin on my phone. Then the next time she asked for the number 2 guard, I thought back to that huge smile on her face, and we got the clippers out. Number 2 guard for the win. She loved it.

After this she went back and forth between presenting male (though I didn't have this language then—she wore her brother's clothes) and presenting female. She was happy and well-adjusted, and we never really questioned any of it. I spent approximately zero minutes really thinking or worrying about any of it. She was expressing herself, and as I said, she was a happy, well-adjusted child. I will say that this new haircut did allow her to jump in on boy games at the neighborhood playgrounds where no one knew she was a girl. She loved this.

Let's jump ahead. My son is transgender. This means my son was born with a male brain and a female body. He was born a girl. (I state it this way for your understanding, but the correct terminology is AFAB—assigned female at birth.) We have been on quite a journey. My eyes and heart have been opened in ways I never could have imagined. My son has led the way, blazed a trail, and shown us how it is done.

A lot of trans teens present their gender identity to friends before talking to their parents and family. They may change their pronouns and even their name with their friends and "try things on" for years. By the time they come out to their family, they have had time to adjust to the idea, test the waters, and make up their minds. They are well along the way before the parents are looped in—mentally and emotionally.

This is where we sat on that fateful night. Shocked and not shocked at the same time. I immediately went into denial. I am her mother. I have a gut instinct. Women's intuition or whatever you want to call it, and I was sure it was a phase. It wasn't real. She would turn around the minute she was faced with a needle.

When the words were first uttered, I looked at my husband

before saying anything, and Tom didn't miss a beat. He said, "Of course we support you. Our number one is that you are happy." I was not surprised by his reaction. I often call him Buddha because out of the blue he will just say the right thing. He'll be calm and centered and unfazed. We told our son, of course he can see the doctor. His face lit up. He had our permission to see the doctor and see where it took him—to start a journey to himself. He was over the moon. I thought I was going through the motions, walking a journey with my child that would result in him going back to the status quo, but the key element is that I was allowing him to explore and find his way and keeping my thoughts about the destination to myself and allowing next steps while I was still processing.

Despite the joy on his face, I still didn't see the opportunity that lay in front of me. He had no doubts, and I had to go on my own journey to trust that. Of all of the things I thought I would navigate as a parent, this certainly wasn't on my radar.

As the process moved forward and with each new appointment, I learned new things. These new things often left me with more questions, more anxiety, and more fear. He already knew the process and all of these things and was ready to discuss them. I, on the other hand, was not. I did some of my own research as this was becoming more real. I talked to him candidly about these things. We were learning together as we went, and we continued to learn. I said and did, and still do, the wrong things all the time, and he gives me grace. We keep the lines of communication open, and when I am not sure how to handle something—or rather how he would like me to handle it—I ask.

When we got new photos of all of the grandkids, I really wanted to keep the old photo up to show how much they had all grown, but since the earlier photo was very female presenting, I wasn't sure how he would feel about keeping that photo up, so I asked him. This is very personal child to child. Some embrace all of themselves and see their younger self as part of their identity, and some completely reject it and don't want to look at photos or have others see photos. I was granted permission to display both photos.

The first step on our adolescent transgender journey is a stop at your primary care doctor. We are lucky to live in a very progressive city that generally is very supportive of the LGBTQ+ community. Some conversation with the doc, and we were off and running with our referral to the gender clinic at Children's Hospital. As a parent I was still freaking out on the inside thinking this wasn't real. *Can't be real. It's a phase. And it is all happening so fast.* I asked my son questions about the validity of his claims (I told you it wasn't easy, and I learned along the way). "The other transgender kid we know came out at like five years old. You're fourteen. Wouldn't there have been signs?" "How can you and other friends of yours also be trans?" "But you wore the pinkest, frilliest stuff when you were young. I didn't pick that out, you did. You wore princess dresses and pink patent leather shoes everywhere." He tolerated my doubt and questioning, and we carried on. I continued to take deep breaths, take the next step, and do more listening than talking.

The change to he/him pronouns was surprisingly difficult. I kept thinking that if he had a more masculine name, it would be easier. His dead name (birth name) was very feminine. I also made the mistake of using this excuse to let other people in his life off the hook. Freshman year of high school he still used his birth name but used he/him pronouns all of high school. He told me that there were a few teachers who still misgendered him, referring to him with she/her pronouns. This felt very disrespectful and intentional to him. He presented male and had done so the entire time he was at the school. I told him that it was hard for people because his name is so feminine, and it made their brains short circuit when they tried to pair it with masculine pronouns. I realized that this excuse was bullshit and said, "You just needed me to say that sucks and tell you I would talk to your counselor at school, right?" Yes, yes, he did. He didn't need me to support the ignorance of others and leave him to hold that pain on his own. Stepping-stones on the parenting journey. I was slowly seeing life through his lens. He was being outed by people of authority in his life. He had asked them to use the correct pronouns, and they were not.

I know what you are thinking. Will there be some counseling? Therapy? Psychiatrist? Does a kid get to just decide they are a different gender, and we just go with it as parents? How could they know at this age? I mean, the short answer is yes, at least in our program, there is evaluation and a diagnosis of body dysphoria. The long answer is much more convoluted. If you had to choose, would you choose to be in the wrong body? If puberty came along and things started shifting in the wrong direction and you were horrified, would you want to do something about it!? Again, I was ignorant to all of this. "Nobody likes having a period." "Every teenage girl has body dysmorphia when they hit puberty." (FYI dysmorphia is not the same as dysphoria, the feeling of distress or discomfort because of the difference between a person's gender assigned at birth and their gender identity.) Closed-minded, everybody-fits-in-a-box thinking. Again, he answered my questions. He explained the differences between dysmorphia and dysphoria. I was allowing him to carry me and my ignorance and my pain. I was putting him in a position to educate me.

Go back for a moment to your own puberty. I know for me the changes to my body were hard to accept. Now imagine for a moment you see yourself as male and you start to develop D-size breasts, or that you see yourself as female and your shoulders widen, facial hair starts to sprout, an Adam's apple forms, and your voice drops. It would be devastating. You wouldn't be able to hide your gender any longer. It would be there for everyone to see. This is a dangerous time for transgender teens. At best, they hide in baggy clothing and become quiet, shy, angry, and withdrawn or lean into their gender assigned at birth and live a life that likely is not true for them. At worst, it becomes unbearable, and they cannot stand to be on this earth. According to a survey conducted by the Trevor Project 2021 National Survey on LGBTQ Youth Mental Health, 52% considered suicide and 20% reported attempting suicide. Compared to 32% and 10% in cisgender (identifying as the gender they were born) youth.[1]

There are many things that come with treating body dysphoria. I won't go into the details here except to say they are all terrifying for a parent. Thoughts of future fertility, possible permanent changes, and potential surgeries. It comes hard and fast. Kids don't want to be in this body, and they don't want to be in it stat!

After puberty started, my son had started to retract into himself. He wouldn't speak up anymore. He wouldn't order for himself. We attributed it to standard teenage changes. We discovered that he had been cutting and was feeling very anxious. He was spending more time in his room and not engaging in conversation during dinner. I was very nervous about the cutting and at a loss for how to handle it. He didn't want to talk to us about it and couldn't articulate to us (or didn't want to) why he did it or the relief or benefit he felt he was getting from it. I started to notice the same telltale signs on the arms of his friends.

All through my doubts and fears and skepticism, we kept taking the next step forward. I did a lot of work on myself during this time. I started to see that I needed to get my mind around this. *This is happening!* I had to find a way to work through my thoughts and feelings about what was happening as we were moving forward so I could be there for my child fully and not be in my head about the future and fear of what was happening. I needed to step out of fear and move into love so I could support my child. This couldn't wait until I understood and accepted

1—"National Survey on LGBTQ Youth Mental Health 2021," The Trevor Project, accessed June 28, 2022, https://www.thetrevorproject.org/survey-2021.

every facet of it. It couldn't wait until I made peace with it or made decisions around treatments that were four steps down the road. I had to make decisions as they came, I had to work with my spouse and my child and all the therapists, social workers, and doctors to take the next right step. My child needed me, and I needed to step up and out of my mind.

My son was struggling to pick out a new name so I asked if I could help. Imagine my surprise when he said yes. I got baby name books from the library—because I am "old" and apparently forgot about the internet. I picked a list of names and he liked a few. I told my sister-in-law about this list and she said Luke immediately popped into her head when we told her. This was a variation of one of the names on the list. I presented it to Luke, and he loved it. And that is now his name. I love this story because of the support of our family! This was one small step for me to take in showing my son that I love, respect, and support him.

I am lucky to have other amazing parents in my life who helped to light the way on this path for me and keep me focused on what matters. My child. There have been many long walks and tears discussing my fears and what-ifs and commiserating over the confusion of it all. These women helped me process my emotions and see where my thinking may be holding me back. They were my safe place to process all of my feelings and emotions and not burden my child with educating me and making it all okay. This is an absolute must. Burdening our children further and asking them to carry our fears and doubts during this trying time is not fair to them. I needed to find a safe place to process all of this so I could be open and available to hear and support him.

It was the support of these women, the doctors, and social workers that helped us get our minds around hormones. He started taking testosterone about three months into this journey. This was a hard step for us to take. It probably seems like we came to this choice quickly, but it didn't feel that way. We agonized over the possible side effects and the changes this meant—big, huge, scary decisions for a teenager to make and parents to sign off on. At the end of the day, we had to plug our noses and jump in the deep end of the pool and trust our child, the therapists, and the doctors. The possible side effects of the hormones seemed minimal compared to the other options: anguish for my son and potential loss of life.

When people question our decision to let Luke take testosterone, I am confident in our choice. "You're not going to let him take hormones, are you? I mean dressing as a boy and using he/him pronouns is one thing, but hormones can cause permanent damage." It is not a proven fact that hormones do cause permanent damage. You know what causes permanent damage? Suicide. After presented with all the facts and learning more of other trans journeys, we were able to move past our fears and give our child what he needed to feel better. This is the treatment for body dysphoria.

Just like the social worker said after he started the testosterone, he was back to being his old self—the vibrant and talkative kid we knew before puberty. Luke opened up more to us in general and about his journey. I'm not sure if that is because of the trust we showed him or the confidence in feeling like he was on his own journey and had some control over his destiny.

In retrospect, I can't even begin to imagine the courage it took for him to come forward. In all of this I hadn't considered the courage he was displaying. He was standing in his truth in all walks of his life! This is something a lot of adults I know don't have the capacity for. This was to be celebrated! He was not only being himself, he was supporting other kids along the way.

This is supposed to be a story about me, but there is no story about me without this story. I am a mother. My children are a large part of who I am. My relationship with my children is a large part of who I am. It is the biggest opportunity for me to practice being who I want to be in this world. How I want to treat people. What values I live by. These have all been tested and continue to be tested along this journey. This has been a grand opportunity for me to pause, take each value and belief, and analyze it and see whether it was truly coming from me or from unconscious programming.

I want to be an open person. I want to be a loving person. I want to be accepting of all beings both similar and different. This is easy to do when all beings "different" are *out there*. When those differences are *in here,* you really get tested. Now the differences (as I am learning) are not all so drastic as gender identity. They can be tidiness, educational acumen, personal interest, intrinsic motivation, desire to please, the list goes on and on. This journey has helped me to look at all of these things and my expectations of myself and others and truly look hard at myself, my actions, my values, and whether or not I am living my values.

My priority is my family. My goal as a parent is to raise loving, happy children whom I have a lifelong relationship with. This takes work. It takes personal reflection and admitting when you react to your past wounds and what you *think* you are supposed to be doing as a parent. To evaluate your motivations. Am I doing this because it is providing the result—a loving relationship with my child—I am after, because it is default parenting based on my childhood, or because I am worried about what *they* (peers, my parents, teachers) may think of me and my family? I now take a long, hard look at what is important to *me*! Does what I am about to say really matter? Does it create confidence and trust in my child, or does it drive a wedge between us? I don't always catch myself, but I always circle back and reconnect. I didn't always do this. I didn't do it because "the parent is always right" or "you can't show weakness or they'll walk all over you."

Well, shit, clearly the parent isn't always right. I assumed I had a daughter!

I have learned to question all the things I previously believed. What boxes am I creating for people? What boxes am I creating for myself? What boxes that others created am I still living in?

I have done a lot of research and it is fascinating to hear stories of other families. It often challenges my default mechanisms. For example, in listening to the story of another family, I saw a pattern in myself that I hadn't recognized. My daughter became my son, and then my son would wear female jewelry and was wearing eyeliner, and my mind couldn't handle it. My mind wanted him to pick a team already. Well, wrong again! There is no team! Male-presenting folks can wear previously labeled female items and vice versa—though let's be honest, ladies, the construct has allowed us to get away with "male" items.

Can you imagine what this might mean for the future? Could this transition loosen the gender inequality? Could nonbinary folks start to really erase that? Could there be an end to getting paid more if you have a penis?

It is time to learn how to think for ourselves. To look at the stories we've been told about the world and ourselves and question them. To really look inside and decide what we think for ourselves. To look at each other and see ourselves reflected back. We have a great resource and example right in our own homes. I am constantly in awe of my children and their peers. They are leading the charge to equality. They are open and accepting, and I feel another shift coming. We can resist this based on their young age and inexperience, or we can help usher it in by listening to our children and supporting them.

I've always wanted to help people improve themselves so *they* could feel better and be successful, but the more I research and see the humanity in us all, the more I really want us to take responsibility for our thoughts and how we show up, not for ourselves, but for each other. For all of our futures.

If you are the parent of a trans teen, you are not alone. Other parents are out there, many of us doubting our choices and fearful of making mistakes. There are resources for you. There are many Facebook groups and in-person support groups. I encourage to you to reach out to these resources, to make connections and find people you can process with. If you are not finding these resources and you are struggling, please reach out. I am always happy and willing to connect!

ABOUT LAURA MOUNT

Parenting is a journey we don't get a map for. When we first find out we are having a child, we don't know what we are going to get! Boy? Girl? Healthy? We can easily map out different scenarios in our minds as to how our lives together will play out—particularly if we discover the assigned gender of our unborn child. It is a natural thing to do. Hopes and dreams are part of the human experience.

We were thrown a curveball that never appeared in any of the various lives I imagined for myself, my children, and our family. One of my sons is transgender. This was a map I didn't even have in the way back of my closet. There was no file in my brain labeled "transgender" for me to access. This was all new territory.

This is the story of how we created our own map with our child as the cartographer.

Laura Mount lives in west Seattle with her husband, kids, and dogs. She is a full-time working mom of teenage twins. The past year has been transformative for her as a mother as she learns how to support and parent her transgender teen. In this captivating account of this first year, she shares the struggles, challenges, joys, and epiphanies she has had on this journey. This process has helped her evaluate everything she believes and the way she shows up in the world.

Instagram: @laura_mount
Facebook: Laura Mount
LinkedIn: Laura Mount
Web: www.lauramount.com

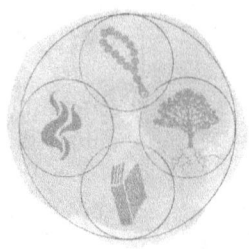

HOW DO YOU GRAND?

Suzette Perez-Tate

"**N**ana is a grandma?" Charlotte says with confusion as she sees images of grandparents that don't quite match what she is familiar with. This is similar for many families out there. My journey growing up taught me how to face adversity head-on and find solutions. That is exactly what I did with *The Grands*. I am the creator and #1 best-selling author on Amazon of *The Grands Modern-Day Grandparent* children's book series. It wasn't easy getting there because it's not always a straight line to get to where you want to go. This has certainly been my experience in life overall.

I am the youngest of four children with a span of five-, six-, and seven-years' difference from my siblings. At an early age, I never quite felt like I fit in, and I always sought acceptance from others, and I also rooted for the underdog. The two don't always go hand in hand, and they're not always the popular choice.

I didn't see it then but many of my life experiences had prepared me for the journey I am currently on. My parents moved us to a small suburban town with the intention of giving us a better life than they had. They struggled to make ends meet in a community that was middle to upper class. I often would have homemade or hand-me-down clothes, and there was no money for extras. As kids we knew if we wanted more, we needed to work for it (babysit, mow lawns, yard work, etc.).

As my parents could no longer make ends meet, they moved us from our comfortable cul-de-sac to another part of town. Time to fit into another neighborhood and adjust to my mother going back into the workforce. This was a pivotal change during my junior high years. With both parents working, I had a lot of unsupervised time on my hands, and my siblings were older and doing their own thing or out of the house.

Soon I would start high school and learn to fit in all over again. High school brought on new challenges in trying to stay focused, which was hard for me academically, and keeping up socially. At fifteen I met a young boy at school, and at the young age of sixteen I had my daughter. I stayed at a teenage maternity home for a few months before giving birth to my daughter. I remember crying the first few nights, but I eventually adjusted as I met young girls from all over and from different backgrounds. My mother never shamed me and was so supportive and nurturing through it all.

I eventually had feelings of outgrowing my daughter's father, and he was no longer my future. I moved on and two months later I met my now husband at the age of seventeen. It was late 1987, so we were met with resistance as I am Hispanic, and he is black. My parents did not want me to date him. As much as I strived to fit in and seek acceptance, I always created my own path. Despite my parents' request, I continued to see him, and our bond with each other grew stronger.

Although I was a teen mom (a label I never accepted), I felt strongly about graduating and then going on to college. After high school, I immediately enrolled in a trade school for electronics, and yes, you guessed it, I did not feel as though I fit in. I must have been one of five girls in the whole predominantly male school. After finishing my associate's degree in electronics, it was time to find a job. I was so motivated to make money to provide a comfortable life for my daughter and me. But doors did not open so easily. Some employers wanted to hire me due to the way I looked rather than the skills I just earned in school. While others rejected me due to my looks, saying that their wife would be mad at them if they hired me. Over the years, I would try my hand at a variety of temporary jobs.

Six years had gone by, and I was still dating my boyfriend from the age of seventeen. I became pregnant with my son, and the resistance to my relationship with my parents was over. They embraced our relationship as though they never had an issue with it.

I remember the day I moved out of my parents' house and moved in with my now husband. Before leaving, my mother asked me if I would leave my daughter with her and my father. I couldn't understand why she would ask me such a thing as I too was close with my daughter and could not imagine ever leaving her. I just couldn't fathom why she would ask me such a question.

Having my daughter at such a young age made my mother a grandmother at the age of forty-two. My mother was such a great example and role model of what it meant to be a modern-day grandparent as she never seemed to fit in the mold. I never met my grandfathers and did not spend much time with my grand-mothers. I had a lot of love and respect for my grandmothers but have very few memories with them.

When people saw my mother and daughter together, they often thought they were mother and daughter. The bond my mother had with my daughter was beautiful. She was always her safe place and much like a best friend and personal cheerleader. I was always the youngest parent at back-to-school night and was even mistaken for a high school student during a tryout event for theater. I always felt that I had to grow into being looked at as my daughter's mother.

As my daughter became older, the bond between her and my

mother strengthened. They talked on the phone daily, multiple times throughout the day and night. They enjoyed short trips together and even went to New York when my daughter was in the twelfth grade. They called this their senior trip.

When my mother turned sixty-two, she was diagnosed with breast cancer. She had beat cancer, and then it returned as it metastasized into her lung as Stage IV cancer. My mother showed us what it was like to *live* with cancer instead of dying from cancer. She didn't miss a beat when it came to being a mother or grandmother. She was full of life, something you just don't see represented in stories or images about grandparents.

Soon it would be my turn to experience life as a grandparent—a concept that I just did not see myself embracing as I could not relate to the one-dimensional character often highlighted in stories and images. I mean, have you seen the emoji that represents grandparents?

I have a blended family, and my stepson had our first grandchild. Loren was a beautiful grandbaby. Now, I wasn't being called Grandma or any other endearing nickname just yet as Loren was still too young to speak.

Loren was just born, and my daughter Ashley was pregnant with my second grandchild. Quinn was born the following year. While I still wasn't sure about being called Grandma, my mother was still showing me how grand she truly is. Still, very close to Ashley, she was very involved with Quinn's homecoming and stayed with Ashley while Quinn came home from the hospital, a moment I will always regret not being there for. I may have taken for granted that my mother was always there for my daughter for major life situations. As Quinn was home and looked upon with much love, tragedy was just hours away. I left my daughter, my mother, and my granddaughter with a bit of an unsettling feeling. Early the next morning I received one of the worst phone calls I could have ever received. Ashley pieced together the words "Quinn is dead." Within a year, I had celebrated my daughter's pregnancy, the birth of Quinn, then a full Catholic mass for my grandbaby's funeral. My heart was crushed for my daughter and mother for the traumatic event they endured together. My mother would always put events in our lives in perspective by saying that they have already experienced the worst thing they could ever experience in their lives.

Another year later came Brooke (Loren's sister). At family gatherings, I was referred to as Grandma Suzette. The name Grandma just had a stigma for me, as it sounded like such an aging reference. I still hadn't quite got my bearings as grandma yet, but I loved the girls so much. When Brooke was born, Ashley was carrying her second child. Come November, Charlotte Rose Smith was born. Being so nervous and unable to forget what happened with Quinn, I stepped into my grandma role as my mother had been showing me all these years. I went to doctor's appointments, smiling from ear to ear over every moment spent with her. I didn't realize that my heart could feel this way. It was truly magic. Everything was about this little girl (as though I had the authority to make any decisions). Here I was for many years trying to just fill my shoes of being called Mom (as many saw me as my daughter's sister) to finally being ready to be called Grandma. It wasn't easy right away, but soon Charlotte was calling me Nana. I light up anytime I hear her call out to me.

But there was still the feeling of not fitting into my role and still remnants of the stigma of being called Grandma, Nana, or anything related to being that one-dimensional character. When reading stories or seeing images about grandparents, I just couldn't relate. I was so actively involved with Charlotte, and I loved being silly without caring who saw me. Over the next few years, my stepdaughter gave us two more grandchildren, Jeremiah and Journey.

Today many grandparents still have a job, career, are active, provide care for their grandchildren, and in some cases live with their grandchildren. I kept telling my mom that I needed to change the stereotype of grandparents. At times I would joke about it, but then one day I became serious about changing the image of what a grandparent looks and feels like in society. As I became a grandmother, I began to really notice other grandparents and how they showed up in their grandchildren's lives. People I observed were friends, family, coworkers, and even strangers. Our stories were all different in how we showed up in our grandchildren's lives, but the focus remained the same as we all had such a deep love for our grandchildren. No one family is the same, and no one grandparent is the same.

My mother's cancer finally took its toll, and she eventually passed away. A few months later, I was driving home from an out-of-town trip with my husband, and I could not shake the feeling of the modern-day grandparent concept. It was as though my mother was right there with me pushing me toward this endeavor. I pulled out my laptop and began to create a presentation of the concept. I had socialized my presentation with a few people and the concept with others. Immediately I received positive feedback and an understanding of what I was looking to do. This was a feeling of validation anytime anyone understood the concept of the modern-day grandparent.

Later that year I was faced with a career decision to take an early retirement package from a company I had been working at for over twenty-five years. My thought was that I would take the package and begin my writing on a children's book about the modern-day grandparent and start the work I had laid out in my presentation. To be clear, I never set out to be an author. This was more about starting a movement where grandparents would be seen for how they show up in their grandchildren's lives.

I eventually made the decision to continue working and started on my bachelor's degree. Passing up the opportunity to retire gave me the perspective that I didn't have to give up the dream of *The Grands* book series. As you can tell I am very much an "and" person. I can do this, *and* I can do that. When you believe in something strong enough, you will figure out a way to make it happen. My husband told me a long time ago if I want something I am going to do it. I had a great teacher in my mother as she always went into what I call fix-it mode. She didn't look for excuses or talk her way out of anything; she would immediately figure out a way to make it happen.

I had no idea where to start when creating a children's book, let alone a series. I just knew there was something I really wanted to change, and the series would be the platform for my message. If I overthink a plan or project, I end up talking myself out of it, easily coming up with reasons why I can't do it. I call this action *getting in my own way.* To move forward, I could not get in my own way. Believe me, I had many reasons I could have used as an excuse to get in my own way. I was still grieving my mother's passing, working full-time, attending school full-time, recovering from spine surgery, balancing time with my family, and traveling back and forth to visit Charlotte out of state.

Soon after I found a coauthor to join in on my passion project to coauthor a children's book, it came time to look for an illustrator. This process was all new for me, and I took it all in and learned so much. I went through about five to six illustrators as I needed the grands to be represented just right. COVID restrictions began, and we had to move to work remotely.

When it came to writing, there was so much passion in this project that we had enough content for two books immediately. No one family is the same, and no one grandparent is the same. This was so apparent as I couldn't decide where to limit my characters and family dynamics within the series. We were so green when it came to learning the criteria for children's books and to publishing. Immediately we learned how generous authors and others in the book industry are. I was introduced to Kate Butler who believed in our story and mission. She helped us bring our dream across the finish line and was so enthusiastic throughout the process.

My hope is that many families will see themselves and feel as though they fit in, in this series, concept, and movement. Getting *The Grands Modern-Day Grandparent* series in households around the world to celebrate the relationship between grandparents and their grandchildren is my *dream*. I went from not fitting in or wanting acceptance to being the creator and #1 best-selling author on Amazon of *The Grands Modern-Day Grandparent* series. Tell me, how do you grand? We would love to hear from you and how you grand @thegrandsmdg on Instagram.

ABOUT SUZETTE PEREZ-TATE

Suzette Perez-Tate is a 52-year-old Modern-Day Grandmother and the Creator and Coauthor of the #1 best-selling Amazon children's book: The Grands: The Race and Time With My Grand. Suzette and her husband have been together going on 35 years and have a blended family with 5 children and 5 grandchildren. Suzette has been working for a technology company for 28 years in business operations and recently earned her MBA, proving to herself that it's never too late. She lived most of her life with a feeling of always wanting to fit in or pleasing others, she is finally living life knowing she is enough.

For over 10 years Suzette Perez-Tate struggled with fitting into the one-dimensional image and characterization of how grandparents are highlighted in children's book stories and society. She couldn't ignore that many family dynamics and the way that grandparents show up in their grandchildren's lives were not being represented and she created The Grands Modern-Day Grandparent series. It is important to Suzette to create an experience through her children's books that provides inclusion and diversity celebrating grandparents and their grandchildren where families can see themselves. No one family is the same and no one grandparent is the same.

You can reach out to Suzette Perez-Tate via:

Email: thegrandsmdg@gmail.com
Instagram: @thegrandsmdg
Facebook: The Grands Modern Day Grandparent
Website: www.thegrandsmdg.com

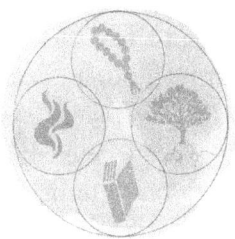

THIS IS *NOT* AS GOOD AS IT GETS

Tracy Richards

I had a whole life. I had built a whole life. I met a man and married him. I had a good job, owned a business, ran marathons and triathlons, had pets, traveled. Over the years, there were some good times and some bad times. To the outside world, it looked like I had it all. My husband and I were the perfect couple, so in sync with each other. How it felt from the inside was something very different. I was suffocating, choking on denial, and convinced that this life was as good as it would get for me. A beginning and an ending would change all of that.

I've never been afraid of beginnings. In fact, they have always excited me. I went to college 2,000 miles from home, I moved across the country two times by myself, and started multiple new jobs. The thrill of something unknown was always fresh. It's the endings that scared me. The finality filled me with fear and made it difficult to embrace the possibilities of a better future. When the chance to begin again was ripe with opportunity, I was always apprehensive.

After fifteen years in the Pacific Northwest, my husband and I moved to northeast Ohio. A job offer for him along with a generous relocation package catapulted us into a new chapter.

We loaded our five dogs and five cats into two cars and made the four-day drive to our new home. I was fearful of the ending that this beginning signified. We were leaving a community and connection behind for a place where I knew no one. The future should have felt wide open, but it didn't.

While our old life had familiarity and safeness to it, it felt lonely. Struggling to find my purpose, I poured all my energy into my animals and my marriage. The only friends I had were those whom my husband and I shared. I gave up my identity long ago, back when we first met, when all I wanted was for him to want me. I gave up my independence when we opened a business that would eventually fail and hurl us into financial crisis. I gave up my peace when we adopted Asha, a dog who was born deaf and blind, with epilepsy and debilitating anxiety. This new location in which we found ourselves would not be able to erase all of that, and so the promise of a new beginning felt empty.

My husband and I were together for seventeen years, married for eleven of those, and through it all, we depended upon each other. I hadn't fallen in love. I had just ended up there and never even bothered to ask myself if that was what I wanted. Our marriage was a partnership, a friendship, a commitment. I believed being married meant stability, affection, and foreverness. My marriage never felt that way to me, instead it was a relentless exercise in bargaining.

I wasn't getting the affection I so desired, but my husband was a solid guy whom I trusted . . . good enough.

I didn't feel passion, but maybe not all relationships were passionate . . . good enough.

I was drowning in our financial struggles, but we were in it together, and how could I ever make my way alone . . . good enough.

I felt overwhelmed with the daily demands of our animals, all of them, but they gave me the love and connection I wasn't feeling anywhere else . . . good enough.

I sacrificed my desires and my dreams, because I worried that if I asked for something more, if I took a chance and tried to find better, I would realize that this was the pinnacle. Then the "good enough" would be a distant memory, replaced by the "remember when" in a life full of regret.

Meanwhile, my husband was making progress in our new environment. He had his job, he found connection in the running community without me, he went back to school for his MBA, he made friends, he found belonging. I stayed at home on the couch with the animals, behind our black curtains with empty walls and old furniture. Our house reflected the way I felt about our relationship. It was sad and dark. No light was able to get in, and I was breaking under the weight of it all.

While I had thoughts of being unhappy and wanting something different, I always pushed them out of mind. Until I couldn't anymore. One day, I collapsed. In one moment, it all changed. I found my voice, and the Universe was ready to match me. It had been waiting patiently all this time. Once I spoke power to my desires, once I imprinted my true feelings on the ether, my whole life shifted.

My husband decided to leave the job for which we had moved to Ohio. He had been there for two years and eight months. Our relocation package required he stay for three years; anything less would result in a financial penalty. I was supportive of his job change because he had been unhappy, and I couldn't tolerate his unhappiness on top of mine. I didn't fully understand the ramifications of the timeline. But I would. Soon enough, I would.

On that day, the day that signaled the line between before and after, I was working in my home office when I got a text from my husband. That text told me that we owed $36,000 in relocation package payback, and we had two months to satisfy that debt. This information literally brought me to my knees. For the first time, I gave myself permission to acknowledge my truth. I had grown tired of living a life of lack, a life of never having enough of anything, a life of emptiness. At the top of my lungs, through body-consuming sobs, on the hardwood floor of my bedroom, I shook the world with my words. "I don't want to live like this anymore."

"I DON'T WANT TO LIVE LIKE THIS ANYMORE."

That's all it took for there to be a seismic shift. I didn't realize it at the time, but I know it now. The Universe heard me. Loud and clear. Over the next year, I wouldn't live like that anymore, not in any capacity. It would all be different.

Three months later, my husband walked down the stairs, sat on the couch across from me, and much to my surprise, told me we were getting a divorce. There was no discussion, there was no counseling, no chance to reconsider. He had decided and that was it. Three months after that night, our divorce was final. I was left with our five dogs and three remaining cats, a house that was falling apart, tight finances, and no local friends to comfort me. I thought I was lonely before, but this was a different kind of loneliness. There was a glimmer of possibility, but it was over-shadowed by the crippling loss that had preceded it.

The end of my marriage devastated me. I was so overcome with fear, grief, and shame that I was unable to embrace the gift of an empty page. I thought my whole world had closed in on me. Who would ever want all of *this*? Who would want a forty-four-year-old, divorced woman covered in tattoos, with a crappy house, no money, and eight animals? I could not imagine any quality person desiring any of that. And because I couldn't imagine it, it stayed impossible.

I spent the year after my divorce making progress in some aspects of my life. I made my way financially by being scrappy. I said yes to everything, I took every job and contract offered to me until I couldn't keep it straight anymore. I found friend-ships by saying yes to invitations, even when I didn't want them because I knew I had to do something different if I wanted a better future. Yet, in one part of my life, I was treading water. I entered a relationship with an unavailable man who would never be able to commit to me. I told myself it was the circumstances not my value that kept this connection from becoming more permanent. This affair allowed me to prove to myself that what I had before was actually as good as it was ever going to get for me.

I had shouted out for a different life and now I had it, but I didn't want this one either. I realized I had never asked myself what I did want. I had never formulated my desires, never expressed the exact feelings I hoped for. I had always created my life by default, by saying "okay, this is fine" when I should have been saying "no, I want *so* much more than this." *Fine* is where dreams go to die. I was further into unhappiness than I ever was during my marriage, and that became unacceptable to me. I opened my journal and began to write.

This is how it will be, I started. I went on to detail how my desired relationship would be. How I would feel, what experiences and emotions would abound. It poured out of me onto the pages, and I felt a lightness as if my vision had reached the intended recipient. I realized I had been saying yes to other things in my life, friendships, financial opportunity, a lifetime of lessons from my dog, Asha, but I was saying no to the possibility of romantic love and connection, the one thing I most desired. I needed to find a way to say yes in every part of my life.

This time, I clearly expressed to the Universe what I wanted, and again, it did not disappoint. Shortly after that entry into my journal, the dead-end relationship dissolved. I was overcome with a sense of relief. *Finally.* I no longer had to convince myself or struggle with the impossibility. It just went away. Because it no longer served me. It no longer provided me the feelings I wanted to feel. It no longer aligned with the clarity of my dreams. The fear I had always felt in endings eased. There was an inkling that something so much better was on its way. It had to be because maybe this wasn't as good as it was going to get. I created space for what was meant for me, and it finally showed up.

One April day, as I parked my car and walked down the street to meet a man I had just recently connected with online, I had to convince myself to say yes. We had texted for two days, and now I was on my way to see him face to face for our first date. *Turn around and go home,* I told myself. I was convinced that what I wanted could not be waiting for me. The chance of a beginning was still buried under the bitterness of an ending. Even though it was uncomfortable and scary, I said yes. I decided to move forward toward the life I wanted instead of shrinking back into the one I didn't. That decision changed everything.

"My God, you're beautiful" were the first words he said to me. And every day since, we have built the life that I asked for, the life that I chose, the life that I created through intention and action. This relationship evolved into the "this is how it will be" relationship that I wrote about in my journal. I asked for it, I got it, and I express my gratitude for it every single day of my life.

As other parts of my life grew cumbersome, I remembered that I could formulate my plan. My work situation had become so stressful, at one point I had twelve email addresses because I said yes to everything that came my way, taking no time to consider if it moved me toward my dreams or not. I wanted a single job that would provide me security, purpose, and flexibility. One afternoon, all my work converged into chaos, and I said, "I don't want to do this anymore." Just then, my phone rang and I was offered a job I had been interviewing for that would allow all the things I had conjured. I was onto something.

I always believed that I was limited financially, that I had a certain ceiling I could never break through. I was a spender, not a saver, and my bank account supported this theory. Until it supported a new idea. I again decided what I wanted, how I would feel when my finances were increasing, what it would mean to have that certainty. I wrote it down, I took action every day, and eventually it became so.

The one thing I couldn't seem to tackle, the single issue that eluded me, was sleep. My dog Asha, the one who was born deaf and blind, the one with epilepsy and anxiety, the one who had stolen my peace . . . she never slept. After years and years of working with veterinarians and all sorts of other practitioners to find a way to ease her restlessness, we still only got three to four hours of sleep at a time. I had gone ten years without a full night of rest. I constantly asked the Universe for sleep. I wrote about it, I dreamed about it, I attempted to move toward it, with no success. Then it occurred to me. It wasn't sleep I wanted; it was the feeling of rest.

I had been asking for something specific, a thing, instead of asking for how I wanted to feel. In all other aspects of my life, in my relationship, my finances, my career, I had created a blueprint for how I wanted to feel. I never asked for the love of my life to look a certain way or have a particular job. I didn't detail what his bank account would hold or what filled his closet. I didn't wonder about investments or think of working for one specific company. All my words, all my visions, all my hopes and actions focused on one thing: how I wanted to *feel*.

I began to approach my relationship with Asha keeping that in mind. I was feeling tired, hopeless, drained, angry, frustrated, and afraid. I thought I wanted sleep, but what I really wanted was to stop feeling these things and instead to be rested and energized, fascinated and in love with this creature who consumed my life. So I did what I had done before. I got my journal and I began to write. It didn't take long for my emotions to transform. Even though my hours of sleep did not increase, I noticed that I felt rested and more loving toward Asha. It became clear. It wasn't the conditions that needed to change, it was me.

There are situations we have control over no matter how much we convince ourselves otherwise. Then there are the things we cannot change. It isn't always the circumstances that need to be different in order for us to realize our dreams. Sometimes it is our expectations, our interpretations, the meaning we assign to the circumstances that create an unwanted reality. What we think becomes our truth. That is the magic, and once you see that, you can't unsee it.

This wisdom is more powerful than any adjustment of situations, and it helped me overcome the fear of endings. It helped me see that whatever the "this" is in my life, it doesn't have to be as good as it will get if I want something more. I believe this lesson is the main purpose of my life with Asha—so much that I wrote a whole book about it. She approaches her life as if it never occurred to her that anything bad could happen. She interprets the world with hope, and she wants to experience all of life. For more than ten years, I have watched her navigate her surroundings, and finally her messages sunk in.

I now approach all my life through the lens of my feelings. How do I want to feel? I no longer exercise to see a certain number on the scale. I do it because I want to feel healthy and fit, strong and powerful. I'm not writing a book to make millions. I'm doing it because I want the heaviness that comes from keeping it all inside to lift. I want to feel light and free, honest and seen. How I want to feel has become my number one priority, and I am intentional about creating a life to match that.

Four years after the life I had built disappeared, after I was paralyzed with fear, I realize that everything I asked for has shown up just as I intended or *better*. I have a wonderful man in my life, and with him I feel joy and love. I have a job that allows me to feel flexibility and purpose. I feel safe and free in my financial situation. I am a creator and feel growth and accomplishment. My world has transformed from dark and empty to full of light.

Every day I continue to formulate the life I want, I imprint it onto my heart, I take action toward it, I feel as if it already exists. I express gratitude for what I currently have and for all the goodness that I *know* is coming. Because I believe that what I want will be mine, I can afford to be patient. That patience calms any fear.

When you know that you will get what you want, or something

even better, there is no longer any reason to be afraid. The first step is to allow yourself permission to acknowledge that you don't want the "this" in your life, the thing that is "good enough." Only then can you alert the Universe that you are ready for the more you are promised simply by being alive on this planet. Determine how you want to feel, believe in it, and experience life through that lens. Take steps every day to move your story forward. The life of your dreams is there for the taking. So it has been with me, and so, I know, it will be with you too.

ABOUT TRACY RICHARDS

Tracy Richards is an author, speaker, Reiki Master, and energy teacher. She has certifications in Animal Reiki, the Akashic Records, and Positive Psychology. Tracy offers classes in vibration, personal frequency, and Reiki attunements in addition to her life-changing workshops. Her book, *Asha: Lessons in Hope and Life,* is scheduled for publication in September 2022.

Tracy helps clients grant themselves permission to acknowledge the "this" in their life, the realities that are not what they want for themselves, and she guides them through the process of formulating how they want to feel in the life of their dreams. Through workshops and individual sessions, she provides a framework that allows clients to become intentional about the life they want and take action to begin living it. She has a unique way of making others feel seen and empowered. Let her help you step into your own light and love.

To learn more about how you can work with Tracy, schedule a speaking engagement or podcast appearance, and to order her book, visit her website www.tracyrichards.co or email her at tracy@ tracyrichards.co.

Facebook: Tracy Richards
Instagram: @tracyrb226
Author Instagram: @tracyrichards_author
Email: Tracy@tracyrichards.co
Web: www.tracyrichards.co

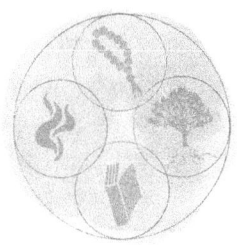

TAKE YOUR CENTER STAGE

Cori Solomon Santone

was seven years old and sang "It's a Small World" a cappella to a packed auditorium of my Catholic school. They had themed the entire finale around my performance, which ended with me standing center stage singing the final chorus surrounded by the other forty children in the talent show. The roar of the standing ovation will go down in Catholic school history.

Little did I know at the time, it set the stage for my life.

Since I can remember, my incredible parents have been gifting me with these mantras: "You'll never know unless you try," "You can do anything you put your mind to," "We will love you no matter what." Parents around the world create these safety nets for their kids, but so many people let fears and self-created barriers stop them from doing what they really want to do. Some people stay close to home, comfortable, living out mundane lives, avoiding challenges or heartache.

Believing that I was invincible, I have been jumping out of my comfort zone my entire life. I've moved nineteen times, changed careers four times, and experienced four great love stories. I've been on countless stages now, quite literally and figuratively, and my belief in taking center stage translated into years of performing arts and taking the lead as a CEO, principal, camp director, fundraiser, consultant, and most importantly, a mom. The inherent problem with putting yourself out there is that it typically comes with a giant spotlight, which invites challenges. New barriers arise and lots of mistakes are made. People judge and criticize, and often, the journey is not all sunshine and rainbows. Like the song says, we live in a world of hope, fears, laughter, and tears. My successes have been clouded with many failures and challenges, but I have honed some valuable coping skills from my experiences that helped me to achieve my dreams.

Some of my coping skills were learned early on. My father was in the US Air Force, so we moved a lot. I learned the value of embracing inevitable change and the power of making friends quickly in new places. My confidence as a young person was unshakable, but like most children, that changed in middle school. In fifth grade, I stopped growing. Not metaphorically, but rather quite literally. Once their equal, I was suddenly different and thus an easy target for the insecure bullies. Short jokes are surprisingly revered as socially acceptable still decades later. After hearing hundreds of these jokes, and enduring three brutally awkward years, I had the opportunity to create a new scene for high school.

With a new setting comes opportunities for new characters and new plot lines. I researched and joined every club possible, sought out new friends, and rediscovered the drama club. On stage, real life didn't exist, and I honed my skills of compartmentalizing and breaking apart people's perspectives. By junior year, I was on top of the world. I was Dorothy in our *Wizard of Oz* production, played varsity soccer, made the varsity cheerleading squad, and fell in love with a star football player. I felt unstoppable, but when you are living life to its fullest, challenges are bound to arise. In the summer leading up to my senior year, my parents separated. It was at a time before people even talked about divorce and certainly before any of my friends' parents were divorced. My parents were each devastated and going through their own individual turmoil and rebirthing after their eighteen years of marriage. Then, I tore my ACL while in gymnastics practice right before our opening football game. The doctor said there would be a surgery—but no cheer or soccer my senior year. While regaining my strength, I realized I needed to change my setting—create a new scene with room to grow. I revamped my college plans and chose a school three hours away that had an incredible study abroad term built into their curriculum. I finished that senior year as third in my class and with bright plans. I was gifted with the superlative Most Talented. Perhaps it was an odd popularity contest, but to me, it was just the right amount of validation that I had turned things around from my middle school self.

I was going to make the most of the opportunities I had in college. Knowing that a key to being successful is having a strong support network, I sought out friends and joined a sorority. I was flung into a world of diversity, new views, and perspectives that my small, conservative hometown just didn't have. I also joined every club I could including the theater and singing organizations. I realized quickly that though I did love performing, the students set on Broadway careers weren't my people. I gravitated toward the teachers. I quickly committed to a career in education with lots of performing and fine arts electives.

My first summer home, I was shocked back into the reality of my parents' divorce with their split homes and the never-ending drama of high school. Using a summer jobs book from the library, my best friend and I secured jobs at an overnight summer camp in Maine. For the next three summers, I was a Theater Director and then Arts Department Director. I loved camp and camp people. My limited acting talents were able to shine on a rustic stage in the middle of the woods. I saw a world where children were able to be whole—embraced for their individual qualities and thrust into safe opportunities to shine on stage. I met people from around the world, fell in love again, and found my two closest lifelong friends.

I finished college summa cum laude with a bachelor's in elementary education and mathematics. Now, being from the South, I had some preconceived ideas that I was also supposed to finish with an Mrs. degree (a.k.a. a husband), which at the time, I had no prospects. I was faced with another opportunity to take a big risk. Create a new scene. The obvious choice to move home didn't feel right, but I didn't have much money since I had been student teaching full-time. Being obsessed with Jane Eyre, I researched teach-abroad opportunities and found an agency that would place American teachers at schools in England. My application was accepted, and the agency set up five interviews for late September. Meanwhile, I had spent the summer back at my camp in Maine and fell in love with a windsurfer from England. At the time, I remember feeling confident that I was again creating my position on center stage. Even watching the twin towers come crashing down while I was packing for England wasn't enough to derail me. I flew out the next week with just five people on my international flight.

The first school I interviewed with offered me a job! My first year of teaching was in a small village town with one church, two pubs, and our little school. I taught twenty-seven little English children ages eight to eleven. I was responsible for their traditional subjects and music, art, religion, and British sports. There were no textbooks or teacher manuals. The kids had blank notebooks and a lot of questions about America. I walked to school with my students during the day and drank at the pub with their parents at night. I learned how to drive a stick shift on the opposite side of the hilliest roads I've ever seen and how to corral wandering sheep from the playground at recess. At the end of the year, the school needed a five-year commitment from me to invest the cost of my permanent visa, and I knew in my heart it wasn't the right choice for me. I hadn't found my people and couldn't see a future where I would thrive. Though it would mean starting over again with so many unknowns ahead, I declined their offer.

I moved back home with my fiancé and found myself an elementary school teaching position. The morale at the school was low, but I found an incredible group of teacher friends, and together, we believed in our power to change things. I always seek out my people. There is no greater bond than those formed by teachers together in the trenches. I also remembered the power the arts had on my learning, so I dove into arts integration and project-based learning. Within just a few years, I was married, leading our district's test scores, and proving to a lot of doubters that through the arts, students could achieve more. For a while, things were okay, but I wasn't finding joy in my life, and I felt a constant pull to make more of an impact in the world. At home, my husband was also feeling lost, so we agreed we needed to make a big change.

Having loved summer camp, I researched and found an arts camp that was based a few states away. We sold our house in just three days at the height of the pre-recession days and made a great profit. Seemed like we were making the right choice. The camp was owned by a couple with two young children, who I thought we would be partnering with for a grand new future. Just a couple of weeks into camp though, I found myself in the middle of a nightmare and realized I had made a terrible mistake. The husband was abusing his wife and children. Our camp nurse taught me self-defense at night in our cabins in case he came after me, and I spent my days running their camp while helping the wife build up the courage to get out of her abusive relationship. Six weeks later, we orchestrated her escape, with great relief and of course police support. I was thinking I must have been meant to come here to help this brave woman. I thought, *This is my path after all*, but the very next day, my husband called me, and before I could share the good news, he said, "I've decided to move back to England. Alone."

Three weeks later, he was gone. I was living back at home and felt like a complete failure. My best friend invited me to Maine so I could get some fresh perspective. I knew I needed to do some research and to reorganize the characters and setting of my world once again to be true to myself and my purpose in the world. I had a dream to work with children in a meaningful way that was authentic to my beliefs. Though I tried and had failed, I wasn't willing to give up.

I did more research and found another arts camp. This time, I researched the camp's history thoroughly, and after my interview, I knew I had found a place I could shine. So, I perhaps did what no other person has done before, and I moved from South Carolina to New Jersey. Alone in this new state, before GPS systems understood Jersey's no left turns/jug handle initiative, I spent a lot of time lost—but only physically, because professionally I had found my place. This camp was eight glorious weeks of children being free to be themselves, having long conversations about their future lives under the stars at night and belting out Broadway tunes on our stage through the day. I trained our staff to work with our campers through an approach I had honed in my many years in the classroom. Rooted in the belief that all children are good, the goal was to form meaningful relationships, establish consistent routines, and use collaborative problem-solving to create equitable and emotionally safe environments for kids to thrive. I spent seven years as a summer camp director, working alongside incredible people, which brought me great joy, not to mention countless plot lines for a TV movie.

One night with a bottle of wine and too many Girl Scout Cookies to count, I created an online dating profile. Online dating is a racket that I embarked upon with a very dear friend, and gratefully, we were both spared by the dating gods from too much suffering by letting both of our first dates be magical men. Picture southern arts ed girl meets Philly music teacher. Tom brought with him two precious little girls (ages three and six), and

I very quickly fell in love with all three of them. He had shared custody of the girls, so we spent half our lives creating the plot of a whirlwind romance novel and the other half making Hallmark-worthy family memories. Of course, there were challenges as I learned about all the ups and downs of being a stepmom, but my relationship with the girls was beautiful, authentic, and full of shared adoration. Tom was my person, and my life's troubled love story had found its magical ending.

Professionally, I was also feeling fulfilled, but the CEO position of my organization opened unexpectantly, and with some encouragement from a generous mentor, I put myself out there. I believed that I could help our nonprofit do more to support children and families. So, I went back to school to get my nonprofit management and financial management certificates, and I was chosen from a national search to be the next CEO.

Little did I know the organization was in dire financial trouble. I had to lay off six people right away, one of whom was a dear friend. Stressful day after stressful day, I worked with a small but talented team to find resources and reinvent the organization. I worked eighty-hour weeks while balancing sleepless nights, crushing pressure, and great unknowns as a young CEO. I made the best decisions I could for the sake of my team and the families we served, but my life was consumed by work.

And then, without sounding cliché, a magical thing happened. None of it felt important anymore; I was pregnant and my perspective shifted. My greatest gift came in mid-September followed by twelve weeks of working from home and processing my new teaching role as a mom. I found myself in an odd position of feeling informed as a mom from having worked with so many children for so many years, including my own stepdaughters, but I also realized what people mean when they say, "You don't really understand until you have your own kids." I was irrationally worrying about everything and wondering how I would teach her those valuable lessons that my parents taught me. How could I teach all three of my girls to take their own center stage roles?

The return to work was filled with the challenges so many moms know: pumping in weird places, exhaustion you can feel in every fiber of your body, and the constant anxiety of making sure your precious little ones are okay while you are away. But, once I got in the swing of things, I had a renewed sense of purpose in my CEO role. I was an advocate for children, education, and the arts, and I knew I had a responsibility to affect real positive impact for the sake of my three girls and children across the region. I didn't know the opportunity would happen so soon, but as I researched our strategic plans, everything started to crystallize.

The organization's campus had thirty-three buildings that sat empty throughout the school year. Opening a school was not only a possibility, it could be the pillar to stabilize the organization. I started to say it out loud: We should start a school. A dream school. A school that integrates the arts with emotional intelligence and true student-centered decision-making. There were many fans, but there were also people who thought it was a terrible idea. We weren't in a good position to take big risks, but I knew in my heart that this was the right thing to do. Over time, I found a group of smart and talented people who shared my vision, and we banded together.

Three years later, we opened the first STEAM curriculum-focused public charter school of the state in an area with few other options for middle school children. My dream had come true. The school opened with great momentum and a waiting list of over one hundred children. The first year brought a lot of challenges, including ending the year with the COVID-19 shutdown, but I'll never forget those ninety-six children in our first classes and the team who worked tirelessly to create a school like no other.

Over the years, I've had the opportunity to connect with so many different leaders, parents, and children. And I've found that the song is correct: it is a small world after all. We share the same fears, hopes, and tears. Generationally, we're all worrying about our children overcoming the barriers we've faced and learning the skills we've used to find our successes. People and organizations are figuring out their strengths to create lives that are fulfilling and impactful.

I used to think my gift was my unshakable belief to create any reality I want. I can dream it and make it come true. I can separate my feelings, self-created "truths" and fears from my circumstances to see ways of overcoming barriers of all kinds.

I've realized over the past year that my true gift is helping others approach their life with this same belief. I've found a way of filling in a gap when people and organizations can't seem to create their desired "new scene." I help them identify and then remove barriers that are preventing them from having the outcomes they want. In helping others, I've finally found my center stage role!

So, to all the women and daughters reading this, remember, you also have a safety net. Find the people who believe in you when you have doubts in yourself, and step into the spotlight as the leading role of your life. Use your gifts to overcome the barriers that life will throw at you and the barriers you've created in your own head. I promise you, the standing ovation at the end of the show will be worth it.

ABOUT CORI SOLOMON SANTONE

Cori Solomon Santone is a dreamer with unshakable optimism and passion for living life to its fullest. She is the founder of Center Stage Solutions, a consulting/coaching firm dedicated to supporting executives, women, and youth to overcome barriers that stand in the way of achieving the life, results, and relationships they truly want. She uses her unique skill set, intuition, and humor to guide others through a collaborative problem-solving process that has allowed thousands to achieve success and take center stage.

Her expertise comes from twenty-three years of successful leadership roles in the nonprofit, education, business, and arts sectors where she's served as a regional nonprofit arts ed organization CEO/CFO, charter school founder, residential camp director, sales director, certified teacher, and school administrator. Cori has raised millions of dollars, launched dozens of programs, and changed the lives of thousands of people. Her involvement in the performing and fine arts, and influential teachers and mentors have played an important role in her life.

Cori's heart belongs to her three talented daughters, Cecilia, Abigail, and Isabella, and superhero husband, Tom. She is most grateful to her parents and three brothers for their lifelong support. When she's not giggling with her girls, she loves sharing her southern hospitality through great parties with friends, cooking, and all things creative.

To learn more about Cori's programs or to work with Cori, visit her website at: www.CenterStageSolutions.com or email her at CoriSolomonSantone@gmail.com.

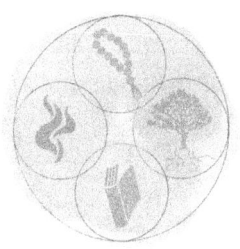

TRANSFORMATIONAL: LOVE, LETTERS, POETRY, AND ART

Ericha Scott, PhD
LPCC917, LAADC, REAT, ATR-BC

People have more grief over unexpressed love than profound trauma.
Tell people you love them!

Meditating on the topic of love through the practice of letter writing, poetry, and art has been the most rewarding and fulfilling discipline of my entire life. Not only have I experienced happier, healthier, and more loving relationships, I have changed. I am more whole and content with myself.

Writing and receiving love letters awakens our consciousness about how much we love and the capacity we have for loving more deeply and selflessly. This is true, even when writing a love letter touches a deep well of sadness inside us and tears flow. One of the gifts of this step-by-step process is that it brings up and releases grief in a very gentle and tender manner. This release helps take down invisible psychological walls, brick by brick.

Psychological issues, such as trauma, abuse, loss, grief, addiction, mental illness, dysfunctional or unconscious attachment styles, and difficulty sustaining long-term relationships in today's world, all negatively impact our ability to feel and express love fully. Therefore, it is no surprise that unexpressed love has become rampant in contemporary society.

We are busy, if not overwhelmed, with work, family chores, a pandemic, climate change, financial upheaval, and social unrest. In our modern world, we reach for a manufactured greeting card when we want to express love to a cherished person. It is an easy solution, especially since the message provided is typically generic and emotionally nonthreatening.

As a result of minimized love, people suffer with a remarkable amount of unexpressed grief. Unexpressed grief fuels indifference, numbing, and emotional distance from the very people closest to us. In an epoch of "social distancing," people need close, loving emotional connections more than ever.

Researcher James W. Pennybaker, an expert in the lie detector test, "found that keeping secrets makes people sick." He also found that writing about secrets, even for only fifteen minutes, can improve physical and mental health.

It seems ironic, but love can be a secret that you do not know you are keeping.

In other words, just as we might have denial about feelings of jealousy or hate, we may also have denial about feelings of love. Receiving and giving love are essential for well-being, and love can feel very vulnerable.

Martin Luther King Jr. said, "I have a dream!" My dream is to help people all over the world create more compassionate, generous, and harmonious intimate relationships through writing and painting about our love for each other.

During the love letter writing retreats, there is an aura, energy, or a subtle light that fills the room while people are painting and writing. Usually, everyone can feel it.

Here Is Feedback from a Few Past Participants

"My husband began to weep before I finished reading the first paragraph, in twenty-five years of marriage, I had never written him a love letter."

"My son said, 'Dad, I didn't know you were that deep.' My son has a point, I never knew I could write like this."

"I have told my wife how much I loved her over and over, and it never seemed to stick, but this letter was different. It touched her heart, and she remembered my words."

"My daughter cried when I read my love letter to her. I have been so fearful, critical, and controlling that she did not believe that I loved her. The letter was the beginning of a change in our relationship."

"I had no idea how much poetry and art could heal my relationships."

Who I Am and Why I Developed a Workshop about Love

Throughout my life-span, challenges and transformational mystical experiences—coupled with decades of professional training and teaching experience—have inspired me to find ways to help people remove, or at least bypass, their creative blocks. What intrigues me is that as the creative blocks are removed, it appears as if hidden blocks to our capacity for loving and receiving love are also removed.

This is my greatest joy: helping people express their deepest thoughts, feelings, and perceptions of life, love, and longing with words and paint.

I am Dr. Ericha Scott. Like many of you, my background is diverse. I am an artist, published author and poet, keynote speaker, retreat and workshop leader, and consultant.

But for this love letter writing process and the creative and spiritual retreats I provide to the public, the most potent offering I have is my life experience.

My personal experience that has shaped what I have to offer you is how I overcame significant early childhood challenges with reading and writing via creativity, poetry writing, and art.

Fourth Grade

I remember sitting in class and looking out the window. I had already failed fourth grade once, and I was just about to fail it twice when I overheard my teacher whisper to my mother, "You know, she really likes art, why don't you find her an art teacher?"

I can remember thinking, *That is a* very *good idea!* This was during the early 1960s, and my mother found a long-haired hippie, who wore jeans, flip flops, and one gold earring to teach me how to paint.

Entering the world of art, color, shape, line, and texture in fourth grade enlivened my life. By the end of fifth grade, after a year of art lessons, I was reading at a college level of competency.

With art as my healer, my life changed from a pattern of chronic failure to outstanding success within a very short period.

A few years later, I began writing poetry. Without telling me, my English teacher entered my first poem in a school-wide contest, and I won.

These events significantly changed the trajectory of my life, and they became directional signposts for my future. Even though I was still a child, I knew that I wanted to help other people experience the same kind of success, relief, freedom, and joy I found through painting, reading, and writing.

As I said earlier, I am a trauma expert, and to my surprise, people in the love letter retreats cry as much, or even more sometimes, than in past trauma and abuse workshops.

Yet, at the end of each retreat, people express relief and they appear to feel giddy with joy.

After giving it some thought, I realized people have as much or more grief about unexpressed love than they do about profound trauma. Almost every single person in the retreats has been moved by the beauty of the letters they and other participants have written. One person even placed the love letter he wrote to his wife in the family vault for future generations to read.

Especially with a world in such upheaval, this is a good time to think about those we love, what we have not said out loud, and what we would like to say.

I hope you will reflect upon the people you have loved throughout your lifetime and select a person who is—or has been—meaningful to you. It could be yourself. It may be a long-time love, someone who remains important to you today. It may be someone who went a different direction in life and you are no longer in touch, and it could be someone who has passed away.

I would like to share another personal experience that is the primary influence for why I have developed this specific retreat. I was inspired by my deceased husband.

In my late forties, I married Bruce Randall Tufts, a NASA scientist, the night before his admission to a hospital for a transplant. Although he was fifty-one years old, he had never been married, and although he was very ill, his joy about our wedding was contagious. Two hundred and forty people showed up to our wedding during a thunderstorm in the desert with very little advance notice.

During our marriage, Randy wrote me a love letter and several cards with handwritten notes. These messages of love and validation sustained and strengthened me over a long period of time, through his leukemia, bone marrow transplant, death, and my grief.

I remain very grateful that this outstanding man outlived his life expectancy prognosis by a year, for the time we were able to be together.

Excerpts From His Love Letter And A Love Note (2001)

In my shaky but loving hand, I must write that I am so profoundly happy that we are married.

You are a wonderful person and wonderful wife. I hope I can approach being as good a person and husband.

So here we are, a year from our loveliest of weddings—what a year of deepening love!

I look forward to continuing strengthening our marriage to each other.

I married you because you are a lovely, intelligent person with a great sensitivity and warmth, and a gleeful inner spark. I love that spark and want to be near it.

I love your ability to come up with good and intriguing ideas and then put them into action. You are one of the smartest and most creative people I know, you truly are unique in this way. You think deeply into an idea and go to the most basic and influential level you can find . . . it is a remarkable quality.

I love your smile, the shape of your head, the curve of your arms, the smooth youthful skin on your face, your graceful bearing and eloquence. Your look can be stunningly beautiful, with your profile like a Greek goddess.

I love your silver hair, and I am glad you did not color it.

I love the light you can bring to a room when you enter.

I love your intuition, your sensitivity to other's needs and thoughts. I love and I am moved by the way others talk openly with you. I love the way you can see many things so clearly yet admit ambiguity.

I love your honesty, your directness, and your diplomacy. (I count on you to talk with troubled friends of ours—you are so much better at that than I.)

I love your creative self, making art so quickly and confidently and beautifully.

I love the you that I see in your baby pictures, so innocent and trusting. I admire the inner work you have done, and respect you greatly for it.

I love your integrity, honesty, and ability to see.

Marrying you is the best thing I have done. I would not miss this for the world.

Love, Randy

Randy became a better husband after writing this letter. It is as if the letter revealed to him how deeply he loved me. I became a better wife because I was able to relax and trust his love.

I hope my story, and Randy's letter, is an invitation for you to join me on a loving and healing journey to deepen the quality of love in any or all your relationships.

Although sometimes it is uncomfortable to speak about, no one escapes illness and death. What if you died, or what if your loved one died suddenly, or what if you have experienced the loss of a loved one already. Do you, or would you, feel confident that you had fully expressed the depth of your love?

You might be surprised by the emotions that emerge while writing a love letter. You might be even more surprised by the emotions your letter will evoke in your recipient or other readers. These emotions are healthy and cathartic. Sometimes people grieve when reading about how much they are loved and why.

I know this sounds confusing. Yet, it is possible for love letters to remind us of periods of time in our lives when we were not loved or truly seen for who we are. It is important to accept love given to us today, regardless of past pain. The old grief will pass as we open our hearts to give and receive love.

To teach you how to write a love letter, I will illustrate a few steps with examples from my personal process of preparing to write a love letter to my husband. You will see that the process is individualized and can be modified to suit your needs.

To help ensure that you are satisfied with the quality of your first letter, please follow my directions below as literally and carefully as possible.

Brief Descriptive Overview of a Few Action Steps

Step 1

Heart-Centered Meditation (Heart Grounding via Somatic/ Sensory Awareness): Please take five to ten minutes to meditate before you start. Allow yourself to notice and feel your heart, and your love, without any judgment. It is very important to feel your heart and your love without trying to ascribe meaning, interpretation, or analysis. There is no wrong way to do this—just notice the sensations of your heart and feelings of love.

Whatever you feel is fine—whether it is warmth, coldness, tingles, pulsing, lightness, heaviness, colors, shapes, symbols, or something else.

Please do not continue this meditation for more than ten to fifteen minutes.

Step 2

Carefully Select Your Letter Recipient (Self, Spouse, Lover, Friend, Parent, Sibling, Child, Mentor): The second step for this process is to select a love letter recipient. It is important to thoughtfully select your recipient, and often, it is the first person who comes to mind. This is true even if that idea is a surprise or it does not make sense to you. The wisdom of the subconscious is not always clear at first.

Feel free to select yourself, or yourself at a younger age. Also, it is okay, in fact it is normal, to have conflicts about the person you select to write to. Please remember, you may write more than one love letter, in fact, I hope you will write many love letters.

Step 3

Make a List of Positive Traits (Positive Traits, Talents, and Strengths): I invite you to write a list of positive traits, talents, or strengths about the person you have selected. Please try to write a minimum of twenty-five to fifty qualities, characteristics, or attributes that you like about the person you are writing. Be sure to be very descriptive and use adjectives and adverbs. These details help your recipient know that the sentiments in the letter are genuine and meant just for them and no one else.

As you write, do so as quickly as you can. Write down everything that crosses your mind, and—for now—do not edit. Following these guidelines will help you bypass the voice of your inner critic and other blocks.

Step 4

Write Out a Shared Vivid Experience with Letter Recipient (When You Felt Loved and/or Loving): I invite you to write via a stream of consciousness or free-association process about one vivid event you shared with your letter recipient. You may select the first event that crosses your mind, or if you think of a more vivid and meaningful event later, go with the more vivid and meaningful.

It helps if you imagine that you are a court reporter and your job is to describe the scene of your event in every detail. Include information about who, what, when, and where, as well as your emotions and loving thoughts. Again, write quickly without editing your thoughts.

Do not use this love letter to slip in a criticism, no matter how well deserved, or even a hint about what behavior(s) you want your loved one to change. That is another type of letter for another time.

Step 5

Haiku Poems: I invite you to write a haiku poem about the event you just described. Haiku poetry is not about rhyming but instead cadence, and so the words and syllables are counted. Haiku poetry is about an actual event, and there is always a reference to nature. The nature referenced might have been true to your experience and therefore literal or it might be symbolic, such as springtime as a representation of new love. But be specific and descriptive instead of just the word "springtime," consider writing, for example, "new buds on the pear tree."

Haiku poems are three short lines. The first line is five syllables long, the second line is seven syllables, and the third line is only five syllables again, and you may change the number of syllables to meet your needs.

It is important to remember that this exercise is about process, and not good poetry or art. When attending a retreat, participants may choose to share their work with the smaller and larger group(s), or not. You may include the poem in your letter or writing a poem may be a warm-up to writing the letter. Notice that this long poem is actually five Haiku, as if the Haiku are stanzas.

LABOR OF DEATH

09/27/2002
The labor of death
brings forth cries of pain and loss,
and winter comes to
the highest point of
the hill. The pinnacle of
his life, hopes, and dreams.
His ash scattered in
the wind, dances before coming
to rest on the sand.
Finally, love lets
go into death, crossing through
a threshold of desire.
Flame turns to ember,
no longer a hot fire
blazing in the desert.

Step 6

Scribble and Doodle Art: I invite you to make a scribble or doodle drawing (which is exactly what it sounds like). You may use any form of crayons, oil pastels, ink pens, colored pencils, watercolors, or acrylic paint. If you have no art supplies, consider making a magazine photo collage, a sculpture with found objects and super glue, or if you are adventuresome, a blind contour portrait (please see my web page for the directions for portraits, https://www.thesoberworld.com/2019/10/31/self-portraiture/).

What is most important is for you to think about your letter recipient, your love for them, and your positive relationship dynamics while you scribble, draw, collage, or sculpt. There is no need to make anything look like an object. Abstracts are great!

If you have anxiety because of a negative or shameful experience in an art class as a child, use your non-dominant hand. This can liberate you from expectations. Allow yourself to be playful.

The playfulness of a scribble drawing is able to help you relax and focus. If you use both hands, at the same time, it will help engage both sides of your brain for optimal engagement and functioning.

You may or may not include the art pieces or a photo of your art piece with your letter or handmade card.

My painting is not included in this publication, yet the soft rainbow colors, hints of gray rainy days, undulating dancelike forms represent the beauty of our relationship and the tragedy of his illness.

I hope you will make your piece at least 16 × 20 in., but feel free to go small.

Step 7

Share Your Letter and Your Art with a Mentor or Friend: If you are not a participant in one of my retreats, then I invite you to share your letter with one safe person before you read it out loud to your loved one. This is one way to be sure that old resentments or judgments do not inadvertently stain the loving energy of your letter.

Step 8

Read Your Letter Out Loud: I highly recommend reading your letter out loud, face to face, in a private and quiet place, to the person you love. It is important for the recipient to hear the letter in *your* voice and observe *your* facial expressions. It is also important for you to witness how your words are received.

Prior to reading your letter out loud, please read your letter to a mentor or a wise friend first, then write out your letter in long-hand on good-quality paper. After you have read the letter to your recipient, please give them a handwritten copy to keep.

If you are not able to meet with the person face to face, you may store the letter in a place where you pray or keep your spiritual books. If not there, then possibly in a keepsake box, or another meaningful location until you are able to meet in person or on Zoom.

Summary

For people living and working in our busy modern world, it can seem trivial or even silly to write a love letter. I can imagine how some people might roll their eyes and think, "That is so old fashioned . . . I don't have time, and what is the point?" I understand. I must admit, I underestimated the potential and power of love letters myself. Imagine, a simple love letter can change your life and the quality of your relationships.

Many people have carefully and successfully followed my directions in order to write beautiful letters. That said, it is much, much more powerful to participate in a love letter, poetry, and art-making group.

Therefore, please call me. If you want to take your ability to express love to a deeper level, I am here to help. If you have any questions, call me at 310-880-9761! I have been creating, designing, consulting, and facilitating creative and expressive arts retreats for over thirty-eight years. I work with individuals, couples, families, groups, and businesses of up to eighty people. When you call, we will brainstorm and create exactly what will best meet your needs, and/or the needs of your family, group, or agency.

ABOUT ERICHA SCOTT, PHD
LPCC917, LAADC, REAT, ATR-BC

Dr. Ericha Scott is an artist, poet, and a published author. She is published in professional peer review journals, textbooks, and popular magazine articles nationally and abroad. Dr. Scott is a Licensed Professional Clinical Counselor (LPCC917) in California and a Licensed Professional Counselor (LPC) in Arizona. She is a licensed psychotherapist and addictions counselor. She is certified as a creative and expressive arts therapist, an advanced diplomat addiction counselor, a Reiki Master, and as an interfaith spiritual director. Dr. Scott has been awarded the honorary title of fellow for the oldest professional trauma agency in the world, The International Society for the Study of Trauma and Dissociation. She has also received the Sierra Tucson Alumni Recognition Award for outstanding service to patients in the sexual compulsivity and trauma program. She offered psycho-educational creative and expressive arts retreats for the medical doctors in Andrew Weil, MD's Center of Complimentary Medicine at the University of Arizona for eight years. Dr. Scott designs original and custom educational, psychological, and spiritual creative and expressive arts retreats and workshops. She provides retreats for personal growth or therapy on topics such as love, wellness and physical health, trauma, spirituality, creativity, emotional blocks, compulsivity, addictions, self-harm, family systems, mindfulness, life goals, sleeping dreams and nightmares.

Please view her web site at http://artspeaksoutloud. org or call at 310-880-9761.

- artspeaksoutloud.org
- linkedin.com/in/ehitchcockscott
- facebook.com/ErichaScottPhD

- facebook.com/erichascott
- twitter.com/ErichaScott
- youtube.com/c/ErichaScottPhD

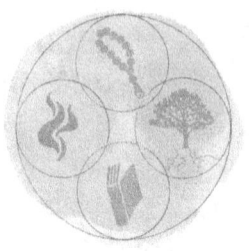

THE PHOTO ALBUM

Abby Steurer

Losing a parent is never easy, but losing a parent at an early age can take on a whole new meaning. When you are little, you may not even realize what happened. You may feel sad, and you may miss that person, but as time passes, you forget what that person looks like, what they smell like, what their personality was like. At least, this is what happened to me. What I did not realize was how the loss of my father would impact my life for many years to come.

When I was just five years old, my father came down with pneumonia and unexpectedly passed away days later due to complications. In just days, my mother's world was flipped upside down and she became a widow with two children. As a mother myself, I cannot imagine what this must have been like for her. I can vividly remember being at a family friend's house, which was across the street from my grandmother's. My friend walked me back to the house, and as the front door opened, I saw my entire family sitting in my grandmother's living room. My grandmother let out a cry, and I believe that is when my mom took my hand, led me into my grandmother's bedroom, and told me that my dad had passed away. We went back into the living room where I crawled onto my grandmother's lap. I was so young, but I remember thinking that I had to be strong because everyone was just so sad.

The next memory I have is of my mom, my little brother, and myself sitting on our couch. I was crying, but not about my dad. Maybe I had gotten in trouble? I cannot recall the exact reason, but I do remember looking at my mom and saying, "I miss Daddy!" She cried so hard when I said that and told me she did too. I apologized, and again, I can remember thinking that I could never say those words ever again because it just made her so sad. From that day on, at just five years old, I felt like I could not talk about my father because it was just too painful for everyone else. I guess I wanted to protect her. I definitely did not want to make my mom feel worse or make her struggle more than she already was. I have never liked making others feel angry or sad in any way. So, I rarely brought him up and neither did anyone else.

It is inevitable that death needs to be spoken about, and every family deals with it differently. We created a photo album of all the pictures we had of my dad and me. All five years of memories condensed into one tiny, handheld photo album. Everything I would remember of my father, for the rest of my life, would be from those few pictures. I slept with this album under my pillow for almost my entire life. This album became my lifeline.

My mom remarried when I was seven, and my two beautiful sisters were born. I do not want to go into much detail about my mother's second marriage since it is not my story to tell, but I can tell you what I learned from this situation and what their eventual separation did to impact my life. My mom was a schoolteacher, and when she was not working, we were always with her. She rarely went out. If she did, it must have been quick because I just remember always being with my mom. All of us. Whether it was the grocery store or the movies or anything in between, she had us all with her.

There was a lot of arguing and fighting within our walls for many years. Most of my childhood. So many nights, I held that photo album of my dad and would dream up stories of what life would be like if only he survived. I became more and more sad about the loss of my father as I became a teenager. I truly do not think I mourned his loss until then. At sixteen, my mom and stepfather separated in what would turn into an extremely messy divorce, and again, I watched my mother struggle. This time with four children. I was sixteen, my brother was twelve, my sister was four, and my baby sister was just an infant. The early days of this divorce were very hard on her. She cried a lot. She worried about shared custody and how she would financially support us, as any mother would. She was very sad and felt like she had failed us.

We left our family home, stayed with my aunt who generously opened her doors for us, and then we moved in with my grandmother. Eventually, my mom was able to purchase the townhouse she is still in today. We moved into our new home with our bedroom furniture, clothing, and lawn chairs for our living room. I can still feel that happiness and excitement, but my mom felt differently. She was nervous, stressed, and sad. I hated watching her go through that. It would take a long time for our mother to regain control of her finances. By the time she was a little more stable, I had graduated from college and was on my way to marrying my husband. I knew that I never wanted to experience even half of what she went through as I started my own family.

My husband and I were married in the fall of 2004. We had our first child, Mackenzie, in 2006 and our son, Nolan, was born in 2008. Before we even became parents, we talked about how much I wanted to be able to raise them. To be home with them as much as I could. I did not want to miss out on any of the special moments. I wanted to be there when they took their first steps. I wanted to be the one to drive them to preschool and to get them on and off their bus, every single day. I wanted to be at the class parties and do all the mom things. But I also wanted to help provide for my family. I never wanted to be in my mom's shoes if something happened that would make me the sole provider. I already knew that no matter how perfect life looked on the outside, many things could happen out of our control that could uproot the life we had. I wanted to be as prepared for that as I could be. I wanted it all . . . being mom, being a provider for my family, and being Abby.

About six to eight months after our daughter was born, I was filled with anxiety. So badly that at one point, I couldn't leave the house. I became agoraphobic. I was afraid of every movement I made. Every thought I had turned into the worst-case scenario in seconds. I could not walk my baby down the steps without envisioning the worst fall in the world. Bathing her was awful. Instead of enjoying the splashes and coos, all I could see was her drowning and me being unable to save her. I know. Believe me, I know it sounds so awful, but I could not stop the racing thoughts. I was stricken with the need to protect and do everything so perfectly so no harm would come to my family that it sent me into a downward spiral of anxiety and panic attacks.

I had very few friends that had children at this stage, so finding someone that could relate to me was difficult. My husband and family were very supportive, but there was only so much they could do. It was something I had to work hard on to get better. I dove deep into why I might be feeling that way, and it all just seemed to go back to the losses I suffered as a child. I was petrified that my children would go through what I went through, and knowing it was all out of my control, that I could not predict the future, was a scary realization. I always swore that if I could get better, I would be helpful to anyone else suffering with anxiety.

A few years passed by, and I was slowly regaining control of my thoughts. I had to retrain my brain to think in a positive way. Any time I started going down one of those scary-thoughts roads, I would try to redirect myself. I found that keeping busy was the best way to distract myself. Not that having two kids under two and a half did not keep me busy enough! But I needed something. Something to keep my mind busy. And I remembered that conversation my husband and I had before we had our children. That I wanted to be mom, but also help provide.

As soon as Kenzie was born, I started capturing every detail of her life with my camera. Every facial expression, every tiny finger and toe. I had my camera on hand everywhere we went. It always came back to that photo album of my dad. I felt the need to capture everything, just in case. I did not even realize I was falling in love with the art of photography. I was just making sure my children had memories. The more photos I took, and the more popular social media became, the more others commented on my photos, and eventually, asked me to take photos for them. That is when it hit me! This was it! This would be how I would help provide while I was raising my family. This is what would help keep my mind busy. I spent about a year researching everything I could on the internet. How to start a small business. What to look for in an accountant. What editing software to purchase and how to use it. How to edit. What computer I needed to buy. How to use the big old camera my husband invested in for me to start with. I researched it all! I wanted to be able to capture memories for everyone. I did not want anyone to go through life without gorgeous moments written down on pictures for generations to follow. I did not want anyone to have to remember a loved one from only a handful of pictures. I did not want anyone to have to sleep with a tiny photo album under their pillow and know it is the only thing they have left of their parent. I did not want my own children to feel that way, and I wanted my future grandchildren to see me and remember me at all stages of my life. The good, the bad, the ugly, and everything in between. I wanted to be a memory keeper.

Becoming a photographer gave me a real sense of purpose. I had a passion. I had something to separate myself from being "just Mom" to being a successful business owner. It kept me feeling motivated and happy and gave me a sense of pride. I noticed I was less and less anxious because I was filtering my energy into photography, and I did not have time to sit and think. The anxiety was still there, but it hovered instead of taking over. I felt so proud of myself for being able to stay home with the kids and bring in that additional source of income. It was a goal I had before even becoming a mother, and I made it happen. I have been a photographer now for over ten years. I went from capturing a few memories for others to winning awards on some of those images. But I was not done.

I began sharing more and more on social media in order to grow. I shared my truth as well as my struggles. I was as authentic as I could be in hopes that it may reach just one person that needed to see they were not alone. I realized the more I shared, the more people felt comfortable sharing their stories back with me. The new connections I made led me to my second business, where I truly feel like I am helping people feel better from the inside out.

Talking to someone about personal struggles can be so important. Sometimes, all it takes is one connection, one conversation, one recommendation. To feel heard and to be listened to is everything. As I get older, I realize that the struggles in my life were there for a reason. I do not allow my personal struggles to get the best of me. Instead, I use them to propel me forward. I try every day to ask myself, "Who am I helping today?" and make an effort to do just that. I feel so lucky to have two businesses that work together seamlessly. I like to tell people that I now get to help people smile on the outside with my photography and on the inside with my hemp wellness business. I would love to talk more with you about hemp and how it can help your body.

Who would have known that a little photo album would have played such a significant role in my life and helped me dream so big? Thanks, Mom and Dad.

ABOUT ABBY STEURER

Abby Steurer was born and raised in the Pittsburgh, PA, area and relocated to southern NJ in 2008. She has been married to her husband, Alex, for seventeen years, and they have two children. Their daughter, Mackenzie, is sixteen and their son, Nolan, is fourteen. Abby has been the photographer and owner of Abby Lynn Photography for ten years. She specializes in family, child, and graduating senior portraits. She has been a finalist in the Shoot and Share photo competition and has had multiple images published in *Shutter Scene Magazine*, including a featured cover artist. Her mission is to capture memories for others with her photographs and to be a listening ear for those struggling with those overwhelming moments in life.

Web: www.abbylynnphoto.com
Instagram: @abby_steurer

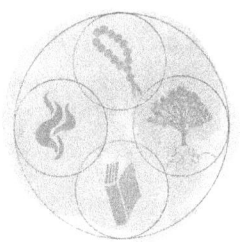

PLANTING THE SEEDS OF PASSION

Teja Valentin

Senior year of high school, we were given an assignment to do about where we saw ourselves in ten years. That was so easy, I didn't even hesitate as I wrote out my wishes on my paper!

Graduate from college as a registered nurse, get married to Mr. Talldarkandhandsome, move into a nice house, have two children—a boy and a girl—and adopt a dog.

Did I get all that? Yes, I did! Life seemed so simple back then. I was pondering this as I sat at my desk unhappy with my life. I had a beautiful home, a handsome husband, a sweet four-month-old boy, and no doubt I would have that little girl too! So what happened?! That painless lump on my neck that I swore was nothing became a cancer diagnosis. It felt so surreal. The doctors told me that this was the "good cancer."

As I started getting over the realization of this news, I began to research thyroid cancer. I learned two astounding facts: thyroid cancer is the most common endocrine cancer and affects women three times more than men! How is this good? What I also learned is that the thyroid is considered to be connected to the throat chakra. I had never even heard of a chakra at that point, and I was immediately intrigued, fascinated. I felt like I was finally putting the pieces together of this incredulous puzzle. What I was reading was starting to make sense to me. Interestingly, the throat chakra is the center of communication. I began recognizing that there was more to me than just my physical body. I was an energetic and spiritual being with a soul. This I believe was a nudge from Spirit. There was a reason this was happening to me. One that I may not have been happy about or understood, but I knew there was a purpose it was showing up.

After six years, multiple neck surgeries to remove my thyroid and affected lymph nodes, and many radioactive iodine treatments, I finally reached a point where the doctors were content to just monitor my thyroid levels and neck ultrasounds. I should have been happy to finally be on the road to better health, except I didn't feel anything. I didn't get angry, sad, or happy. I was flat, numb. Only existing. My husband at the time said it best, "They are basically killing you slowly to make you better." It didn't matter what was happening in my body, my expression to everything was the same. I kept waiting . . . but for what ? I thought, *Okay, when is this going to be over?* It seemed nothing was ever going to change. The light in me seemed to have gone out. Now my only goal was to get my chores done each day, and my reward was to sink into my bed at night and fall into deep sleep.

I felt like such a horrible mom. I never had the energy to play with my children, and my patience was short. My husband was always working twelve-hour shifts or traveling for work and then would be busy on the weekends. I often felt very alone and isolated. My childhood best friend was the only one I could really talk to, and even then, I held back a lot of what was really going on. "I'm fine" was always my automatic response whenever someone asked.

My mother had always told me to shut up. Unable to defend myself or speak my mind, I learned to stay silent. As I grew to an older child though, it was rude not to respond when adults asked me how I was. My mother told me to just say, "I'm fine."

I couldn't really hide the fact that I wasn't fine anymore. In essence, I felt powerless, helpless . . . just so tired all the time. I had been used to my son being easy to entertain with his blocks or videos or just about anything you placed in front of him. He would be so fascinated with the most minute details. My daughter, however, was my "spirited" child. I could not keep up with her curiosity, and her sense of adventure was endless. She did everything with such gusto. Inside, I was so envious of how she was always fully into whatever she was doing. Passionate. Full of life. I knew something in me had to change if I was to be her mother.

One day, I don't even know how to describe it except there was this shift in my energy. I was feeling sick and tired of feeling sick and tired, and I just got up from the couch, put my sneakers on, walked out the front door, and ran to the corner stop sign! I felt excited and invigorated when I did! Next day, I did it again, and again! Soon I was running one mile, five miles, ten miles. I felt alive! I could feel my heart pumping, my stride taking me further and further from my troubles. On my runs, I could completely detach from all my pain. I could dream, plan, and create. I could be me. Cancer could not define this version of me.

I walked into the house one day after I completed a ten-mile race. Riding on the wave of endorphins from finishing one of the hardest and longest runs, I decided I was going to run a marathon! I joined the Leukemia Lymphoma Society Team in Training to train for the marathon and raised four thousand dollars for the 2008 Walt Disney Marathon in Florida. I couldn't run very fast, but I was there in Disney World, "where dreams come true." I made the most of it as I ran through Epcot, Animal Kingdom, Cinderella's Castle. From the moment the horn blared, I never looked back. Somewhere around mile sixteen, I happened to see my coach. He ran over and, probably seeing how exhausted I was, he said, "You will cross that finish line if I have to carry you over it." I looked him in the eye and said, "I will cross over that line on my own two feet!"

I did indeed cross that line. This is one of the first times that I became aware of my grit and perseverance. Despite it all, I managed to cross the finish line on my own two feet. My big toes were black-and-blue, and my four-year-old daughter seemed to keep stepping on them the rest of our vacation. In Reiki lore, there is a myth that when you stub your big toe, you are on your way to an awakening . . .

In 2014, I was introduced to gentle yoga, and it was great but I wanted more. A friend recommended that I go for a Reiki session. The Reiki Master saw my spiritual and psychic potential. He gave me much more than Reiki, he gave me friendship, support, hope, and a newfound sanctuary where I was free to be me. There were people there like me!

I had felt like an outcast in my own home. The big flat-screen had taken over, and conversations ceased. The heaviness in the living room was stifling. Still I said nothing.

As I began Reiki Level two, my third eye began to open. I could suddenly see colors so bright, auras and visions. My dreams became even more vivid, and it felt like I was experiencing an awakening. Upon describing my many dreams, especially those with snakes, he explained what I was experiencing was Kundalini energy. Sure enough, a beginner's Kundalini workshop was being offered at the studio. It felt so foreign and weird. I felt so weak and inadequate. My arms and shoulders hurt and were shaking and seemed to weigh a ton. Though, the amazing thing was that after each class, I felt so awesome and pumped; energy was flowing through my body. I wanted to go dancing after each class! The seventh week, our second-to-last week of the Intro to Kundalini course, I shared with my teacher that I had this amazing dream where I was able to destroy a huge dragon-like serpent that was wrapped around my neck trying to choke me. She was horrified, but I was excited! I had a very good feeling that this was good news coming.

I continued with self-Reiki and Kundalini Yoga on my own every day. The following month after the Intro to Kundalini class was over, I found out that my latest lab work showed the thyroid cancer was undetectable! I felt like my body, spirit, and mind were freed.

Listening to Spirit, I heeded the call to take the Kundalini Yoga teacher training.

I began my training in 2016. Many times I felt like I couldn't keep up, but it was like I had to become undone to put myself back together again. "I'm fine," my mind would echo. I found myself in tears often. This in itself was very healing for someone who always had to hold it in. The support of my teachers and classmates and my "sisters" was unmatched. We were all battling something, mostly ourselves.

During this time, I became my dad's caretaker while he was suffering from Alzheimer's disease. Every time I would go visit him, we would go on our "walk and talks." He always seemed to know what was on my mind. He knew before I did what I was feeling. Four months after Kundalini Yoga teacher training, I had a hysterectomy and I was climbing mountains . . . literally. I had joined a few of my Kundalini sisters in the Women's Hero's Journey. However, there is this thing I have called fear of heights, but these mountains I climb figuratively and physically keep calling me. One day during our walk, my dad said, "You are on a quest." Immediately that resonated. Yes, I was . . . but for what?

The day arrived that I was standing at the base of an almost five-thousand-foot mountain, the highest point in the Allegheny Mountains and Appalachian Plateau. It was very challenging, but I managed to find my next step and pull myself up over and over again. I was staring at the rock in front of me for hours. As we neared the end, we approached the back of the mountain and also the steepest portion, but the top landing was so close. I literally lost all strength in my arms and shoulders by this point, and I could not gather any more. I started to panic that I was going to end up dangling there forever. Luckily, I had two experienced women with me on that back section—one in front of me and one behind me. They each breathed with me and gave me words of encouragement along with instructions. I was there praying to God and everything holy, especially my father who had crossed over by this time as I begged for strength. Once again, life was flashing before my eyes. The women all before me were at the top and had started to sing to me. In complete surrender, I followed the instructions to clip myself and let myself dangle and rest. Finally, I found my footing and gave it my all, and I made my way to the top. It took some time to process all that occurred on that mountain, but I was astonished that the strength in me had been there all along. On that day, I contemplated the untapped power in each woman. We may not have the physical strength or size, of other experienced climbers but the power of their voices, and their compassion and grace carried me through. I had overcome a lot up to this point, but I still was not living my best life. It was as if I was being kept in this castle with comforts of food, clothing, shelter, vacations, and no worries regarding money, but where did my husband go? Whether he was traveling for work or in the same room as me, he was absent. His lack of presence pierced my heart deeper and deeper. I knew it was time to move on, and I knew that I had to do what I had been putting off for many years. I struggled each day feeling unhappy, not enough, and lonely. My marriage had become a façade. My husband and I became strangers sharing a home and children. Sex was nonexistent.

It was devastating to me to think what it would mean to our kids if I asked for a divorce. There was a fear that I would be burdened with all the blame of wrecking our family. My children would hate me. Fear took over and I kept my mouth shut. After a couple more years of working on myself, noticing the patterns, the stories, the beliefs, and programs that I had, I realized it wasn't my fault for being afraid. It was a result of my upbringing and inner child trauma. Staying in this marriage meant that I would be safe. The known was better than the unknown. Finally, an intuitive that I confided in about wanting out of my marriage explained that by staying I would actually be doing a disservice to my children because I would be modeling for them it was okay to stay in a loveless marriage. Well, that hit me like a ton of bricks because that is exactly what my parents did. They finally divorced after thirty-six years of marriage and kept it secret from me for five years! Finally, I got the courage to tell my husband what was on my mind and my heart.

One of the most fascinating things I had learned in my discovery of the chakra system was how closely the female sex organs (pelvic floor and uterus) resemble the throat center (vocal cords and larynx). Hence, it is very likely when you have issues in either one of these energy centers, you most likely are having issues in the other as well. This really spoke to me. Not only was my voice and true expression shut down, but my sexuality and passion had been shut down too. Through the divorce, I finally found my voice. I allowed myself to get angry. I made myself heard. I had to be my own advocate and literally speak up for myself. I moved out of the house, and for the first time in a long time I felt I had a purpose. I already knew what my weaknesses were, and now it was time to lean into my strengths.

During COVID, I joined an online coaching program to become a love, sex, and relationship coach. I began going through the motions but still there was some doubt. What will people think? What do I tell my kids? Who am I to talk to others about sex? Can I actually start a successful business doing what I love? Well, it turns out that people are actually fascinated by what I do. It was a scary risk to give up my nursing job, but I am proud of what I do. Proud that my children accept me regardless of what I do. Turns out I am exactly the right person to be talking about sex because most of my clients are just like me!

While on my way to becoming a coach, I helped heal myself of my own disempowered attitude toward sex, love, self-love, and relationships, which I realized I desperately needed. I wanted to learn how to have sex without pain, to be able to relax and enjoy the intimacy, to just receive pleasure, let myself be heard during sex, and of course feel passion! It wasn't until I was in a relationship after my divorce that it was possible to be intimate without any pain, to feel safe to be seen and heard. Connecting with my sexuality felt like a key to this new untapped potential within me. It was truly a spiritual experience. The passion I felt was not just for love but for life. Though the relationship was brief, this beautiful experience gave me the confidence I needed to make some strides in reclaiming my sexuality and liberating the shame and undeservingness I felt in relationships and in myself. I was feeling good with myself even after the breakup with my on-again-off-again partner because this time I was feeling much more secure in myself and realized I had outgrown that relationship.

Now with more time for myself I couldn't deny some discomfort in my mouth. Chewing was very uncomfortable and even painful on my gums. I was shocked when I found out that the treatment was surgery. After feeling devastated, I went inward and decided that I was not a victim and that this was not happening to me but for me. I knew that this occurrence was another manifestation of an unbalanced throat chakra issue. The process was really tough and it almost felt like a joke—coaching clients with a swollen face and a huge gap between my front teeth! I continued to date, and a few men I went out on dates with were kind, but there were a couple who were cruel. I thank these men now because it forced me to really look at myself in the mirror literally and figuratively. If I could not accept myself 100% then how could I expect anyone else to accept me? It was a constant test of self-love, self-confidence, and deservingness. It took me a while to understand that yes, I had learned to express myself but there was still more.

How am I showing up in my life? Am I able to really express my truth to the world? I knew I was still holding myself back. I continued focusing on my coaching program while recovering and healing from the surgery. My healing started to become a metaphor of what was happening in my life. Through the surgery, expander, and braces, I saw that space had to be created, then supported, and finally aligned.

Working through the lessons and practices in my curriculum, I discovered empowered and disempowered parts of myself that I didn't even know existed. I sent love to my wounded inner child, honored my inner feminine and masculine, celebrated my priestess energy, befriended my witch energy—all the while using the many integration practices to soothe my nervous system. I feel more whole now. I can now say I love myself and really mean it. The work that I do is life fueling. I didn't know this work would be a dream of mine until I actually just started doing it. I realized that this is where I am meant to shine and share my message.

At the time of writing this story, I again had another health scare. My lab work showed that it appeared the cancer was back. The next few months were a blur with the amount of testing I underwent. The happy ending I had planned vanished just like that. There will be more follow-up necessary, but the good news is that what was found does not appear malignant at this point. I will continue to take matters into my own hands and work with a variety of healers—from modern science to ancient wisdom.

Sometimes the shortest way is through. I followed my intuition to go to Costa Rica and embark on a spiritual retreat to receive healing transmission with plant medicine. I went in the first night of ceremony with Ayahuasca with the intention to see who I had become. I saw that I was a little girl who felt unwanted, unloved, and never enough who then became a woman who still felt unwanted, unloved, and never enough. Mama Aya appeared to me as a beautiful white Flower of Life pattern. In Mama Aya's loving embrace, I could feel her love fill me, and I began to channel light language . . . until I was told I was too loud by one of the ceremony helpers. The visual ended abruptly and I was upset. I took my blanket and went outside to the hammock under the almost full moon.

I began trying to understand what just happened. I realized I had never been accused of being too loud, but I have always been shut down by people in my life. Interesting! Wrapped up in the blanket, I made myself comfortable and lay in a fetal position. I then started to feel her again, but this time she was the moon and I was in her womb! I felt so cherished, desired, loved, and wanted.

On the second night of plant medicine, my intention was to merge me back to my soul at all costs. It quickly became very scary. It appeared I was having an ego death. I had no choice but to surrender. Mama Aya once again held me as I died over and over and over again. I would see her moonlight streaming in through the window. I would keep adjusting my body to align with her light. She merged me back with my soul. With each death, there was that first breath of life until finally morning came and then I was alive again, filled with such a love for everybody and everything including myself. There was a song in my heart and I began to sing. It did not matter how I sounded because I know this was what she was showing me was necessary . . . to flow in love and not hide my song. My song is meant to be shared.

The third night of plant medicine, my intention was to heal my heart. It felt like nothing was happening, but a lot was actually happening behind the scenes. I slept most of the night but still kept insisting I should be doing something or having an "experience." Once again, I realized I was trying to control my fear of the unknown. I welcomed sleep the best I could to allow integration and healing.

The last night was the longest ceremony—and so worth it! It was a beautiful ceremony with many shamans who performed a healing. One shaman in front of each of us and one shaman behind each of us. They fluffed us with their feather wands, their incantations, holy water and oils, gentle blowing and healing caresses. It moved me to tears knowing that whatever had been showing itself in my body as disease was no longer viable in my body nor welcome because of the vibration of love and light. My heart was healed. I have no proof, but I feel healthy, healed, and whole. We danced and sang and welcomed the morning. No need to sleep.

Once home, I had a wonderful dream where Mama Aya showed me that all my gifts and talents come from the "jewels of my throat chakra." She showed me a beautiful image of blue crystals and gemstones surrounded with light. It was magnificent. This was the confirmation of what I felt all along . . . there will be more to discover on my quest.

The seeds of passion have been planted.

ABOUT TEJA VALENTIN

Teja's thirst for growth and self-actualization fuels the ability to facilitate growth and actualization in others—body, mind, spirit. Through her nonjudgmental and receptive spirit, lighthearted and playful, yet respectful of the serious and sacred, she helps empower you to reclaim your pleasure, passion, and vitality.

Teja Valentin is a proud mom; love, sex, and relationship coach; RN, KRI certified 220-hr. Kundalini Yoga teacher; certified 200-hr. Ayurveda Yoga teacher; certified chair and restorative yoga teacher; certified Usui Reiki Master; sound/energy practitioner; and ordained minister.

In addition to her coaching practice, Teja offers Kundalini Yoga classes, Reiki healing sessions, and Reiki Training and Kundalini/Gong meditations. Words of wisdom that she follows is to "Follow your heart, your One True Teacher." It is her desire and commitment to help plant the seeds of passion in others and guide them on their own path of healing so they may plant their own seeds of passion and bloom hard!

Connect with Teja here:

Web: http://tejavalentin.com
Facebook: https://facebook.com/tejashanti.kaur
Instagram: @teja_valentin

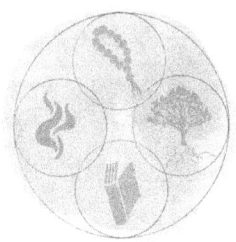

DREAM OF THE FATHERLESS

Jennifer Weaver

"You're nothing. You came from nothing. You'll always be nothing!"

No seven-year-old girl should hear those words spat in her face by a frustrated second-grade teacher, but I did. I remember coming in from recess in tears that no one would play with me. I ran straight to my desk, put my forehead down on my folded arms, and sobbed. Snot was running onto the plastic top of my chrome desk, and I was hyperventilating with heaving gasps. My teacher was saying something, but it wasn't anything I could make out over my distress.

She grabbed me under my armpits and yanked me out of my chair, sending it flying out from under me, as she pulled me across the classroom into her office. She threw me in her chair, leaned into my face, and demanded to know why I was crying. I couldn't respond. I was in hysterics and still gasping for breath through sobs and utter shock.

Not responding to her made her even angrier. While red-faced and enraged, those ten words she left me with alone in her office after slamming the door are seared into my brain like a branding iron leaves on a sixty-day-old calf. They've stayed with me my entire life.

What I wouldn't have given to have my father rescue me at that moment. Upon seeing me being ripped from my desk, dragged, and thrown into a chair, my dad would've burst through my teacher's office and yelled a few choice words and expletives while scooping me up into his arms and storming out of that class full of mean-spirited kids and witch of a so-called teacher. That is if I had a dad. But I didn't.

I was the child of a single mother. My brother was fourteen months younger than me, and we looked very different. He was blond, freckle-faced, and had fair skin with blue eyes. I had a solid olive complexion, dark brown hair, green eyes, and my ears poked out like a little elf.

We both had the same last name as my mother, so I didn't ever question paternity. Why would I? I had no reason to think otherwise. Besides, I looked like my mother with my dark hair, except for my tanned skin and nose, which had a hump and slightly dropped tip that became more prominent with age. But still, something didn't feel right.

I felt out of place as a child. That discomfort was coupled with insecurity and loneliness. There wasn't ever a time in my life that I remember having a dad. My mom was divorced when my brother was two months old, so I wasn't even a toddler when the man whose name is on my birth certificate left.

I only knew him by name as a child. And that name always felt foreign and strange. However, the tall, muscular man who bested all wicked witches I dreamed up in my imagination and always loved and protected me was familiar. He was my hero—whoever he was.

Years passed with me still dreaming about a father I wished I'd had. We moved away from the only stability I had with my grandparents in rural southern Utah to Salt Lake City a few weeks before my tenth birthday. (If I had a father, we wouldn't be moving away. He'd make sure of that!)

There we were, my brother and I as latch-key kids, home alone as my mother worked double shifts to keep a roof over our heads. But my head was in the clouds with thoughts about what my life would've been—should've been—had I only had a dad.

My dad would go to work in a suit and tie, briefcase in hand, while my mom would help as a teacher's aide at school so I could still see her every day. He'd then come home to our ranch and put on his jeans and cowboy boots, and we'd go outside and ride the horses. That was my dream, but my reality was being in a cockroach-invested apartment, dishes stacked in the sink, and barely any food in the refrigerator. I ached for my father.

Eighth grade rolled around, and I was taking a journalism class. An assignment given was to do an interview with your parents about their marriage and divorce if they had split. With notebook and pencil in hand, I sat at my mother's feet on the floor as she sat on the couch and asked her questions about how she met my dad, when they got married, and why they got divorced.

She explained she'd met my father at the deer hunter's ball in college in the fall of 1969, but she veered off about getting married in March 1970. I was born on June 27, 1970. The accounts didn't add up in my brain, so I asked, "Was I five months premature?"

My mom's outburst of laughter stunned me. Her reply was, "Haven't you figured it out yet?" Dumbfounded, I shook my head no. She continued to explain that my brother and I had different fathers. My father was tall, had brown hair and big hands, was a good dancer, and his name was James, but he went by Jimmy, she said.

Then her demeanor plummeted into sadness, and she looked away, put her hand to her chin, and asked me not to bring it up again because she'd heard that he had gone to fight in the Vietnam War. She didn't know if he was alive or dead. I picked myself up off the floor, went to my bedroom, crawled into bed, put the covers over my head, and cried.

I kept my word and didn't ask my mom any further questions about my father until I was twenty-one. I had dropped out of college after being told by a communications professor that I was "too ethnic looking" to be a TV anchorwoman, a dream I had since I learned how to write and type. When I was eight, I would use my mom's black typewriter to write stories.

I loved the sounds of the metal slugs with raised letters hitting the white paper. The printed marks on white sheets of words I formulated filled me with glee, so much so that I even squealed with joy as my fingers hit the lettered keys. That is until I made a mistake and had to use the Wite-Out correction fluid. But ultimately, I'd have my story!

I'd take my script and sit in front of my bedroom mirror with a hairbrush in my hand as a microphone to report the latest on the cookie bandit who'd switched out sugar with laundry detergent, destroying any hopes of a successful school bake sale as people burped bubbles after biting into supposed chocolate chip cookies.

The desire to tell stories motivated me to enroll in that eighth-grade journalism class, which also led me to major in communications and broadcast journalism in college. After being told I had no hope of being the next Barbara Walters, I was lost. Another dream of mine had been crushed. I didn't know what to do . . . All I wanted was my dad.

I was in a deep depression, not knowing my identity or what I wanted to do with my life. However, I managed to get myself to work doing inside sales for classified ads. Until one day, I had the strong urge to jump out of the third-story window. My supervisor stopped me and immediately referred me to human resources to get help. I was referred to a counselor who advised me to talk to my mother about my biological father. She thought knowing more about him would help me learn more about myself.

Talking to my mother about my father wasn't easy. But I did

it. She didn't tell me much more about him than when I was thirteen, but she did say that they had a class together, and they recognized each other at the deer hunter's ball. That's how they connected. After the holidays, she never saw him again. She'd heard he'd gone to Vietnam only through other classmates, but she didn't know for sure.

I don't know why that information appeased me for a few more years, but it did. Then, my twenty-fourth birthday was soon approaching. My mom asked me what I wanted for my birthday, and I blurted out, "I want my dad." The dream I had of knowing my father was alive and well. I wondered all the time if I looked like him. Was he a war hero? Did he crinkle his nose like I did when he laughed? Did he work with those big hands that my mom described? I had so many questions, and I wanted them answered.

I got my birthday wish. My mom took a trip back to her college in southern Utah and met with the alumni association president. They reviewed some records and found Jimmy's family's phone number and address. They called, and his father answered the phone.

The alumni association president explained they planned a college reunion and wanted to invite Jimmy. Much to his dismay and my mom's worst fear, Jimmy's father told them he'd been killed in Vietnam. A helicopter he was in crashed from mechanical failure, and he'd died on May 10, 1972.

It was tough waiting to hear from my mom. I was anxious, nervous, and excited all at the same time. That all changed when I finally got the call. He was dead. My dad had died, and so had my dream of ever meeting him. My mom and I decided to write a letter to Jimmy's parents and included some photos of me.

Months later, my mom received a reply from a woman she used to work with, who coincidentally had married Jimmy's brother. She arranged a barbecue, and I met an entire family of grandparents, aunts, uncles, and cousins . . . and they had dark hair and green eyes like me.

Having another family that I'd never known before was joyous but terrifying and uncomfortable at first. Jimmy's parents, four brothers and sister, and their children were the most down-to-earth, hardworking people I'd ever met. They loved each other and supported each other in everything they did, including a long-standing family business in heating and air conditioning.

They did not shy away from hard labor and loved outdoor recreation like camping and fishing. Though I still felt a loss from being fatherless, I felt more connected to him than before meeting his family. A dream was realized, just not as I had hoped.

Numerous years later, that connection would extend to a man who had fought in Vietnam with Jimmy. He was the chair of the Vietnam memorial that was being erected in my hometown. I had given a classification speech at the Cedar City Rotary Club and shared my story of finding my father only to learn of his sacrifice overseas. Unbeknownst to me, one of the Rotarians shared my story to the memorial committee to ask consent for a paver to be etched in memory of my father as part of the memorial. It was unanimously approved.

As the dedication date of the Vietnam memorial drew near, the chair of that committee, who went by the nickname Doc, visited me at my office. He wore army green and a black baseball cap with the embroidered POW/MIA logo. He explained that his role during the Easter Offensive was to draw out mobile enemy units for ambush since he "had the face of the enemy," being half Chinese and half Japanese.

He talked about a soldier who smoked Camel cigarettes and disobeyed orders, and brought his unit supplies at a volatile time when they were all being asked to surrender during the North Vietnam siege in An Lôc. He said he witnessed the helicopter that soldier was in upon its departure from a supply run get shot down by a PT-76 tank of the Soviet Army.

I was perplexed about why Doc shared this information with me, but I listened. He concluded by extending an invitation to the dedication ceremony of the Vietnam memorial, and he emphasized that I should make sure to bring my children. I accepted the invitation and brought my children to the dedication event that paid tribute to the eight resident soldiers who lost their lives during the war.

The emotional dedication was fitting for the memorial with seven black granite tablets containing information about the war and a five-foot statue in the center of the new Rotary Centennial Veterans Park. After the ceremony concluded, Doc beckoned me to follow him.

With my children in tow, Doc led me to an engraved paver with my father's name, rank, and date of death with the added letters *KIA* (killed in action). My disbelief turned to utter shock when Doc took my hand, put it to his heart, and said, "James Christian Jensen, killed in action, May 10, 1972; I knew your father."

Now Doc's office visit weeks earlier made sense. He was adamant that Jimmy's helicopter didn't crash from mechanical failure but that it was shot down. He was also resolute that from that day forward, he was my father, and I was his daughter. It was the least he could do for the man he said saved his life. That was a dream come true that I didn't even know I had. Since then, Doc has been an integral part of my life. We have shared dinners and lengthy conversations. We've celebrated holidays and birthdays. We've also shared loss when his wife died and renewed hope when he remarried. We were family.

Family doesn't have to be blood related. That truth became even more profound when my cousin and I decided to do an AncestryDNA test. I was forty-nine and wanted to know more about my heritage on my biological father's side of the family because what I knew was that his ancestry emigrated to the

United States from Denmark. They even named the township in Utah that they settled Elsinore after the Kronborg Castle.

The results of that DNA test would change my life forever. I didn't have one drop of DNA from Denmark, Sweden, or anywhere close to those countries. And I didn't match at all with my cousin, whose DNA markers were heavily from Denmark. Devastation does not begin to describe my heartbreak.

I contacted a professional genealogist who analyzed my DNA markers. He said I was clearly Spanish. Hearing those words instantly surfaced a memory of a conversation I had with my grandmother as a teen after I found a wallet-size photo of a man in her projector slides.

On the back of the photo, handwritten in cursive was the name Jose Luis de Dios. I was thirteen and had been told by my mother a few months earlier that my brother and I had different dads but not to discuss it further. My grandmother explained that she'd kept the photo of the foreign-exchange student because she thought he could be my birth father since my mother had dated him.

The same feelings of anxiousness, nervousness, and excitement I had when waiting for that phone call from my mom twenty-five years earlier about my father were coupled with absolute dread. But I did it. My mom cried, "No, no, no, no!" I responded in a whisper, "Yes."

My mom then divulged a relationship with Jose that was not approved of by her father. She corrected what my grandmother had told me and said Jose was from Madrid and had come to the States to do mining and engineering. She said they met at a college party. Their dating consisted of him playing the classical guitar and being intimate.

She went on to say that Jose had asked permission from her father to take her to Lake Tahoe with some friends, which he responded to with disdain and disgust. The answer was obviously no. While Jose was away, my mom encountered Jimmy. She thought Jimmy was my father. My dreams, once realized, were now shattered.

I picked up the pieces with introspection and prayer. For me to heal, I needed to reveal the truth to people who'd accepted and loved me. My cousin, who did the DNA test with me, accompanied me as I went to my uncles' homes and told them that Jimmy was not my father. Telling my grandfather was the most devastating because he was in a nursing home. I could only talk to him through a window screen amid the COVID-19 pandemic restrictions.

Sharing with him the DNA results were something my ninety-one-year-old grandfather didn't comprehend. I just had to come out and say it. "I'm not Jimmy's daughter," escaped my quivering lips as tears fell down my cheeks. My grandfather put his hand on the screen, so I touched it with mine. He then said, "You're a special girl."

The word *special* is something I fixated on. I was healing, and it made me realize what I longed for in my dreams throughout my life—my father—I already had but in other forms. I did have loving grandfathers and uncles on both sides of my family. I had teachers and mentors. I had Doc. And I always had my father in heaven, who'd been with me my entire life. Divine inspiration told my heart that I was loved and always had been.

Dreams are lovely to have for inspiration, motivation, and in my case, the deliverance of truth. Also, in my case, dreams changed and even came true, but not in the way I thought they would. They also got crushed. But what matters is that you still dream.

My seven-year-old self didn't know it then, but I know it now after a lifetime of dreaming that all of us are not defined by our DNA. My second-grade teacher got it wrong. This is what she should have said: "You are valued. You come from the divine. You will always matter!"

ABOUT JENNIFER WEAVER

Jennifer Weaver is an award-winning journalist and mother to three grown children. She earned a bachelor of science degree in human development and family studies from the University of Utah and a master of management and public administration degree from the University of Phoenix, where she also graduated as a member of the Lambda Sigma Chapter of the International Business Honor Society, Delta Mu Delta. She currently operates her own business, girlcodeandcontent.com, and resides in South Jordan, Utah.

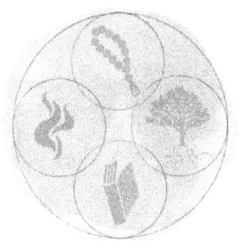

THE LITTLE BARN THAT COULD

Michele Gambone

A brief introduction is probably in order with the understanding that this story in and of itself is a journey down the road less traveled with myriad choices leading to spiritual awakening and enlightenment. This odyssey has elevated my life beyond what I believed to be my limits and continues to amaze me each and every day.

My name is Michele Gambone, and my life originated in small town Westville, New Jersey, where I still reside with my family. I have always had passion in everything I have done and always believed that my life takes me exactly where I need to be in every moment. I spent many years working in animal rescue and still consider it one of my passions, but a few years back in fall 2014, a new passion came knocking, and it has become an all-encompassing voyage fraught with epic highs and demoralizing lows.

It was just before Thanksgiving in 2014 when I found out about a woman that was eight months pregnant and living in a minivan with her husband and children. We have all heard horror stories about life on the streets, and this story was no different from the countless stories that preceded it—but somehow, for some unknown reason, I felt compelled to help this family. I believe without a shadow of a doubt it was the Holy Spirit moving me to act and help someone who really needed it. By accident, but absolutely not by mistake, the Unforgotten Haven was born on that day.

The Unforgotten Haven, which today is a nonprofit 501(c)(3) and is now one of the fastest growing charitable organizations in the country, started with extremely humble beginnings with its sole mission statement stated simply as being "the wind beneath the wings of all living things."

I have to take you to the beginning and probably explain the name of this story. As you can imagine, the first family I wanted to help planted a seed deep inside, and the idea and belief started to grow that no one should ever be overlooked or neglected, and each person truly deserves dignity and respect and should always have a safe refuge. The Unforgotten Haven by definition means exactly the idea that was planted that day back in November 2014. It wasn't long before this idea blossomed and donations from angels started to overrun my living room, my kitchen, my porch—well, you get the idea. I found myself needing a space to contain and disperse the blessings we were receiving. In my travels, I happened upon a run-down little barn on the back end of a residential property that was being offered for lease. Now when I say run down, I mean it had no heat, no electric (or none that worked), no insulation to keep out the cold as it was now December, and it had no running water or bathrooms. It was absolutely perfect!

I signed a month-to-month lease, and the little barn had now become my new headquarters. The donations were pouring in. We started with collecting food and toiletries along with clothing by the truckload, and furniture also was fair game. After only eight short weeks, this little barn, which was now packed to its rotted little rafters, was also filling up with volunteers that were fast becoming the life blood to push this growing relief effort beyond what I was able to do alone. The time spent in this little barn was difficult at best with the winter upon us, and snow often blocked the entrance, and the brutal cold made it almost untenable. I still remember pulling up to the barn after work, using my headlights for light so we could sort donations, and stuffing our gloves with hand warmers as vapor came out of our mouths due to the frigid temperatures. I remember my husband coming to slide open the old, extremely heavy door for us to get inside. It may seem odd to look at this building with fond memories given the physical hardships that everyone endured, but that building helped support an idea and gave hope to a brighter future for everyone. I suppose the symbolism of that building fit right into our mission. It was overlooked and neglected, but it became our refuge, our haven.

The little barn was the springboard for an organization that propelled a belief in helping others.

We, as an organization, had to bid farewell to our beloved barn and move forward to be able to help more people. The next step was at best a leap of faith in which I signed a yearly lease for a much larger and more modern space that could accommodate future growth exactly five months after helping our first family. I say *leap of faith* simply because we had exactly zero funding. If I was to tell you that it was a little scary, that would be a massive understatement. My fears were quelled by my belief that if I put it in God's hands and it was meant to be, we would certainly succeed. I know that there are many nonbelievers, but from where I stand, it's virtually impossible to deny that our survival as an organization was steeped in faith. We have witnessed many miracles and have reached over 1.5 million souls that desperately needed to feel the blessings of a merciful God. This includes people and animals.

The Unforgotten Haven has benefited from the blessings bestowed upon it and thereby has helped more and more people and animals along the way. I am the founder, and yes, that requires more hours than there are in a day. I have continued to work as a manager of an engineering firm for the past twenty-five years as well and have devoted a minimum of an additional forty to fifty hours per week to this labor of love. Fortunately, as an organization, we have been able to garner corporate as well as private sponsorship from businesses and individuals that can see the value in what we are trying to accomplish. We have amassed a team of volunteers with a passion and belief in helping others and truly have seen this organization bring out the best in everyone. We are now a team of forty individuals that have compassion and love and the belief that we can make the world a better place for all living creatures.

We operate as 100% volunteer based, seven days a week, and the haven is a well-oiled machine. Each supporter and volunteer is the oil to that machine. We are called "The Blessing Hub" as we are the hub filled with donations and we share with churches, schools, and other organizations to spread the love.

The Unforgotten Haven was founded on the fundamental belief that we as an organization can not only make the world a better place but we can elevate those who have lived through some of the most incredibly difficult times ever known. We have seen devastating loss and wept with families that have lost everything and everyone that mattered in their lives.

Each and every day we have seen the best, and yes, the worst that exists in our local communities and all around the world, and we are dedicated to easing the grief and sense of loss from all disasters, man-made and natural.

During this journey, God placed a very special little boy into our lives at the Unforgotten Haven. His name is Nico Cassabria, and he fought Stage IV high-risk neuroblastoma. He fought from age three to age ten. We were the lucky ones to have been able to meet such a hero walking among us here on Earth. Our entire team and the entire community came together despite any differences to embrace Nico and his family through his journey here on

Earth. This is one of our devastating losses, and we still speak of him daily. The work we do is not always rainbows and butterflies. It's often filled with tears and heartache. We often grieve, but we love hard. When you open your heart, it is susceptible to being broken. Nico made everyone want to be a better person during his ten years here. He is part of the Unforgotten Haven family and part of our story. As promised to his family, he will *never* be forgotten. We honor Nico by having his very own project, Nico's Power-Up Packs, which are bags made up with arts and crafts and other items given to children in the hospitals and also to children's infusion centers.

The Unforgotten Haven continues to grow, and with growth we found that we needed even more space to support over twenty individual projects intended to pinpoint specific needs within our communities, such as support for terminally ill cancer patients or for victims of domestic violence as well as our homeless out-reach initiative serving hundreds of homeless in Philadelphia, PA, and Camden, NJ, each Sunday. We found ourselves supporting victims of natural disasters during the Louisiana floods and hurricane relief in North Carolina, Texas, Florida, and Puerto Rico. We supported the victims local to New Jersey who lost everything in a tornado September 2021. Our most recent support has found its way directly to the Ukraine in an effort to ease the atrocity inflicted on a war-torn nation.

With our rapid growth, we found that we needed a building that would better enable us to support the needs of everyone. Volunteerism is very important to us, and we ran out of space at our current building we rent, so we started searching for a larger building in the beginning of 2021.

We asked and prayed for God to once again provide what we needed, and once again he provided. Our supporters rallied and donated $75,000 toward the purchase of a new building. A family of angels gifted us a half-million dollars. Let me introduce you to the Radwell family! This is the first time the family has been announced. We wanted it to be special. What better way than to put this miracle into a book. This gift allowed us to purchase a larger building and ultimately gave us the leverage to aid even more people in need.

The Radwell family will never know the impact they have made in this world. Our gratitude can't be expressed in words. As we searched all over South Jersey for a building, many obstacles occurred. It was very difficult to find a commercial property. Then it happened! Directly across from where we rented, a massive building went up for sale for $575,000.

Exactly what we had to the penny.

Who says God isn't listening!

We are expanding, and the building we purchased will be a volunteer headquarters in the near future. The building we rent will remain our pantry where families can stop in anytime we are open for *free* nonperishable food, toiletries, diapers, wipes, formula, baby food, feminine products, and cleaning supplies (depending on what we have donated to us at the time).

Hours and more information can be found on our website: www.theunforgottenhaven.org.

I will leave you with this. When you have faith the size of a million mustard seeds, those seeds spread quickly—just like when you blow on a dandelion. I am thankful every single day that God put faith in my heart and provided me with the best family, team members, and friends a girl could wish for (my dandelion seeds). Without God, my family, and my team, this beautiful organization would not exist.

ABOUT MICHELE GAMBONE

I am happily married with two skin children and six fur children.

I reside in a small town in South Jersey (Westville, NJ) where my family has been rooted for over 100 years!

I have managed an engineering firm full-time for the past twenty-five years (Hydrographic Surveys) and recently went part-time to be more hands-on at the Unforgotten Haven.

I have been a certified colon hydrotherapist for the past fifteen years.

I am a photographer and an animal activist. I enjoy the beach and hope to retire there one day.

I have worked hard since the age of fourteen and would say I am a workaholic. Each day starts at 3:00 a.m. (seven days a week). I enjoy helping others, and it does the soul good.

I am a faithful servant of God, and not a day goes by that I don't pray or give thanks to my father in heaven.

My faith is the size of a million mustard seeds. My favorite quote:

"No one has ever become poor by giving." —Anne Frank

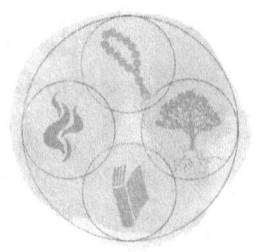

SOUL ANSWERS

Lauren Oberly

Ever since I was a little girl, I've always believed in universal magic and the unseen. From unicorns, imaginary friends, Santa Claus, the tooth fairy—you name it, I believed it. Throughout my childhood years is when these beliefs started to change. I lost a bit of the belief in magic. This is when I started to question everything about myself: my inner truth, my self-worth, self-love, and self-confidence. I always used to think, *How could my parents tell me to believe in anything, when I found out everything I thought was real is a hoax?* Thinking back on this as an adult, it's very clear that my inner child is where my limiting beliefs came from and how I was built as an adult.

I began sitting quietly in contemplation on a daily basis in my late twenties. I began to notice my own thoughts. Many beliefs I held—both negative and positive—came up. One very heartfelt and emotional moment for me was when I made a life-changing decision for my daughter Lily and me. It was Monday morning, October 26, 2020, I experienced one of the scariest and proudest moments I had in my life. I was walking into the courthouse with my sister-in-law to put a stop to the marriage that I knew wasn't serving me any longer. At that moment, I had an overwhelming number of emotions and thoughts running through my mind. *Can I do this for my daughter and me? Is this the right choice for us? What am I going to do next?* After following my true instinct, a huge sense of calmness came over me. I finally was able to feel and receive the message God was guiding me to see.

Now one of the affirmations I say every single day is, *I am open to the fullness of my power and know that I am perfectly enough exactly as I am.* You have the power to heal your life and I feel that is something everyone needs to believe. We often doubt ourselves and think we do not have the potential to achieve what we want. What people don't realize is we have the power of our minds—claiming and consciously using your power. Trauma is never your fault, but healing is your responsibility. Your ability to love yourself is mirrored in the love you accept from others. If you're seeking a deeper love, look within and seek a deeper love within yourself first. Being true to yourself while loving who you are during the journey is the most courageous thing you will ever do.

I grew up a daddy's girl. I always wanted to be the center of attention, and most of all, I wanted his attention. My dad was born in the 1940s, and back in that time, it wasn't socially accepted to have a voice or express emotions, which means it was all stuffed deep down in his body as trauma. After the passing of his mother when he was seventeen years old, my dad had to grow up fast to help his own father provide for his other siblings, instead of having the freedom of enjoying his teenage years.

It wasn't until about eight months ago that I realized my dad was emotionally unavailable during my childhood. This is where I believe I learned my low self-esteem from. I came to this realization through a coaching session with one of my mentors, Melanie Wilson, an anxiety and trauma coach. I asked myself one day, *Why do I feel a sense of jealousy as I watch my daughter Lily and my dad read books together?* The valuable lesson that I was able to learn in that current moment, was having the ability to look at it from a different perspective. Shifting from the egotistical version of self, I was able to see this as a blessing in the purest form.

I learned this through my own self-healing and connecting with my intuition. When I feel an emotional trigger, I need to *pause* and identify why I might be feeling this way. What inside of me needs more healing and exploration? If I didn't allow a space for my own healing, I might have missed this pure blessing God put right in front of me. My dad, seventy-three, has been the closest thing Lily has had to a father figure. I am grateful that my dad is able to fill that void for my daughter, as her own father wasn't willing to be present in her life at the time. I've always believed you have children when you need them, not when you want them. God knew I needed change in my life, and Lily is the reason I am the woman I am today. I pray that one day her own father can see how much of a blessing Lily is to us both.

After becoming a mom myself, I felt my relationship with my mom was very important to me. I have always viewed my mom as a caring, loving, strong, independent, hardworking woman. Growing up, I always felt like it was very hard to connect with her. So I prayed about it in hopes of some answers. I needed to get to the root of why I was never able to connect with her. I wanted to learn more about her childhood and her teenage years. So, I was able to come from a place of love and compassion. Just recently, I asked my mom if she would be more open to telling me about her childhood and teenage years. During our conversation, she shared with me her struggles with her own inner peace and past trauma. She also told me she masked all of this for years to make sure my dad, my brother, and I were all taken care of first.

As a child, I saw this as her being controlling, manipulating, and always worrying about everything. In turn, it put a wall between us. I was the type of kid that never liked to be controlled or told what to do. As an adult, this was a hard habit to break and still shows up for me at times. My parents always had very high expectations of me even as a little kid still learning. Knowing this,

I am just the product of my past experiences and trauma, but I am the one who is responsible for healing this. I am responsible for how I show up for myself. I can't blame people for who they are when they are hurt. Just because I was led to believe certain things in my childhood doesn't mean I wasn't safe or protected as a child. If I couldn't believe what my heart and soul believed in, how was I supposed to believe in myself? That's where the limiting beliefs in myself came from.

As a child and teen, I judged others for having big emotions because I couldn't understand how to deal with my own in a healthy way. That is why I was always drawn to codependent relationships. I confused self-sacrifice with self-preservation. Today, my parents are my best friends and my main support system. I am so grateful to have been able to help heal our relationship bond.

Until I had my own daughter, I lived my life just trying to survive day by day. I wanted to get to the root of why I was suffering. I was just a bottomless pit of toxic emotions—fear and shame mainly. I was drowning in my negative emotions about not being enough. This prompted me to start my own shadow work, so I could heal the wounds from my childhood and past relationships. The "shadow" is most apparent in strong emotions. Being able to identify and see what those emotions and sensations are can help you see your life patterns.

Three key parts of starting my shadow work were identifying my life patterns, triggers, and projections with people and relationships in my life. Some of the questions I asked myself while journaling were: *What is the trigger attached to that pattern? What family patterns do I fear I am repeating? How do I present myself to the world?* I did all of this through journaling, self-reflection, and childhood analysis.

After doing my own shadow work, it made me come to the realization I needed to break this generational trend to not subconsciously pass it to my own daughter. I was so sick of what was happening in my life, sick of all the people I let hurt me, so sick of the pain. I was not going to shrink myself down so someone else was comfortable with me. I would use my voice and be as powerful as I wanted to be. I stopped caring if people thought I was too much. Because I know I am enough. I stopped caring if I asked too many questions, if I seemed too passionate, or if others thought I was too sensitive because I am in touch with my emotions.

I was done ignoring my feelings for the comfort of someone who couldn't handle it. I knew that it was possible to be a misfit in one group and fit in perfectly in another. This is the time I explored my true passion and dreams. Continuing my shadow work, I realized I was the only one who got to decide how I was going to live my life. No one else was going to magically show up and do all the hard work for me. It wasn't until I hit rock bottom, at the darkest and lowest point in my life, that I decided I needed a change, sitting on my kitchen floor packing up boxes alone to move out of the first house I bought on my own. I was so sick and tired of feeling like I had no purpose in this universe. I wasn't strong enough to change for myself at the time, so my daughter became my why. I decided to put in the hard work no matter how hard it felt at times. I chose to believe in the magic you can't see, because this is where my inner belief came from.

Once I chose me, I could not stay in a marriage that wasn't serving my highest good and purpose here on Earth. I have since learned that in a relationship, you either grow together or you grow apart. That doesn't necessarily make you or the another person a bad person. If you don't love yourself, you can't love another person. You're just using that person as a bandage to cover up what you are hiding from yourself.

I started to work through all my trauma and feel my emotions from my past hurt. I had to go through this process alone. I had to show up 100% for myself first to heal so I could show up as a better mother, daughter, sister, friend, niece, and cousin. But most importantly, God's higher purpose here on Earth was as an energy healer.

As I gained more self-awareness, I learned to trust myself more. I can now even use that introspection in relationships. Starting my self-love journey and becoming whole again, I owe a huge amount of gratitude to my very close and dear friend Tara Lepera. She saw me for what my soul had to offer this world. She walked alongside me, holding my hand and guiding me each step. I wouldn't be the woman I am today if it wasn't for the belief she saw in me. After identifying the negative self-talk, the limiting beliefs, and the ego-driving narrative others projected on me, I changed.

One of the biggest lessons was getting out of my own ego and connecting with my higher self. I started to look at my life from a different perspective. This is the evolution of the journey: the reflection of my childhood, limiting beliefs, and negative self-talk. While also working with Melanie, she helped me realize I had to surrender to myself. I worked with her in a very intense twelve-week program, which was meant to help me rise up from my anxiety and trauma. She helped me develop new beliefs, break the chains to my anxiety, and start to live my life unapologetically. Ultimately, I discovered the only way to fully love myself was to surrender—even though I left a marriage, had to move back home, lost money, had to leave my job, singly provided for my daughter all while building myself back up.

My ultimate lesson was all of these things had to happen in order for me to fully surrender. Honestly, I think it's one of the most helpful perspectives one can cultivate now. I had no idea a passion for spiritual study, creativity, writing, and deeply connecting with nature would be ignited within me. I shifted my focus toward being of service to others. So I was able to walk in my soul's purpose here on Earth. Surrendering isn't about giving up, it's about recommitting. It is not to force the desires of your lower ego mind. It's giving up control for peace. I decided on a new direction while being gentle with myself as I practiced this new way of being. I am no longer in a mental prison fighting against myself. I am fully living my soul's purpose. In turn, this led me to realize what I had always known my whole life: I am a healed empath. This allowed me the opportunity to tap into my universal energy through Reiki healing, an amazing journey of my soul's destiny for my sacred calling.

Through my own hard work, I found new meaning in my soul's purpose. Your life will change once you discover your passion, spiritual path, and tribe to support you on your journey. If you want to dig deep and uncover your dreams and visions, I invite you to connect with me. I will walk alongside you and guide you to find your own inner light so you can finally live in peace. If you listen to your heart, all things are possible when you are able to dream!

> *"You can't go back and change the beginning, but you can start where you are and change the ending."* —C.S. Lewis

ABOUT LAUREN OBERLY

Lauren Oberly is the founder of Mermaid Light. Lauren is a single mama of a two-year-old girl named Lily. After having her daughter, Lauren always knew there was more to her soul's purpose on Earth than just being a mom. She was tired of working for someone else's dream and decided to stop living in the matrix. Lauren is an energy healer and discovered using her gift as a Reiki master, intuitive life coach, and author. She guides her client's step by step in uncovering their dreams and passions. After becoming the CEO of her own life with the power of prayer and the universe, she helps empower women to find their own soul's purpose on Earth. Lauren believes every human has the power within them to heal. Lauren is just your personal cheerleader to help guide you to see your own inner light.

So I invite you into my world to learn more on how you can work one-on-one with me, visit www. themermaidlight.com or connect with me on social media:

Facebook: Lauren Oberly
Instagram: @LaurenOberly

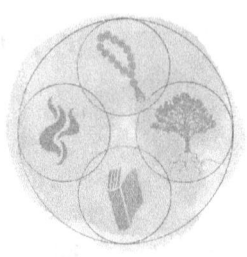

UNSEEN

Dawn Schimke

My legs dangled, childlike, in midair as I shivered on the examination table at the hospital. It was early December, and I was clad in a skimpy and revealing hospital gown, but it was the words that had just been uttered that sent a chill down my spine. "Prepare for a miscarriage." The doctor standing before me was absent of emotion and barely gave me a second glance when he made the definitive proclamation. The shock of that prognosis silenced me. How does a person prepare in advance for their dreams to be crushed?

The reality of his words hit me on the subway back to my upper Manhattan apartment, and I fought to hold in the storm of heaving sobs until safely away from the dead eyes of the other commuters. A soggily incoherent call to Ken, my fiancé, at his office failed to garner any reassurance. What did *he* know about being the owner of an incompetent cervix and the barbaric threat of having "a stitch" put in place to stave off what seemed like an inevitable outcome.

After three emergency room trips in the six weeks since my pregnancy was confirmed, I was getting used to sharp needles, invasive questions . . . and wild assumptions—was I actively using crack? For patients who are uninsured and reliant on Medicaid as I was, the medical system often can be a brutal inquiry into their lifestyle and an intrusion on their very autonomy.

Enter Dr. Xu! He was an acupuncturist and well-respected doctor of Traditional Chinese Medicine (TCM) who I had visited occasionally before I learned I was pregnant. Ken was a big fan of so-called alternative medicine and was keen to get me on board. But I knew from my *What to Expect* . . . book that acupuncture is not recommended during pregnancy, so it was with reluctance that I tagged along for my fiancé's Saturday visit. Dr. Xu asked where I had been and beckoned for me to extend my arms so he could listen to my pulses—in TCM there are six, and they each provide information about the systems of the body. A moment later, he flexed his arm triumphantly and said, "I give you strong baby."

His wife, the apothecarist, prepared a bundle of paper packets containing a dusty powder that was to be mixed into hot water every night. My introduction to medical herbalism was via some of the most obnoxiously bitter plants that have ever crossed my palate. I had recently received my diploma in classic pastry arts, and that flavor profile was profoundly offensive. I cried every night before gulping down the potion, but the effects were noticeable in days. The terrifying hemorrhaging that had been happening for five weeks dwindled, then disappeared; the cramps that doubled me over: gone. I finally started to put on weight.

I was feeling better, and my curiosity had been awakened. How did he know what plants my body needed to tune it to the frequency of "baby"? What secrets did he discover by feeling for a barely discernible vibration deep in my wrists? How was this shift even possible? Given the prognosis of my previous doctors, it felt miraculous. Why did they give me the shrug? Why the resignation, the "there's nothing we can do"? Clearly there *was* something to be done, and it was very effective, but how did it work? Over the next several months, I received a different, personalized formula during each visit, and the dream of baby started to feel like it was going to come true.

During that time, I was added to my husband's excellent health insurance, and I learned something else. Having that coverage makes a massive difference in how people are treated by providers in the allied health professions. I interviewed several OB-GYNs to find the right fit. What a luxury! I had my pick of potential pediatricians, all of whom took a significant amount of time to answer my questions. Would this have happened if I had stayed on Medicaid? Probably not. The system is jammed with people who are not in a position to afford the basic right of healthcare, and there are simply not enough doctors to go around.

In the current medical paradigm, an encounter with the doctor should last fifteen to twenty minutes—this ideal first gained a foothold 1992, based on a complex Medicare calculation.[1] That is very little time to properly assess and diagnose a complex patient with any degree of nuance or accuracy. There is a saying that is heard in medical circles: "When you hear hoofbeats, think horses, not zebras."

In principle, this makes sense—common conditions are prevalent, hence their name. Yet this leaves 3.5 to 5.9 percent of people (approximately 300 million worldwide) who have rare conditions . . . unseen.[2] Beyond that, almost 60 percent of adults in the United States have one chronic condition, and 40 percent have multiple conditions that affect their day-to-day life and functioning.[3] Often, the most complex patients have challenges

---

1—Roni Caryn Rabin, "15-minute doctor visits take a toll on patient-physician relationships," PBS News Hour, April 21, 2014, https://www.pbs.org/newshour/health/need-15-minutes-doctors-time.

2—Hlawulani, "New Scientific Paper Confirms 300 Million People Living with a Rare Disease Worldwide," Rare Diseases International (website), October 15, 2019, https://www.rarediseasesinternational.org/new-scientific-paper-confirms-300-million-people-living-with-a-rare-disease-worldwide/.

3—National Center for Chronic Disease Prevention and Health Promotion (NCCDPHP), "Chronic Diseases in America," Center for Disease Control, accessed June 28, 2022, https://www.cdc.gov/chronicdisease/resources/infographic/chronic-diseases.htm.

accessing providers and find their symptoms minimized or attributed to another issue (being overweight for instance), after months and even years of waiting for an appointment. Unseen and unheard. Getting insurance authorizations for required therapies and treatments is another hurdle that prevents people from accessing appropriate care; there are people employed by insurance companies who "manage patient expectations around bureaucratic hurdles"—people who are paid to tell other people why they get to be unseen.

Moreover, there is a massive resistance within the medical system against working cooperatively with practitioners of integrative and complementary modalities. Using plants to support wellness is sometimes portrayed as quaint, ineffective, hippie-era folk medicine. At the other end of the spectrum, some consider it to be risky, irresponsible, and even quackery.[4]

While the technological advances of the past century are nothing short of astounding, our ability as a society to navigate how to actually provide comprehensive care to humans has not caught up to the machines and diagnostic and surgical tools we have available. The New York Academy of Medicine, founded in 1847 to recognize highly skilled physicians and to bring credibility to a troubled profession, in an inaugural move voted that practitioners of homeopathy (which is not at all the same as herbalism) be barred from the medical field. This was almost *two decades* before Louis Pasteur developed modern germ theory.

How (and why) did the use of pharmaceuticals overtake the use of botanical remedies so quickly? In a nutshell, they are easy to standardize and dose appropriately. Aspirin was originally derived from the bark of the white willow tree. Prior to it being commercially available, a person would need to find the tree, harvest the

---

4—People who practice herbalism call it traditional medicine because it has been used effectively for thousands of years. The world of medical and pharmaceutical research is starting to catch up, and currently there are well over one hundred plant-derived compounds used in medications for anything from a headache to lymphoma.

bark, make some type of extraction, and then decide when and how much to take. That requires a lot of work and the knowledge to do it. It is much simpler to buy an effective anti-inflammatory at the store. It's not formulated so differently from the tree bark, plus it's convenient, and the side effects are manageable.

In some cases, a medication might be very strong and upset the equilibrium of a person's system in a more significant way. Antibiotics undoubtedly save lives; they are also well-known for disrupting the gastrointestinal tract because they do not discriminate between the unwanted bacterial visitors and the microorganisms that keep our digestion functioning smoothly. Naturally, it is important to address illnesses or conditions that may be life-threatening. And in modern medicine, sometimes the solution is akin to attacking a fly on the windowpane with a baseball bat. It will probably kill the fly, but the window won't be in great shape either.

One of the advantages of using the whole plant (with exceptions for those that have a degree of toxicity) is that it gives us access to all of the constituents that already work together harmoniously, rather than separating out the chemical compound that we think is doing the heavy lifting. Herbs that are known as "tonic herbs," "adaptogens," and "amphoterics" often are very effective at toning imbalances, helping the body adapt to stress, and even have the wisdom to normalize a system of the body that is expressing symptoms. I think of these more subtle actions as an embroidery needle, precise and much better for the overall health of the organism than knocking the daylights out of it. Plants used properly both remove the fly and result in a windowpane that is a little cleaner and shinier.

Moreover, facilitating and empowering the individual to implement health strategies that work for them increases and broadens wellness accessibility and autonomy. Empowering the consumer to make decisions with gentle guidance toward best practices rather than insisting on compliance builds trust and expands the opportunity for effective intervention.

I need to emphasize that accessibility is critical and fundamental. Wellness is not an elitist sport. Nor is it a moral issue. Wellness is a sign of a body in harmonious equilibrium. Rippling outward, the state of health of the people indicates the state of health of the larger society. The phrase "getting to the root cause" comes up often, and the individual "puts roots down" into the soil of their communities. There is no healthy garden if the earth is unattended or undernourished in any area. That is because land, plants, humans, communities will compensate for their imbalances and deficiencies in any way possible.

Years ago, I attended a lecture given by Henry Niese, an artist and herbalist in the Lakota tradition, in which he described a certain plant gradually creeping closer and closer to his home. After tuning into and listening for the energetic messages of the plant spirit, he discovered that the constituents and actions as determined by scientific exploration were helpful for a health imbalance or condition he was challenged by. I, too, have found that the plants that "approach" me are springing up for a reason. Just this morning, on my daily walk, I had a thought: *I haven't seen many Cleavers[5] this year.* A moment later I turned my head to the left and spotted a healthy patch by the creek.

Nature intelligence has sophisticated communication capabilities that go beyond what can be seen and heard. We do not exist apart from nature, despite all of our efforts to protect our vulnerable bodies. Tapping into that massive potential unleashes the body's ability to readjust itself to equilibrium and harmony. This can co-exist with deepening our understanding of the known scientific information about the effects of the plants as we continue to have more revelations about matter at the microcosmic level. There are over 120 medications derived from plants, and

---

5—Galium aparine, a wonderful lymphatic that proliferates in April and May, which, not-so-coincidentally is considered a good time in TCM to focus on releasing any stagnation that has built up over the winter.

research continues to expand. We have the capability of maximizing health on all levels by acknowledging that traditional and integrative care techniques can work synergistically with the system we have created for now.

The privilege of being an herbalist is immense, as is the responsibility—to our clients, to the earth, to the plants, to our colleagues. I am using my expertise to be a passionate advocate for those who are unseen by the medical system and on the vanguard of a new wellness paradigm. One where healthcare consumer is offered an array of modalities within a cooperative and collaborative framework. One where there is a trained herbalist accessible in every medical office and a living apothecary in every medical center. One in which the medical system has the capacity to fully see every human that they care for, ensuring better wellness outcomes for all.

In case you were curious, the baby from the beginning of this story got to have a gentle and joyful birth and is now twenty-four years old fiercely pursuing her own dreams in the world.

ABOUT DAWN SCHIMKE

Dawn Schimke is an herbalist, wellness coach, and advocate for her clients. Her first life-altering experience involving herbs was when a skilled practitioner of TCM saved her high-risk pregnancy in 1997. She shared the story at a TEDx Charlottesville open mic event in 2019.

Her formal herbal education began in 2007, with her mentor, Teresa Boardwine of Green Comfort School of Herbal Medicine. Dawn initially focused on applying her training as a pastry chef to formulating in the apothecary. Gradually she developed clinical skills and a love for research. She interweaves storytelling, nature metaphors, and a keen eye for energetic patterns into her work.

Dawn provides support and coaching for people who experience complex conditions helping them have more good days so they learn to love and trust their bodies again. She also offers mini workshops to HerbCurious people who desire simple, delicious techniques to upgrade their wellness autonomy.

Diagnosed with Ehlers-Danlos syndrome in 2013, Dawn uses her knowledge and insights to help medical "zebras," neurodivergent people, and those unseen by the dominant medical paradigm.

To learn more about how you can work with Dawn, please visit her website www.leafandpetalalchemy.com.

Facebook: Leaf and Petal Alchemy
Instagram: @leafandpetalalchemy
Pinterest: Leaf & Petal Alchemy

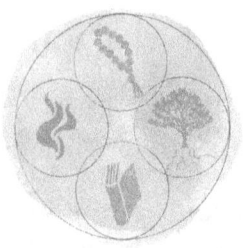

FROM WISHES TO DREAMS

Bobbie Jo Yarbrough

As I sit in our Sacred Circle drinking my cacao, I clear my mind of expectations. My gaze follows the flames, dancing in the center of the beautiful mandala, calling in the Four Directions, the Universe, and the heart-centered connections from above and below. The beauty of being present in myself now. My body begins flowing in the music and the movement of my Shakti energy—connecting to my life force, my Divine Feminine, in ways that feel like the first time.

Settling and silent, I listen to the sacred words guiding me as I walk through my portal door to merge with my future self in the sacredness of the quantum realms. Here, my beautiful highest spiritual self and I are integrated. *I Am* her and she is me. *I Am* loved and safe. *I Am* seen and heard. All my dreams, all my desires, everything *I Am* creating and more is now. I'm filled with the truth, that each day I will expand more, desire more, and love my family and myself more. My soul shines brightly and fills me with more joy. I know that my dreams are meant to be created and lived. Living my dreams is the embodiment and integration of who I truly am. *I Am.*

———

Now I didn't always believe dreams were real. I think as small child, I would associate them with wishes and prayers. I would make wishes and say prayers every night hoping that my life would be better. I was scared to fall asleep and have literal dreams because I would always have nightmares. When I closed my six-year-old eyes every night, I would play out scary scenarios of being abandoned, unloved, and unsafe. I would be running and running, so very scared, and no one would help me. I still said my wishes and prayers and tried to give myself hope, but when I opened my eyes, everything was still the same.

I was learning at the very core of me, during my crucial developmental stages, to be silent and to be invisible. As I grew up, I immersed myself in books and music. I would lose myself in the stories and lyrics. I would stay up all night just to finish a whole book. I would constantly think about the characters and who they were while I was going about my days. I loved book series like, Carolyn Keen's original Nancy Drew young sleuth stories and Stephen King's The Dark Tower series. These adventurers and heroes helped others, led others, close friends with them, and most of all were who they wanted to be, no matter the challenges they were facing. I would think about the characters so much, it was like they were in my actual world. I longed to go on adventures and see the world, but most of all, have the freedom to be myself. Every now and then I would bravely write songs, poetry, and journal about my wishes and dreams, but it never made my life better. I never felt like I could share the creative stories and parts of me that I felt needed to be shared. Some feeling or small whisper made me believe deep down I wasn't alone in how my life was. I knew there were others who lived or felt the way I did, but in my youth and before social media, I never knew how to find or reach out to them.

I was popular in school and had some good friends, but growing up, I went to small-town schools where everyone knew everyone. We were the foster kids and the kids who had ethnic hair and darker skin, but were "white" too, so we usually, naturally stood out. I was nice and well liked; however, inside I was awkward, ashamed, and hidden. I wished my life was like the kids I went to school with, who seemingly had parents who loved them, money to do all the fun things, and more than a few outfits for school clothes. I just knew deep down this wasn't truly how I was supposed to feel about myself. I was just riding out time till I could get out of foster care and be on my own. I knew this couldn't be my life forever. I was still just making wishes, not knowing I was actually dreaming my future life into creation.

As I was thrust into adulthood, I was naturally forced into new challenges. I was in a new part of the country, with all new people, trying to figure out who I was and where I would fit in, all at once, no time to take breaks or have introspection. At this point in my life, it was all about survival, and there was no time to dream or make wishes. All of those were put on hold while I tried to work or start college so I could set myself up for some distant future that I couldn't connect to. I lived in my car at times, sleeping in the parking lot of my work so I wouldn't waste gas or have to worry about being attacked. I became friends with some people who weren't always the best to be around so I had a sense of protection from the scariness of the streets.

At some point, actually living a better life became just as important as just surviving it. I took a job in another city, I was still just asking and dreaming, but now I had more freedom to seek out how to get the life I wanted. I loved where I was and who I was with. I finally felt like I could be understood more and breathe. My new best friend and I did everything together: we spoke about our dreams, we lived in various cities together, we struggled together, and we supported each other in every way. In retrospect, I can see one of the most powerful aspects to our friendship was our mutual support for each other. We both believed we could achieve the futures we both wanted, no matter how long it took.

Then my life took a very unexpected turn. The events of 9/11 happened, and within two days I had signed up to serve in the US Navy. There was something that happened or changed inside me while watching the events unfold in the next few days. I was shocked, scared, and sad for those who couldn't find their family members. The call to help others feel safe was stronger than I had ever felt before. I had to do something.

So, the little girl who grew up feeling abandoned, the teenager who dreamed of being on adventures helping people, now was the young adult doing just that. My first four years in the military were spent living overseas at various duty stations, two of which were islands, one of those in the Middle East. Later while stationed in Italy, I got to visit many other countries, such as Germany, Amsterdam, Ireland, etc. I got to explore Rome, Pompeii, and beautiful off-the-coast getaways. I had fun and created friendships that are still strong today. I'm not sure if I knew then; however, now I can see how all my wishing, prayers, and dreams growing up became parts of my real life as an adult.

When a traumatic event happened to me while serving overseas, it felt like my happiness was halted. I was catapulted into the space of feeling scared, abandoned, and shamed. When I got stationed back home in the US, I was in a different mindset. Being myself wasn't safe. My coping skills were all over the place. I didn't understand at the time how my anxiety and depression were being masked every day to help me seem normal. I felt like I stopped dreaming again and was just longing to feel happy. Like being happy was something I had to find or just accept was out of my reach. Even being part of a group of friends, I never felt like I fit in or was wanted. Internally, I was always questioning everything and everyone. "Fake it till you make it" does not happiness make at all. I know—I lived it for a lonely long while.

———

When I reflect now, I still couldn't tell you how I came to find the path to the journey I've been on for so many years now. I could say that my friend and I went to a metaphysical mixer one evening out of curiosity and found out about a magical, esoteric, sustainable-living community in rural San Diego. Then I was introduced to an intuitive school that tapped me into all my natural spiritual gifts and self-healing. And for years to follow, there has been more intensive self-healing, learning various powerful healing modalities, and intentional living every day. That is the easy explanation. It's true, it's simple, it's to the point. This journey has been so much more than that though.

As I was taught how to tap into the magic of who I truly was, I could connect with my higher self. I was learning to trust my intuition and have the discernment to know what wasn't mine to feel. I remember when I was learning Pranayama breathing and setting a timer to meditate in silence, how uncomfortable and scared I felt. I remember when we would have Karma yoga together in silence for hours, working side by side together, how anxious I would get, thinking everyone was thinking I didn't belong there. Sometimes I would want to just run away from everyone or leave. Sometimes I wished I could do that to myself, just leave myself and live my safe, pretend life.

As I dove more and more into accessing myself so deeply and spiritually, I still didn't realize that all the fear, shame, and invisibility I had wrapped myself in for so long had actually become me. This is how I saw myself and believed others saw me too. The shifting was so uncomfortable because I was seeing my true self, I was connecting to my highest self, I was healing and rewriting my new stories; however, I wasn't believing yet who this me was. I was learning how to pause and sit in my stuff, weed out the lies, and believe in my dreams, but I wasn't in alignment with me. Literally, I was struggling with which me was going to be the real me moving forward. It is so mind-blowing to think about not resonating with your true self so much that you are not sure of who you really are and it feels safer to stay miserable. I wanted to be in alignment with my true self more than anything now. I knew it was time for me to choose my true self. I was top priority. I was learning how to make my dreams, of truly being me, bigger than my fears.

And I dreamed big. I was dreaming bigger than ever before. I believed what was inside of me could be healed. I believed that I didn't have to hold on to old identities, beliefs, contracts, relationships, etc., that no longer felt good or resonated with me. I dreamed I could help people transform their lives in different sustainable ways. I believed in self-healing. I believed I could heal all of me. I believed I could help others do the same. I believed I could be a mom, after being told by my doctor I wouldn't be able to carry a child. I believed I could have a completely different family life than I had growing up. I was listening to Abraham-Hicks daily, and I truly believed that I could figure my life out and find true happiness. I finally believed that dreams were not just wishes. Dreams were more than just my wishes; they were my big asks to the Universe—of the life I believed I wanted. The life I knew I could have.

What I didn't clearly understand at the time was I couldn't just bypass the deeper healing that still needed to be done in order to have all the things I wanted. Being that my identity was shame and hiding for so long, and now I wanted to be my authentic self and live a fun life with my children, there was a huge disconnect I wasn't even aware of yet. I was going in cycles of standing in my power, using my voice, and still not being heard, valued, or treated with integrity. This went on for a few years and was very confusing.

I was asking for a very different soul-led life, but I was picking the same environments, friends, and situations that put me in situations forcing me to go home and yell in discord, "This is not the life I want. Universe, please help me." Even as I type this.

Universe, please help me. There is calm. A quiet among the tears. A belief. A hope. A dream. A knowing that there is better. I am better. My life can be better. I can have a soul-led life of abundance, soul family, healing, ascension, expansion, and most of all, love. I can have a heart-centered, love-led life. Breathe that in. Pause. Exhale that out.

Yes, I am still learning. I am still healing. I am still learning my value, my worth, and my voice. I am learning what and who I can let go of. I am learning how to create new beliefs every day. And I never stop creating new dreams. Every day the kiddos and I talk about what we want or where we want to explore and who we want to visit. My children are growing up in a house of trial and error as I navigate through my personal healing journey. And also, they are learning healing, they are learning not to give up, and they are learning unconditional love. They are learning to dream big, to ask the Universe for the things they want, and we celebrate and give gratitude every time we receive.

I continue to put myself in rooms, connect in ceremonies, and tap into my personal energies and flow in order to bravely be more and more of my authentic self. When I need to integrate, process, and rest, I rest. Each day I remind myself that I know my dreams are meant to be created and lived. Living my dreams is the embodiment and integration of who I am. *I Am.*

ABOUT BOBBIE JO YARBROUGH

Meet Bobbie Jo, founder of Bravely Authentic, LLC. An intuitive alchemist, master healer, spiritual teacher, artist, and coauthor of the bestseller *Faces of Mental Illness: A Journey from Stigma to Health.*

Bobbie Jo graduated from San Diego State University, school of social work, after serving in the US Navy. She is a graduate of Intuitive Insights: School of Intuition San Diego, certified Sacred Soul Alignment Advanced Practitioner, and Usui Reiki Master.

Bobbie Jo assists people to heal their heart, body, mind, and soul from the inside out. She uses a combination of powerful quantum energy healing modalities, essential subconscious reprogramming techniques, and advanced intuitive techniques to create heart-centered spaces of growth and healing for those that want to live in their joy again.

If you are ready to take a new course of action in your life or just want to start feeling better in your day-to-day, then she can help you. Bravely Authentic also regularly sponsors various PTSD trauma healing programs.

By healing ourselves, we create ripples of healing for the whole world.

How you can connect and work 1:1 with Bravely Authentic:

Linktr.ee: /bravelyauthenticliving
Instagram: @bravelyauthenticliving
Facebook Group: Bravely Authentic Conversations

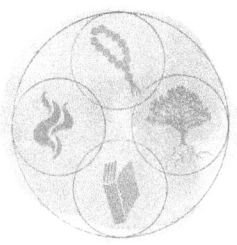

Have you ever dreamed of
becoming a published author?
Do you have a story to share?
Would the world benefit
from hearing your message?

Then we want to connect with you!

The *Inspired Impact Book Series* is looking to connect with
women who desire to share their stories with the goal of
inspiring others.

We want to hear your story!

Visit www.katebutlerbooks.com to learn more
about becoming a Featured Author in the #1 International
Best-selling *Inspired Impact Book Series*.

Everyone has a story to share!
Is it your time to create your legacy?

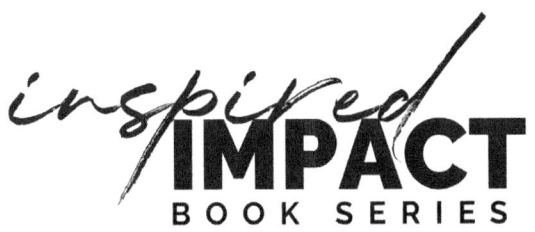

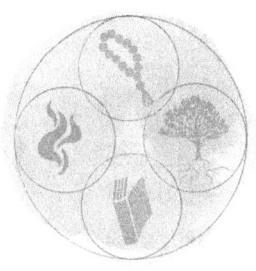

May Your Soul be uplifted, and the words of these pages inspire
you to continue to DREAM your infinite light living the fullest
expression of your divine life.

the women who dream

REPRINTED WITH PERMISSIONS

Abby Steurer
Addy M. Kujawa, CAE, DES
Amalai
Bobbie Jo Yarbrough
Candice Shepard
Christina Macro
Cori Solomon Santone
Dawn Schimke
Ellen M. Craine
Ellie D. Shefi
Ericha Scott, PhD
Erin Bonner Hudyma
Erin McCahill
Jennifer Weaver
Keri Gavin
Laura Mount
Lauren Oberly
Linda Gonzalez
Linda Yang
Lori Anne De Iulio Casdia
Mary Gervais
Maya Comerota
Melissa Malland
Michele Gambone
Susan Meitner
Suzette Perez-Tate
Teja Valentín
Teri P. Cox, MBA
Tiffany Donovan Green
Tracey Watts Cirino
Tracy Richards